# CHINESE COOKING
## FOR THE AMERICAN
## KITCHEN

# CHINESE COOKING

## FOR THE AMERICAN KITCHEN

# KAREN LEE

## WITH AILEEN ROBBINS FRIEDMAN

*Illustrated by Sidonie Coryn*

WITH A FOREWORD BY MME GRACE CHU

## ATHENEUM

NEW YORK

ATHENEUM
Macmillan Publishing Company
866 Third Avenue, New York, NY 10022
Collier Macmillan Canada, Inc.

Library of Congress Cataloging-in-Publication Data
Lee, Karen.
Chinese cooking for the American kitchen.
Includes index.
1. Cookery, Chinese.   I. Friedman, Aileen, joint
author.   II. Title.
TX724.5.C5L543        641.5'951        76-11858
ISBN 0-689-70596-4

Macmillan books are available at special discounts for bulk purchases
for sales promotions, premiums, fund-raising, or educational use.
For details, contact:

Special Sales Director
Macmillan Publishing Company
866 Third Avenue
New York, NY 10022

First Atheneum Paperback Printing February 1980

10   9   8   7   6

Designed by Kathleen Carey

Printed in the United States of America

# FOREWORD

Nearly everyone, I think, likes Chinese food. But for the most part, without a course of lessons, these people can enjoy it only in restaurants; they are denied mastery of the techniques for preparing Chinese food at home. Now Karen Lee, whom I am proud to claim as a former student of mine, has written a book that will, I think, open the pleasures of Chinese cooking to many more American families than have had access to them before.

She is a natural cook and a gifted teacher who has spent years in learning her craft; what she has so carefully learned—including sympathy for the novice faced with an array of strange utensils and ingredients—is shown here in a way that will appeal to both novices and the most sophisticated cooks.

I would not hesitate to commend to anyone this thorough, clear, well-illustrated guide to the pleasures of cooking and eating Chinese food, and I wish its users many hours of pleasure with it.

Grace Chu
New York, New York
1976

# ACKNOWLEDGEMENTS

A good cookbook, in my opinion, can not be accomplished by one person. The source of this book is my knowledge and experience as a cook, teacher, and caterer over the past seven years.

The clear format was made possible by my editor, Aileen Robbins Friedman, who was and is a constant source of motivation.

The contents are largely in response to my students, who have supplied me not only with questions and demands but also with the enthusiasm and positive feedback I needed to complete this project.

Karen Lee

# CONTENTS

---

# SOUPS 123

# POULTRY 138

# SEAFOOD 166

# DINNER PARTY PLANS

# ILLUSTRATIONS

# ΛUTHOR'S PREFΛCE

The story of how I became a professional cook is a short one. Most cooks you hear or read about grew up surrounded by glorious food, prepared by their mother or grandmother. They have recollections of wild raspberry pie cooling on the window sill of their Vermont summer home. My mother was, and is to this day, a confirmed dieter. My brother and I grew up on sirloin steak, whole or chopped, and French-cut string beans. The only enticing smell I can recall was the sautéing of onions in the apartment next door.

It was not until my freshman year at college, where I was exposed to inedible institutional food three times a day, that I began to want to prepare not only edible but also exciting food myself. In order not to starve to death, I purchased and smuggled into my dormitory room a highly illegal device called a Roto-Broiler. At one point the housemother, investigating what seemed to be the most unlikely odor of frying onions, knocked on my door and demanded to know what was going on inside. I unplugged the unit and hid it in the closet, had to confine my cooking experiments to late hours, and avoided onions. Eventually, however, it was confiscated.

Around that time I began reading continental cookbooks at a

rate that cut into my more academic studies. I also grew addicted to Julia Child's programs on television, which contributed to my growing fascination with French and then Italian cooking, and tried out recipes whenever I had the chance.

I was married at twenty and obsessed with cooking. At the suggestion of my husband, who adored Chinese food, I signed up for a course with Mme Grace Zia Chu to study the Art of Chinese Cooking. I returned home with exotic recipes from her homeland which were not my husband's idea of Chinese food. He was more interested in having me duplicate the dishes he was accustomed to eating in Chinese restaurants. As a self-taught French cook, I thought I knew what I was doing, and proceeded to stir-fry shrimp and snow peas. I was determined to please. Two weeks later, after having scorched ten pounds of snow peas (at least they were crisp) and rubberized five pounds of shrimp, we were losing weight rapidly. I decided to stick to the recipes we were taught in class until I had mastered the basic techniques. He was quite tolerant of trials and errors: ducks hanging in the shower, holes in my Chinese pancakes, and smoke permeating the apartment. Nor did he object to habitual midnight dinners, which was lucky, because organization did not come easily for me. I remember the first time I made fried rice: there was more rice on the floor of the kitchen than in the wok. I was becoming very discouraged. With continued support I persisted and eventually, by cooking Chinese food every night, was able to produce edible dinners before my husband had fallen asleep. We started having friends over regularly. I blatantly ignored the rule that you should never experiment with a new recipe for guests, and did exactly that with excellent results. My husband loved my cooking at last. As it turned out, that was the only thing he loved about me. Four years later he left. But my urge for cooking and feeding people persisted. The more I cooked at home, the more dissatisfied I became with restaurant food, and the more interested I became in calories, nutrition, and variety.

I continued the Chinese cooking course with Mme Grace Zia Chu for the next year and a half. She was, and is, considered the most informed teacher in America. I now consider myself a disciple of Mme Chu. She is an extraordinary teacher, who encourages her students to go out on their own as professional teachers and cooks, if they are really interested. Most women in her position would not have done this, but Mme Chu was concerned with more than just her share of the glory; she wanted more Americans to understand and appreciate the methods of preparing Chinese food themselves. For her attitude and influence she can never be given enough credit.

My studies with Mme Chu were interrupted by a most inconvenient move to Poplar Bluff, Missouri. Soon after I recovered from the shock of living in a town with a population of ten thousand, having spent the majority of my first twenty years in the heart of New York City, I planted a garden in my backyard. I selected and ordered a variety of seeds from the Burpee catalogue and was able to grow my own snow peas, bok choy, and Shantung cabbage. I also had a steady supply of mung bean sprouts growing in the drawer of the buffet in the dining room. I was able to order dried, canned, and bottled Chinese staples from St. Louis, which were delivered by bus. I started making Chinese food regularly in a town that did not have a Chinese restaurant. The summer soon ended along with my supply of Oriental vegetables. By now, however, I was too hooked on Chinese cooking to let the lack of a fresh snow pea hold me back.

That winter, when I no longer had access to fresh Oriental vegetables, which I had assumed were a prerequisite to preparing good Chinese food, I considered the possibility of substituting American vegetables, such as broccoli, celery cabbage, green peppers, onions, zucchini, mushrooms, and carrots. I was surprised how beautifully they worked, and that discovery motivated me to investigate further the relatively unexplored area of Chinese-American cuisine.

After a few months we started to invite people over for dinner. Our guests never knew what to expect when they came to our house, since I usually prepared Chinese meals which included dishes and styles of cooking they had never experienced. Few of them had ever been exposed to authentic Chinese food, and everyone seemed to be amazed and delighted at such creations as a duck roasted without its bones, noodles made from shrimp and egg whites, and barely cooked stir-fried vegetables. Several people expressed interest in learning how to cook Chinese, and I gave some informal classes.

I spent a total of a year and a half in Poplar Bluff, but ironically it proved to be a very fertile time, because it gave me a chance to experiment and develop a way of adapting American produce to Chinese cooking. It gave me confidence in the realm of Chinese-American food preparation, considering the enthusiastic response I had received from the residents of a typical midwestern town.

I returned to New York City with a mission. Mme Chu supplied the source of inspiration; Poplar Bluff, the challenge; and Karen Lee, the interest and determination. Upon my return to New York City, I renewed my studies with Mme Chu, and soon after became her assistant.

Once a week I taught an evening class in Chinese cooking at Saint Bartholomew's Community Club. During the day I worked at the Dione Lucas Gourmet Center, where I learned an enormous amount about every conceivable kind of kitchen utensil on the market. Eventually the store requested that I run a series of Chinese cooking demonstrations.

It was also at that time that I began catering. I put an ad in New York magazine and soon landed my first professional assignment as a Chinese cook: a nine-course dinner party for twenty-five people. Needless to say, that was no small undertaking for a first job, and I was slightly hysterical imagining the infinite variety of things that could go wrong. As it happened, however, all the dishes were enthusiastically received and the party was an unqualified success. The only drawback, as far as I was concerned, was the assumption on the part of the guests that the meal had been prepared by the Chinese high school boy who was working as my assistant!

The assistant soon relocated to Texas, however, and I was left to cater the next few parties on my own. Each party required every ounce of strength I could muster, and I finally broke down and engaged another assistant.

Although catering became easier as I became more and more organized, I have always found teaching far more gratifying. By the end of that year I had acquired enough private clients, from demonstrations and parties, to teach on a full-time basis, which I continue to this very day.

In my six years of teaching experience, I have found my classes to be an invaluable aid, helping me to clarify and simplify my approach to Chinese cooking. I have also become aware of the specific problems that Americans have in learning to cook Chinese food. As a result of my enthusiasm and its reflection in my students, there has been a growing demand for a book based on my recipes and instructions. This cookbook is my response to that demand.

My enthusiasm convinced my students that Chinese food was not just to be eaten on Sunday nights; after a few lessons, they agreed that it could become a regular part of their diet.

I eat Chinese food at least five times a week. My students ask me if I ever tire of it. The answer is an emphatic *no!* There is perhaps no other cuisine in the world with greater variety. It is possible to study with every teacher of Chinese cooking in America, and still be lacking in many areas. The list of Chinese ingredients is endless, but for the westerner many ingredients are difficult to learn about or impossible to find.

Once, while shopping in Chinatown, I came upon a vegetable which I had never seen before and was anxious to try. I asked the grocery store clerk how he would prepare it. "Somebody like it with bacon and somebody like it with pork," was his reply. I have often gone into a restaurant and ordered a dish which I found myself excited about and wanted the recipe for; most times, however, the recipe was unobtainable from the chef or any cookbook. I was then inspired to experiment at home until I could approximate the dish myself.

Chinese cooking thus answers the need to be creative and adventurous, perhaps more than any other cuisine. What started as a hobby for me is now a preoccupation. It was a sense of mystery that attracted me to Chinese cooking; it is mystery that keeps me interested after more than 10 years of exploration. To study Chinese cooking is to be in a constant state of discovery.

My own interest in Chinese cooking, which began in the early

1960s, anticipated the current trend. Today there are many Chinese cookbooks to refer to; there are many supermarkets and health food stores which carry fresh Oriental vegetables, and Chinese cooking courses and demonstrations are springing up in cities all over the United States. There are many reasons for its current popularity. Generally speaking, it answers many of the important needs of Americans: it is high in nutrients, low in calories, and extremely economical. The basic cooking technique, stir-frying, retains all the flavor and vitamins in vegetables, as opposed to boiling, which robs them. The ratio of vegetables to meat is proportionately higher than in American cooking, which accounts for the low cholesterol. You can also use inexpensive cuts of meat and save up to 50 percent on your food bills.

I have two main objectives in this book. The first is to show you how and when to use whatever produce is fresh and available, and convert it to Chinese-style cuisine. My students are always surprised and relieved to find there are many different ways to plan a Chinese meal, and that a trip to Chinatown is not necessary every time they want to prepare Chinese food. My approach to this cuisine is open and adaptable. I believe that once you have purchased the necessary staples, many of which last for over a year, and can find fresh local produce, you can cook Chinese.

My other objective is to show you how to coordinate a multi-course Chinese dinner. Other books have hinted at suggestions, or given bare outlines; I will give a detailed, step-by-step plan of the preparation and presentation of a dinner. It will answer the question that so many of my students ask me: "How can I prepare a Chinese dinner party with all its last-minute cooking, and still join my guests at the table?" This book includes different types of dinner plans, from those that are easy for the beginner to those that are challenging for the expert; from those that require a trip to Chinatown to those that need only a trip to the nearest supermarket. After reading this book, with a little patience and experience, you will be able to give a Chinese dinner party for any where from four to forty people, and be able to enjoy yourself as well.

# THE
# FUNDAMENTALS

# INTRODUCTION

## FEAR OF FRYING

I can clearly recall my feelings of helplessness, bewilderment, and panic when I first started Chinese cooking. It seemed as if there was a great deal of information being thrown at me at once, most of which was unfamiliar and mysterious. There were new utensils, new ways of cutting, new types of raw ingredients, new seasonings, and new techniques for cooking.

My advice is to take it slowly, learning one thing at a time. First, familiarize yourself with the basic implements: the cleaver and the wok. The more you use the cleaver, the easier it will become; I now find it the single most efficient and handy implement in my kitchen, and I use it for everything from mincing garlic to shredding beef.

Practice the different types of cuts (straight-cut, slant-cut, roll-oblique-cut, shredding, mincing, dicing) with a vegetable such as zucchini until you understand the movements involved and what the finished pieces should look like. Those basic cuts can be applied to a wide variety of foods, from vegetables to meat. Part of the unique and subtle beauty of Chinese cooking lies in the preparation of the food in unusual shapes and uniformly sized pieces.

The first cooking technique which you should practice, ideally until it becomes automatic, is stir-frying. It will seem difficult and different at first; it requires speed and steady rhythm, which come with time. The wok will seem unwieldy at first also, because of its size and shape; you will soon realize it to be the most versatile instrument you have ever put on a stove, since you can use it to stir-fry, deep-fry, braise, blanch, stew, and steam. Once you become adept with your metal spatula and wok, you will see how remarkably fast and efficient the technique of stir-frying is, and you will want to experiment on a wide variety of vegetables; vegetable-meat or vegetable-seafood combinations; and noodle combinations.

You must also be unafraid to experiment with new ingredients —not only raw and canned vegetables, but also unfamiliar spices, seasoning sauces, and dried ingredients. Don't be put off by an unusual name, look, or smell; many ingredients change textures or absorb other flavors when cooked. Try the variations and substitutions listed under the recipes; if you find you prefer hoisin sauce to bean sauce, make the substitution.

Once you have gotten over your fear of mastering the cleaver and the wok, you can begin cooking with confidence and imagination. After a few weeks you will begin to understand and appreciate not only a new cuisine but also a new culture—new to us, but older than our own.

# COOKING UTENSILS

In the realm of Chinese cooking, the equipment needed is far less numerous and less costly than for the European cuisines such as French or Italian. There are two crucial items: the cleaver for preparation, and the wok for cooking. Expensive heavy copper pots and a range of Wüsthof carbon-steel knives are not necessary. The total cost of Chinese cooking equipment will be under eighty dollars, as opposed to the hundreds or even thousands of dollars necessary to set up a kitchen equipped for French cooking.

The following is a list of the required utensils:

1. Two steel woks: two 14-inch, or one 12-inch and one 14-inch, with two dome-shaped covers.
2. One steamer with 2 or 3 levels, at least 12 inches in diameter (each level should be at least 3½ inches deep), or a large roasting pan with tight-fitting cover.
3. Two cleavers, one for slicing and one for chopping.
4. One boning knife.
5. Butcher's steel and carborundum stone.
6. Bamboo chopsticks (20 pairs).
7. A rubber mallet.
8. A chopping block.
9. Two wire strainers, approximately 6 to 9 inches in diameter.
10. Two steel spatulas for stir-frying.
11. A rack that will fit into the 14-inch wok (for steaming).
12. A Taylor deep-fat-frying thermometer.
13. A heavy dutch oven for braising, made out of cast iron or enamel, with a tight-fitting cover.
14. A heavy pot for steaming rice, also with a tight-fitting cover. The heavier the pot, the more even the heat distribution.
15. A dozen small bowls and a large number of disposable paper cups (3-ounce size) for organizing ingredients on trays.
16. Four to six trays, cookie sheets, or shallow roasting pans.
17. One or two racks for roasting.
18. A stock pot.

## WOKS

Stir-frying is most easily accomplished in a wok, although a cast iron dutch oven, an aluminum paella pan, or a high-sided sauté pan are viable alternatives. Originally in China the wok was placed on the coals of a fire made by the cook. Later, when stoves were introduced, there was a special top designed to meet the needs of wok cooking, which differed radically from the top of an American stove. The wok was placed on a hearth, a concave metal disk permitting the flames to reach up and around the sides. The rounded shape of the wok fits perfectly into this arrangement, and with a maximum flame, stir-frying is performed at its best. Chinese restaurants in America today still have this arrangement. The size of the hearth varies according to the size of the wok, keeping the round-bottomed wok stationary so the cook is free to stir-fry with a spatula  in one hand and a ladle or chopsticks in the other.

The traditional rounded wok was not designed for American stoves and poses problems for the American cook. The round-bottomed wok wobbles on the flat burner and could slide off the stove if not anchored by at least one hand. The situation can be remedied, however, by placing a ring over the burner, which balances the wok and keeps it stationary. The disadvantage of the ring is that it elevates the wok from the flame, thus reducing the intensity of the heat. There are several solutions to this problem, depending on what type of wok you are using. There are three main types available:

1. A round-bottomed wok with two steel handles.
2. A round-bottomed wok with one wooden handle and one steel handle.
3. A flat-bottomed wok with one wooden handle and one steel handle.

If you are using a round-bottomed wok with two steel handles, since the handles will soon be too hot to touch, you should wrap a dish towel around one of the steel handles or use an oven mitt. That will enable you to hold the wok with one hand while you stir-fry with the other hand. With that type of wok it is not only necessary to hold the wok throughout the entire stir-frying process; it is also necessary to stop the stir-frying while you add each new ingredient.

If you are using a round-bottomed wok with a wooden handle, you do not need the dish towel or oven mitt, which simplifies the process of stir-frying. In both cases you need no ring to balance the wok on the burner if you continue to hold on to the wok with one hand.

Neither situation is perfect, however, for two reasons: first, you may have to reach for an ingredient, which interrupts the stir-frying; and second, the method is much more efficient if you have both hands free for stir-frying. That way you can hold the metal spatula in one hand and chopsticks in the other, and keep the food in motion at all times.

It is possible to balance the wok with the handle resting on your stomach while you stir-fry with both hands, but it is tricky.

The perfect way to adapt a wok to an American burner is to buy a flat-bottomed, wooden-handled wok which rests securely on a gas or electric burner without a ring. With that type of wok you can stir-fry with two hands and can even leave the wok on the burner for a few seconds if necessary. The flat-bottomed wok is not authentically shaped, but it is designed with the American stove in mind and makes stir-frying fun and exciting, not agonizing and nerve-wracking.

The flat-bottomed wok is made and distributed by Taylor and Ng, P.O. Box 200, Brisbane, California 94005, and can be purchased at specialty shops on the Coast. If there is any problem locating one, write to Karen Lee Chinese Cooking School, 142 West End Avenue, New York City, New York 10023.

You can buy woks made of different materials, such as steel, cast iron, aluminum, stainless steel with a copper bottom, and all stainless steel. The best metal for a wok is heavy-gauge steel. If properly maintained, it will last a lifetime and improve with age and use.

*How to Season the Wok*
1. Scrub the wok both inside and outside with a steel wool soap pad. Rinse well and dry.
2. Over a very low flame, rub several tablespoons of peanut oil over the inside surface of the wok with a clean rag for 2 to 3 minutes.
3. With a vegetable brush, soap, and water, wash out wok with very hot water.
4. Repeat Steps 2 and 3.
5. Run your finger over the inside of the wok to see if a grease film still remains. If it does, repeat Steps 2 and 3 again.
6. Wash wok with vegetable brush and hot water. Never again use soap or the food will stick. Dry it over high heat for about 20 seconds.
7. For the first few months, rub a teaspoon of oil in the wok before putting it away to avoid rusting. If the wok does rust, it must be reseasoned.

As your wok becomes seasoned, it will gradually turn black. A well-seasoned wok is a source of great pleasure to a cook because food will never stick to it.

If you cannot wash your wok immediately after using it, pour several cups of water into it so the remaining particles of food will not harden and make cleaning difficult.

Wok covers are dome-shaped and are made out of aluminum. The shape is important because it allows the wok to be covered securely when the wok is full or contains a whole bird, as in the case of Soy Sauce Whole Chicken. Since the cover is made of aluminum and does not come in direct contact with food, you can use a steel wool pad to clean it. Oiling the cover is not necessary because aluminum does not rust.

### STEAMER

A roasting pan can be converted to a steamer if you don't want to buy one. (For detailed instructions, read the section on Steaming.)

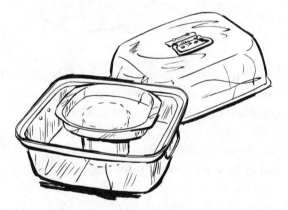

If you do wish to buy a Chinese steamer, there are two types from which to choose: bamboo or aluminum.

A bamboo steamer is more pleasing esthetically, but it is difficult to clean and will not hold up as well as an aluminum one. To use the bamboo steamer, fill the 14-inch wok with 2 to 3 cups of water and bring the water to a boil. Then place the covered steamer containing food inside the wok. Use a vegetable brush and hot soapy water to clean the steamer.

Aluminum steamers, which are the same shape as the bamboo but are sturdier, come in three different sizes. If you plan to give Chinese dinner parties, buy the large size. The medium-size steamer (12 inches in diameter) is the smallest one you should purchase,

with at least 2 levels for steaming. The levels should be 3½ inches deep or more. Some styles are even deeper, which is better for steaming fish if you put the fish in a bowl which has deep sides.

To use the aluminum steamer, fill the bottom of the steamer with water up to the first bolt, bring to a boil, then place the first level containing food on top of the water. Continue with as many layers as you have filled. Cover and steam as the recipe directs. If you are steaming a fish, place the thicker half in the bottom of the steamer, so it will cook at a slightly faster rate. If you are making Pearl Balls, set the timer for the midpoint of the allotted cooking time; when the timer goes off, you should check the water level, replenish with boiling water, then place the top level on the bottom and the bottom level on top. If you buy a steamer with more than 2 levels, which enables you to steam more than one kind of food at a time, remember that the bottom layer receives more heat than the top layers.

To clean the aluminum steamer, use a steel wool pad.

## CLEAVER

A cleaver may look threatening at first, but if used properly it will become your favorite cutting instrument for all types of preparation. Many of my students tell me that they have abandoned all their knives for the Chinese cleaver. Equip yourself with two different cleavers: a light, slicing cleaver with a thin, 2-toned blade, used for slicing, dicing, shredding, mincing, and slant-cutting; and a heavier, thicker cleaver, used for chopping through raw fish and poultry bones, cooked and raw. Do *not* buy stainless steel. Both cleavers should be made of carbon steel and should have wooden handles. After use, wash it with a vegetable brush and warm water. Dry it immediately so it does not rust. Never leave any type of carbon-steel blade in the sink. If rust does occur, it may be removed with an abrasive cleaner such as Ajax and a cork (from a wine bottle). You could use a steel wool pad to remove rust, but it will scratch the blade. Oiling the cleaver is not necessary if it is properly dried.

You can buy cleavers in many stores in Chinatown in New York City, such as Wo Fat, 16 Bowery, or the Chinese American Trading Company, 91 Mulberry Street.

## BONING KNIFE

The best composition for a knife, in terms of a fine cutting edge, is carbon steel. A carbon-steel knife requires the same treatment as a cleaver. It should be stored where it is least likely to receive nicks, such as a magnetic knife rack or a section of a drawer. Be sure to wash and dry it soon after use to prevent rust.

A 5-inch carbon-steel Wüsthof boning knife with a wooden handle is extremely useful for boning chicken breasts, and whole chickens or ducks. It is not always available, but can be found at or ordered from The Bridge Kitchenware Company, 212 East 52 Street, New York City, New York 10022.

### Carborundum Stone and Butcher Steel

Cleavers and all knives are best maintained and kept sharp with a carborundum stone and a butcher's steel. The stone can be stored in its original box or in a plastic bag. The butcher's steel can be put in a rack or drawer. The stone is used to sharpen the cleaver, which should be done once a week if you are using the cleaver every day. The butcher's steel keeps the edge on the blade and should be used every time before the cleaver is used.

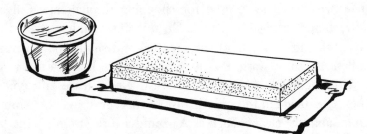

*How to Sharpen Cleavers and Knives*: There are two sides to the carborundum stone, rough and smooth, similar to an emery board. Place the stone, with the rough side facing up, on a paper towel on a chopping block. Drop a little water on the rough surface of the stone. Take the cleaver in your hand and, with the blade almost touching the stone, draw the cleaver sideways and toward you, using a fair amount of pressure and making sure the entire blade is covered by one sweeping motion. That is important in order to sharpen the blade evenly. Turn the cleaver over and sharpen the other side of the blade. Keep adding water as necessary.

Do 20 to 30 strokes on each side of the blade. Wipe the cleaver with a damp paper towel, dry it, then use the butcher's steel to remove the shavings from the blade. The function of the stone is to sharpen the cleaver blade; the function of the steel is to hone, or keep its edge. Both are important if you wish to maintain your knives properly. Before replacing the stone in the box, rub it with

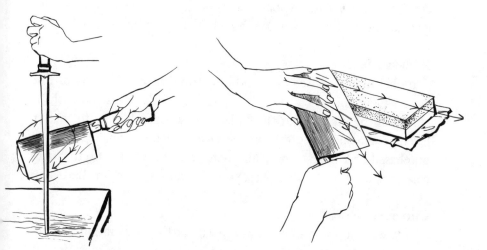

a little cooking oil in order to avoid rust. A razor-sharp cleaver will help make you an efficient Chinese cook, considering that more time is spent preparing than cooking the food. A dull cleaver will frustrate you and double your time in the kitchen.

## CHOPSTICKS

Chopsticks are made from many different materials: bamboo with no finish, bamboo with a lacquered finish, ivory, and silver. Bamboo is the easiest to work with and the cheapest. You should have at least 20 pairs on hand. They are extremely useful to work with in the kitchen, and once you have developed the proper dexterity, they are fun to eat with. They are used for a great variety of tasks: beating eggs; measuring level tablespoons of dry ingredients, such as water chestnut powder; turning ingredients that are deep-frying and stir-frying. They are also handy for lifting pickles or olives out of bottles. Do not let them soak in water for too long, because they will warp; it is best to clean them with hot soapy water and a vegetable brush. Ivory chopsticks are the equivalent of a sterling silver flatware set. They are elegant, expensive, and very slippery. After washing, they should be dried and stored flat with nothing on top of them; otherwise they too will warp. The same treatment applies to the lacquered bamboo chopsticks. Silver chopsticks are given as a wedding present in China but are not used for eating.

### RUBBER MALLET

A rubber mallet is used as an aid in cutting through poultry or fish bones. Place the heavy cleaver on the part of the food you wish to cut, hold the mallet near the end of the wooden handle for better leverage, and pound down on the cleaver. Rubber mallets can be purchased at kitchen-supply and hardware stores. If a thin, slicing cleaver is used for this purpose, you risk causing nicks in the blade.

### CHOPPING BLOCK

A wooden chopping block is as crucial for the preparation of Chinese food as a cleaver. Buy as big a block as you have room for, at least 18 × 24 inches and 2 inches thick. Keep it out on a counter top so it is ready to be used at a moment's notice for any last-minute preparation. A counter space near the stove is an ideal place to keep it.

Proper home cleaning and maintenance is important. The block accumulates and spreads germs, and should be cleaned regularly and thoroughly. A wooden block is best cleaned with hot, soapy water and a hard vegetable brush, a plastic pad, or a copper scouring pad. Always make sure the board is dried well to avoid warping. Once a week, rub cooking oil into it to avoid cracking. If water spills and comes in contact with the board, dry it immediately. Once a month, pour a layer of salt over the entire surface of the board and let it remain overnight. Brush off the salt in the morning. That will remove any germs and bleach stains out of the wood.

### WIRE STRAINER

A Chinese wire strainer is extremely useful. It can be used for Chinese, American, and European cooking. For Chinese cooking it is used for a variety of tasks, such as removing wontons from boiling

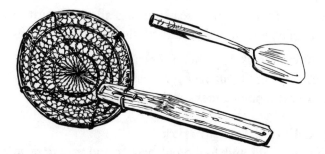

water; removing spring rolls and pieces of meat or poultry from oil; and, when a sauce is not thickening properly, lifting the vegetables and meat out of the wok and placing them on a serving dish while the sauce reduces to the desired consistency. For western cooking, a wire strainer is extremely useful for lifting noodles or vegetables out of boiling water. Two wire strainers are necessary if you are going to prepare multicourse dinners. A good size to have would be between 6 and 9 inches in diameter.

### Spatula

A Chinese steel spatula fits the contours of a wok and is ideal for stir-frying. It is wise to buy 2, one for each wok. Use a steel wool pad for cleaning, and dry them immediately after washing to

avoid rust. If rust does occur, it can be removed with a soapy steel wool pad and hot water. Seasoning the spatula is never necessary. When buying the spatula, check to see that it is free from nicks which might scratch the wok. Do *not* buy a stainless steel spatula, since it will scratch the wok. It is necessary to scrub a new spatula with a soapy steel wool pad in order to remove the grease.

### Racks

Racks are used for steaming, roasting, and allowing meat or poultry to cool. Ideally, you should have the following assortment:

1. A round rack, to fit in a 14-inch wok for steaming
2. An oval or oblong rack for roasting
3. An extra oblong rack for the cooling of meats

### Deep-Fat-Frying Thermometer

The only accurate and fool-proof way to judge and maintain the correct oil temperature in deep and shallow frying is to use a deep-fat-frying thermometer. There are several different types available on the market. I prefer the Taylor deep-fat-frying thermometer, which works on the same principle as a mercury fever thermometer. To use it properly, place the thermometer in the oil after the oil has heated a minute or two and watch the mercury rise until it reaches the required temperature. While the food is frying, check the temperature occasionally to see that it is maintained and adjust the flame accordingly. After deep-frying several times, you will be able to judge the temperature of the oil visually by the rapidity of the bubbles.

# CUTTING TECHNIQUES

Since the emphasis in Chinese cooking is on preparation rather than cooking, it is important to learn well the techniques of cutting. In a very good Chinese restaurant, there are several chefs, each one of whom has a specific task; it is not uncommon to have 14 cooks working in the kitchen, many of whom deal only with cutting meats and vegetables. It is common for an apprentice cook to spend years developing skill and speed with a cleaver. The result is not just a technique but an art, in which the Chinese take great pride. There are informal competitions among Chinese chefs, for instance, to see who can slice the thinnest piece of meat.

Accurate cutting is important for 2 main reasons: one is decorative—the appeal of the dish to the eye—and the other is functional—all pieces should be cooked to the same degree of doneness. For instance, if you are slicing zucchini for stir-frying, and some of the pieces are ¼ inch thick, while the others are ⅛ inch thick, the finished dish will contain some pieces that are overcooked (soggy) and some that are undercooked (too hard). Also, if the pieces are different sizes and shapes, that will detract from the esthetic appeal of the dish.

A good example of a dish in which all ingredients are uniformly cut is Szechuan Shredded Beef, in which the vegetables and meat are shredded to the same size and shape.

The easiest and best way to learn how to use a cleaver is to watch and imitate someone who is adept, who can correct any bad habits or misconceptions you may have in the beginning. If such a person is unavailable, try to learn from the following instructions.

The best way to hold a cleaver is to grasp the wooden handle with 3 fingers (the pinky, ring, and middle fingers), placing the thumb on the inside part of the blade and bending the index finger on the outside of the blade.

### STRAIGHT-SLICING
This is the simplest and most basic cutting technique. It often serves as the basis for other more complex cuts. It is best to practice on a long vegetable such as a carrot or zucchini. Hold the cleaver

in your right hand and anchor the carrot in your left hand, with your fingertips curved slightly on the top of the fat end of the carrot. The knuckles of your left hand will serve as a guide. Hold the vegetable perpendicular to the blade of the cleaver and start the slice approximately 1 inch from the end of the cleaver blade, continuing the slice about half way across the blade. Push forward from the shoulder, moving your whole arm, with the elbow bent but the wrist

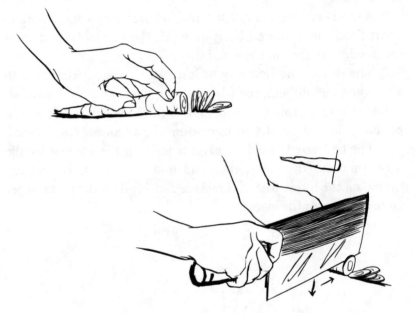

and hand steady. The movement of the cleaver is always forward; set up an even rhythm for yourself, pushing the cleaver forward in one motion to make the slice, lifting it up slightly, then pushing forward again. There should be two opposing directions going simultaneously: the movement of the cleaver blade toward you, and the movement of the fingers slowly pushing the carrot stalk away from you. Although barely perceptible, those rates should be coordinated equally.

Two common mistakes often occur when you first practice slicing with a cleaver: sawing and sidestepping. They should be avoided from the start in order to learn the most efficient method of cutting.

*Sawing* is the backward and forward motion of the cleaver, involving 2 blade strokes when one is sufficient. It is the most common mistake, and means that you expend twice the energy and time necessary to make a slice. To correct it, think of the motion as consisting of one and a half beats, with the strong accent coming on the first, forward-moving motion. The lifting up of the cleaver and returning it would be the half, or the "and," of the "one-and" combination.

*Sidestepping,* the other bad habit to avoid, consists of the superfluous action of pushing a slice aside after you have completed it. Every time you push the blade to the right after completing a stroke, you are not only throwing off your rhythm and wasting time, but you are also dulling the edge of the cleaver blade. You can look at the outside of the blade while you are slicing to gauge the accuracy of the cut. It is important to make thin and even slices. Though it may seem difficult at first, it can be mastered with some practice. The cleaver feels a little awkward and unwieldy in the beginning, but it is a remarkably adaptable and efficient tool which can save time and energy in preparing all types of food.

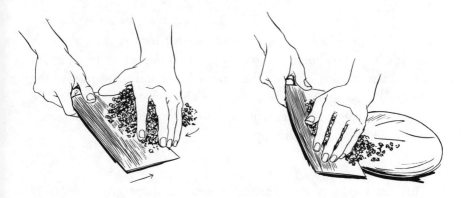

Another function of the cleaver is as a shovel to scoop up a pile of vegetables or pieces of meat. Place the blade almost parallel to the chopping block and use your free hand to push the vegetables onto the side of the blade; then use that same hand to sweep the vegetables off the blade into a bowl.

### Slant-Cutting

The slant-cut is the next most common cut, used for all types of vegetables in stir-fried dishes. To practice, try a long vegetable such as a carrot or zucchini. Place the vegetable parallel to the length of the chopping block. The angle between the vegetable and the

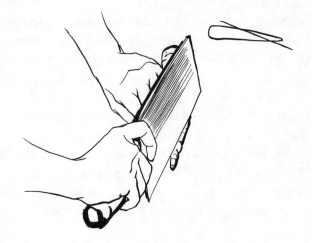

cleaver blade, which was 90° (a right angle) for the straight cut, is slightly wider; it should be about 135°. It is important to maintain a constant relation between the cleaver blade and the carrot, so the slant is the same. If the angle changes, the shape and length of the slice will change. It is desirable to have uniformity of size for both even cooking and esthetic appeal.

### Triangle-Cutting

This cut produces an esthetically pleasing shape. It is primarily used for hard, flat vegetables such as fresh peppers. It is an interesting alternative to dicing, and can dress up many seasonal stir-fried vegetable dishes as well as beef, poultry, and fish dishes.

Start with a sweet red or green pepper. Cut the pepper in half and remove the seeds. Then cut each half, lengthwise, into even strips, about ¾ inch wide. Take a strip and start by making a diagonal slice (slant-cut). Then swivel the strip with the fingers of

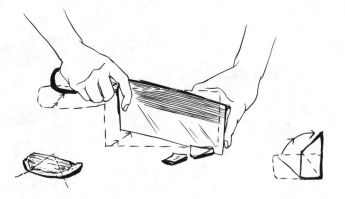

your left hand so the blade of the cleaver forms an equilateral triangle with the freshly cut edge. Make this second cut and then swivel the remaining portion of the strip so the blade again forms an equilateral triangle with the slant edge. Set up a one-two movement, swiveling the strip of the pepper first toward you and then away from you, keeping the triangles as similar as possible in size and shape.

ROLL-OBLIQUE-CUTTING

The purpose of this cut is to expose the maximum number of sides of a raw ingredient, so while cooking the piece will absorb as much of the flavor from the seasoning as possible. It is also a very decorative cut, slightly more complicated than the triangle-cut. It is used with long or large vegetables such as carrots, members of the squash family, asparagus, and bamboo shoots.

A good vegetable to practice on would be a carrot. Start by making a slant-cut in the carrot. Leaving the blade in place, roll the carrot one-quarter turn toward you. Then make another slant-cut so the blade forms a triangle with the cut edge of the first slice.

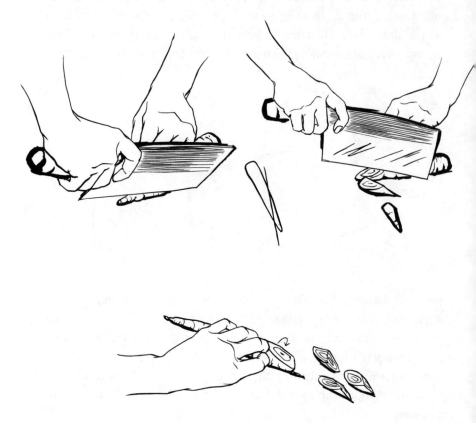

Now roll the carrot another ¼ turn and make a new slice, forming a new triangle. Continue rotating the carrot, forming polygonal pieces which have triangles on some, but not all, facets.

### DICING

This is a technique used to cut food into small, squarish, quickly cooked pieces. Practice on a carrot. Start by making several slices, which can be either straight or slant-cut. Then pile 2 to 4 slices on top of each other and with the length of the slices parallel to the cleaver blade, make *thick* slices. Then turn the long slices perpen-

dicular to the cleaver blade, and make widely spaced cuts in the other direction to form squares.

## SHREDDING

This common technique is used for meats as well as vegetables. Practice with a vegetable such as a carrot or zucchini. First slant-cut a few slices, and then pile them on top of each other. Then, using the straight-slicing motion, push the cleaver lengthwise through

the piled slices, creating thin shreds known in other cuisines as "matchstick" or "julienne." It is important to note how the position of the thumb differs in this particular cutting technique. The blade in the right hand continues to push lightly against the knuckles of the left hand, with all 4 fingers of the left hand on top of the pile of carrot slices while the thumb is behind the pile, pushing the slices forward to meet the blade. Do not pile up more than 3 or 4 slices at a time, or else they will slide off each other.

## MINCING

The purpose of this technique is to cut the ingredients into the smallest pieces. It is used in the preparation of fillings for wontons and dumplings, as well as in the creation of sauces (the ground pork

in Shrimp with Lobster Sauce or the dried shrimp in Dry Sautéed String Beans, Szechuan Style). It is also used to prepare the ubiquitous ingredients, garlic and ginger, which are strongly flavored and are used sparingly. You can practice with a carrot. Start by making slices; then make shreds, and pile the shreds in a little heap, all facing the same directions. They should at this point be perpendicular to the cleaver blade. Go over them a second time with the straight cut, pushing the shreds away from you while the cleaver blade moves toward you. Make sure that the shreds form the same right angle with the blade as in the straight slice.

## MINCING WITH TWO CLEAVERS

This technique doubles the speed of mincing by using two cleavers, one in each hand. It can save time if you have a large quantity of vegetables, fish, or meat to mince. It is used to make a filling, such as for wontons; a topping, such as for Shrimp Toast; or a stuffing, such as for Cantonese Stuffed Bean Curd or Pan-Fried Stuffed Peppers.

Hold two cleavers at once, grasping each handle with all fingers and thumb. In the case of carrots and other hard vegetables, cut first in slices and then in shreds. Mince once; then go over the pieces a second time with the two cleavers, setting up a fast and even rhythm, alternating the right-handed and left-handed strokes.

In the case of mincing shrimp, it is not necessary to slice or shred first; you just cut the shrimp into small pieces and then work through the pieces with both cleaver blades.

## PEELING AND MINCING GARLIC

Put one or more separate cloves of garlic on the chopping block. Put the flat side of the cleaver blade parallel to the block on top of the clove, and tap the blade once or twice with the heel of your free

hand. The gentle tap serves to loosen the skin of the garlic, but will not damage the clove, which should remain whole if you intend to slice or mince it. Do not smash down on the side of the blade unless the recipe calls for, or you desire, a crushed clove of garlic.

After removing the dry outer skin, cut off the hard, flat end. Hold the clove in your free hand and make 3 or 4 lengthwise cuts in the clove, parallel to the chopping block. Do not go all the way through the clove; leave part of the far end intact. Then turn the clove around 45° and make as many cuts as you can, about 4 or 5, so the incisions form a grid pattern. Turn the clove another 45°, and chop through into a fine mince.

To remove the odor of garlic from your hands, rinse them in water and then rub with lemon juice.

### Chopping Scallions

Scallions are most commonly prepared for cooking by straight-slicing. Cut 4 to 6 scallions in half once, and pile them alongside each

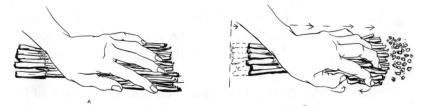

other. Hold them together with your left hand, at a slight angle, and make straight-cuts forward at intervals of about ½ inch. Because of the slender size and shape, the result will be a chopped scallion, even though the motion used is a simple slice.

### Scoring

Scoring serves several purposes: it helps to tenderize meat; it helps a marinade to penetrate whole or cut portions of fish or meat; and in steaming and deep-frying it helps produce even cooking. It consists of a series of criss-crossed diagonal cuts made in the outside of the piece of meat or fish at about 1-inch intervals, at a depth of about ½ inch.

# COOKING TECHNIQUES

### STIR-FRYING

Stir-frying, the most commonly used and characteristic technique in Chinese cooking, evolved from an economic cause: the shortage of fuel. If food is cut into small pieces and cooked over intense heat, it requires less cooking time and therefore less fuel.

It involves four important factors:

1. Small pieces of food in a little oil
2. Intense heat
3. Continuous tossing and turning with a spatula
4. A short duration of time

The sizzling you hear when you stir-fry is an important sound, because it lets you know the heat is intense. Have the local handyman adjust your stove so you can have the maximum amount of gas released.

Stir-frying can be mastered with some practice and concentration. The most important part is to set up a steady rhythm for yourself, so the spatula is continually tossing the contents of the wok every few seconds.

Be very sure that the spatula moves all the way through the food in the wok, and that you reach the center; otherwise the food will stick to the bottom. The movement is from the shoulder and involves the whole arm, so this technique will be tiring at first. If you do it on a regular basis, it will become quite normal, fast, and efficient.

Stir-frying can be done in a dutch oven or even in a skillet, but it is much easier in a wok. It's the difference between tossing a salad in a plate or in a bowl.

*How to Stir-Fry*

1. Place the dry wok over an intense heat for 10 to 30 seconds.

2. Add oil with a tablespoon in a circular motion, starting at the top of the sides of the wok and continuing around, so the oil coats the sides as well as the bottom of the wok. Do *not* lift the wok away from the burner or turn it to circulate the oil (as you would a saucepan) because the wok should at no time be lifted away from the source of heat. You can slide the oil on the spatula in order to distribute it around the sides of the wok. Do this for about 30 seconds, or until the oil is hot but not smoking. If the oil is not hot enough, the food will stick. Until your wok is properly seasoned, the food will stick anyway; this will improve after the wok has been used at least 12 times.

3. Add any one type of ingredient (vegetables, meat, fish, or poultry) all at once, no more than 3 inches from the inside of the wok. That will help keep spattering down to a minimum. Start stir-frying immediately, following the order of the recipe.

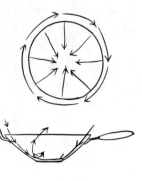

4. After the contents of the wok have been emptied, wash
   the wok immediately with hot water and a vegetable
   brush. Do not use soap. Dry the wok over a high flame
   and for the first few months, rub a teaspoon of oil into
   the wok, to prevent rusting and protect seasoning.

Use the highest flame possible at all times except when the recipe
indicates to lower it. Watch carefully when you are stir-frying vegetables, because they may begin to scorch, in which case you should
turn the flame down immediately. When stock is called for in a
recipe, bring it to a boil in a separate saucepan before adding it to
the wok. It should be added around the sides of the wok, as is the
case with all liquids. That way it will come to a boil much more
quickly, and the final dish will be superior. All sauces and dry
spices should be distributed evenly over the contents of the wok.

You can rewarm stir-fried dishes the next day, but they are
never as good because the crispness of the vegetables is lost. If
you do have leftovers that you don't want to eat cold, there are 2
ways of rewarming: one is the double-boiler method; the other is to
put the food in a preheated oven at 350° with a loose cover for
about 10 minutes.

Mastering the art of stir-frying requires time and much practice. The most important part of putting together a dish is *organi-*

*zation*: get in the habit, from the very beginning, of putting all the ingredients for a recipe, in the order in which they will be added to the wok, on a tray or in a designated area on a counter or table top. Read the recipe over several times before you start to stir-fry; if possible, post a copy of it on a wall or cabinet at eye level for easy reference.

Since it is impossible to rapidly adjust the heat on the burners of an electric stove, you must preheat as many burners as there are temperature changes in the recipe. Preheat one, two, or three burners to low, medium, and high. If the recipe says to turn the flame from high down to medium, remove the wok from the high burner and place it on the medium burner. It is always a good idea to read through the cooking procedure to see the total number of temperature changes.

If the sauce is not thickening or is too plentiful, remove the vegetables and meat (fish or poultry) from the wok with a wire strainer. Let the sauce drip down into the wok, then boil it down, stirring constantly until the proper quantity and texture are achieved. Then pour the sauce back over the vegetables and meat. This emergency technique prevents overcooking of ingredients.

Vegetables should be dry before adding them to the wok to avoid spattering.

Meat and vegetables are always cooked separately for 2 reasons: first, they require different cooking times; second, the vegetables contain moisture which would hinder the browning of the meat and the sealing of flavorful juices.

## DEGLAZING

Although this is a French cooking term and technique (*faire un déglaçage*), I find it to be most useful in Chinese cooking, especially in certain stir-fried recipes, since it adds valuable flavors which enhance the final dish. This technique can be used in all stir-fried and sautéed dishes, for meat, poultry, or fish.

Here is an example of deglazing in a shrimp recipe. After you have stir-fried a pound of shrimp and emptied the contents of the wok into a serving dish, there remains in the wok a crust of hard-ened juices, or browned bits. Splash in about 3 tablespoons of sherry or any type of stock (chicken, pork, beef), and use a wooden spoon to gently scrape the bits so they become incorporated with the liquid. Boil the liquid down, letting the boiling do most of the work, not the spoon, until the liquid is reduced to a thick syrupy glaze. Pour this deglazing liquid over the shrimp (or the meat or poultry). Then wash out the wok and dry it well before proceeding with the next step of the recipe, which is the addition of oil and then vegetables. The shrimp with the added deglazing liquid are added to the wok again at the end of the cooking procedure, along with the binder which serves to thicken the sauce. If you omit the deglazing process, you will be missing important essences which contribute to the flavor of the dish.

When doubling a stir-fried recipe, never *double* the oil or stock. The purpose of the oil is just to coat the sides of the wok. Any liquids would be increased, but slightly; if too much liquid is added, it will take too long to boil down and will produce too great a quan-tity of sauce.

If you are doubling the recipe and are using more than 1 pound of meat, you have to deglaze after stir-frying each pound of meat. You may find that even 1 pound of meat is too much for the inten-sity of your stove's flame; when there is too much, the meat begins to stew instead of fry (you can tell by the accumulation of excessive moisture). The flame on some stoves can't handle more than ½ pound of meat at a time. As a way of cutting down on time in the kitchen after your guests have arrived, you can stir-fry the meat, fish, or poultry and then deglaze the wok, pouring the juices over the meat several hours ahead. Then at the last moment all you have to do is stir-fry the vegetables, adding the meat at the very end to heat and blend all ingredients and flavors.

MARINATING

The marinade recommended in this book (consisting of egg white, water chestnut powder, and sherry) affects the texture and not the taste of the meat, fish, or poultry. It functions as a tenderizing agent and gives the raw ingredients a velvety texture. This differs from the usual western concept of a highly seasoned marinade meant to affect the flavor. (There are a few exceptions, such as Roast Pork and Barbecued Roast Duck, whose marinade affects taste as well as texture.) In western cooking, the meat is submerged in a large quantity of the marinade, whereas in Chinese the meat is barely coated.

If the egg white is beaten lightly, it is easier to divide in half. A whole egg white is really too much coating for less than a pound of meat, but too much egg white is far less harmful than too much water chestnut powder; it may make the marinated pieces stick to the wok.

It is important that the water chestnut powder be measured accurately: level off the measuring spoon with a chopstick or knife as if you were measuring baking soda for a cake. Too much water chestnut powder or cornstarch will cause 3 undesirable effects: the meat will stick to the wok; the sauce will be too thick and lumpy; and the meat will have an obviously thick coating which can be felt as well as tasted.

Use 2 chopsticks and stir in 1 direction in order to mix the marinade thoroughly.

It is also very important that the oil is sufficiently heated before the marinated pieces are added to the wok in order to avoid excessive sticking.

### EMERGENCY BINDER

Always have these emergency ingredients at your fingertips: soy sauce, stock, and—most important—a mixed binder. It should be by the stove, ready to be restirred in case the sauce is not thickening properly. Dissolve 1 tablespoon water chestnut powder (or cornstarch) in 2 tablespoons water or sherry. You may not need it, or you may need only some of it, but it is an excellent precaution to take.

It is also a good idea to keep a wire whisk near the stove, to be used when adding the binder to any large quantity of sauce. It will help prevent lumps in the sauce.

Most stir-fried dishes are very delicate and cannot be kept warm without deteriorating; even slightly overcooked vegetables soon lose their crunch. In each recipe, I will indicate how long the dish can be kept warm. If it is essential for you to keep a dish warm in which you have used a binder, substitute cornstarch for the water chestnut powder, since the latter will break down sooner and lose its thickening ability.

### DEEP-FRYING

The Chinese are very fond of deep-frying, because it produces interesting textures, and seals in flavor and juices. For several reasons, a wok is the best utensil in which to deep-fry. First of all, it is excellent for your wok, because it speeds up the seasoning process. The wok absorbs some of the oil, which makes the whole inner surface smoother and will help prevent all food pieces from sticking. Second, the high sides of the wok prevent the oil from spattering all over the stove. Third, a heavy wok is a good conductor of the heat, which aids in the browning process and produces even browning. The oil temperature is extremely important in deep-frying. The most accurate way of judging it is with a Taylor mercury deep-fat-frying thermometer. Many Americans are fearful of deep-fat-frying because of burns and grease spatter, but if handled in an organized fashion it can be an efficient and desirable way of cooking.

Make sure the wok is dry before adding the oil to the wok. The amount of oil needed will depend on the size of the wok: a 12-inch wok will require 2 to 3 cups of oil; a 14-inch wok will require 3 to 4 cups of oil. The oil can be used 2 or 3 times, if it has not become too brown and if it is strained through a sieve lined with cheese-cloth and then refrigerated. It is healthier to use fresh oil every time, but quite expensive.

If the proper oil temperature is maintained, the food will not absorb any more oil than will stir-fried dishes. Once the oil registers the correct temperature on the thermometer, carefully lower the food into it with tongs, chopsticks, or a wire strainer. The food is then either gently stirred or turned with chopsticks. Stirring is done with the pair of chopsticks in one hand. Turning is done with one chopstick in either hand. When removing food from the oil, hold the food over the wok for at least 5 seconds to allow some of the oil to drain off. Then drain on several layers of paper towels.

When reheating the oil to the desired temperature before adding the food, turn the flame to high. If the oil begins to spatter, place the cover on the wok for about a minute or until you hear the spattering stop. Oil will spatter more when reheated. Before adding the food, turn the flame down to medium. Add no more than 1 pound of meat at a time. Never crowd pieces of meat, since they will create too much steam and cool down the oil temperature too quickly. If the required oil temperature is 325°, preheat the oil to 350° to allow for the cooling down of the oil temperature once the food is added. Avoid heating oil to the smoking point, because at this point it becomes saturated.

Food that is to be deep-fried is usually marinated first, then coated with cornstarch or water chestnut powder. The marinating helps to tenderize as well as to flavor; the coating of starch serves to seal in juices, to prevent the food from absorbing too much oil, and to create a crunchy exterior. Two examples are Cantonese Fried Chicken and Peking Spareribs.

*Twice-frying* is frequently required. One frying is done first at a lower temperature; that actually cooks the food. The food is then removed from the oil, drained well, and allowed to cool. The second frying is done at a higher temperature, and its purpose is to create a crunchy exterior. The first frying can be done several hours ahead, which significantly reduces the time you have to spend in the kitchen once your guests have arrived. Always have handy several cookie sheets lined with paper towels before you start the frying process. While the food is frying, keep checking the oil temperature with the thermometer, raising or lowering the flame as necessary. After you have deep-fried several times you will be able to tell if the temperature is right by the movement of the bubbles. The food should always be dry before being lowered into the fat to avoid excessive spattering. If the oil spatters, cover the wok for a few seconds until the spattering stops.

Another form of deep-frying is called *passing through*. In this technique, the marinated pieces of meat are first deep-fried in a low temperature of oil (280° to 325°). It is very efficient to stir the pieces by holding a pair of chopsticks in either hand, making figure eights in opposite directions. Then the pieces are removed from the oil and allowed to drain in a strainer. Later the meat is stir-fried with vegetables and a seasoning sauce. This technique evolved out of practical considerations. First, refrigeration is not as available in China as in America, so if the meat is partially cooked, it does not require refrigeration. Second, if the meat passes through the oil once and is partially cooked, when it is stir-fried later it does not stick together. For the American cook this is a time-saving device, making it possible to complete preparations as well as part of the cooking procedure several hours in advance, which decreases the time spent in the kitchen and increases the time spent with your guests. Two examples are Lamb with Hot Peppers and Scallions, and Szechuan Diced Chicken.

#### SAUTÉING

This technique is common to westerners through French and Italian cooking, in which the food is fried until well browned in a pan with enough oil to generously coat the bottom and sides. The purpose is to brown all sides and to seal in the juices, but the flame is not as high as in stir-frying, which requires intense heat. It is not very common in Chinese cooking; two examples are Cantonese Stuffed Bean Curd and Pan-Fried Stuffed Peppers.


## ROASTING

Roasting is another important part of Chinese cooking. It is, however, rarely done in Chinese homes, simply because most Chinese families do not have ovens. This lack is due to the scarcity of fuel. There are central ovens (both in China and in Chinese communities all over the world) where roasted meats are prepared and can be purchased by the pound or piece, such as a whole roasted duck or a portion of a roasted pig.

For the American, Chinese-style roasting at home can be accomplished in the following manner. Always marinate meat whole first. Then put the meat on a rack in a shallow roasting pan which contains about ½ inch water, which provides moisture and prevents the drippings from burning. It is crucial to elevate the meat from the pan and the water, so the heat can circulate all around the meat. In China and in Chinese communities elsewhere, where the ovens are as large as closets, the meat is hung up on hooks, with a pan of water underneath to catch the drippings. An example of roasting on hooks is illustrated in this book by Roast Pork.

Poultry is submerged in boiling water, hung in a cool place by the neck if it is fresh-killed, or by the wings if the neck has been removed, until the skin is dry. A good example is Peking Duck. It is then marinated before roasting. The purpose of submerging the whole bird in boiling water is to remove some of the fat. The purpose of hanging the bird is to dry the skin, which insures its crispness even after the bird is allowed to cool.

A seasoning liquid is sometimes placed in the cavity of the bird, which is sewn up before roasting. The liquid is removed before the bird is cut. Several grocery stores in Chinatown sell poultry prepared in this manner, along with other cooked meats, such as roast pig, roast pork, duck, chicken, and many of the organ meats.

American stoves are too small to roast whole fowl or large cuts of meat in the authentic Chinese fashion.

## WET-STEAMING

Steaming is a technique frequently used in Chinese cooking. It is an easy way of preparing food, low in calories and cholesterol, and it creates a very different texture than stir-frying or deep-fat-frying.

It is necessary at the start to clarify the difference between steaming and poaching. Poaching is the manner of cooking in which a fish, for example, is totally immersed in a court bouillon (a seasoned liquid) and simmered until done. The fish is thus cooked by coming in direct contact with the seasoned liquid.

In steaming, the fish never actually touches the boiling water; it is cooked by the steam created by the boiling water placed in the bottom of a steamer. The seasonings are placed on the fish itself. The steam rises up and around the fish. Therefore you can't use a French fish-poacher, because in it the fish would touch the water.

Once your steamer is set up, it takes care of itself and requires no attention. That fact allows you to stir-fry one or two dishes while the third dish is being steamed, meaning you can easily handle a three-course dinner without any help.

Many different foods are steamed either whole (such as a whole fish or duck) or in small pieces (such as Pearl Balls or dumplings). Rice is also steamed. In most cases the food can and should be cooked and served in the same dish. You have many choices for dishes, ranging from ordinary Pyrex or Corning Ware to your best china.

The dish that you choose does not have to be fire-proof or oven-proof; the type of heat created by steaming is not great enough to damage good china. The important factor is the size of the dish, not its composition. It must be at least 1 inch smaller, on all sides, than the vessel in which it is placed to steam, so the steam can circulate all around the food. It must have sides of one inch, or sides that slope up; otherwise the juices that collect around the ingredients being cooked will spill out. The food should be cooked on a medium-high flame, and the water level below should be checked every 15 minutes to see that it has not evaporated. Just keep setting the timer.

*Types of Steamers*: Many improvised steaming arrangements are possible, all of which are just as effective as an authentic Chinese steamer. For instance, a roasting pan or a dutch oven is easily transformed into a steamer by placing an empty can (approximately 3 inches high × 4 inches wide), top and bottom removed to form a cylinder, in the bottom of the pan. Fill the pan with water to a depth of 2 to 3 inches. Stand up the cylinder, vertically. Then place the dish in which you cook and serve the fish on the opened top of the can. Cover with the top part of the roasting pan (or dutch oven). When you preboil water, the cover should be on, so that some steam builds up.

Steaming in a wok is another possibility. Fit a round rack in the lower half of the wok, fill with water to just below the rack, and place the dish on top of the rack.

If you plan to buy a Chinese steamer, there are two kinds from which to choose: bamboo or aluminum. The bamboo steamer will fit into a 14-inch wok which has been filled with 2 to 3 cups of water. A bowl or a Pyrex pie plate are the only dishes you can use, however, because of the round shape of the steamer. I prefer the aluminum steamer since it is easier to clean and lasts longer. Fill the

333443334333444444

lower part of the steamer with water, then place the layers on top (usually 2, sometimes 3). If the fish is too long, and the pieces do not fit side by side when cut in half, place the thickest half in the bottom layer, the other half in the second layer. If that is done, both halves will cook in the same time, since the thickest portion is closest to the source of heat.

### SIMMERING

Simmering is a technique of slow cooking in which the liquid is kept just at or slightly below the boiling point. It is used to make sauces, because simmering helps blend flavors; it is also a way to cook meat. After the boiling point has been reached, the flame is turned down to a low setting and the meat in the liquid is allowed to cook slowly until tender. The saucepan or wok should be checked occasionally to make sure the liquid has not evaporated.

### RED-COOK SIMMERING

This technique's name is rather misleading and is based on a Chinese preference for the color red over the color brown. In this manner of cooking, whole pieces of meat, fish, or poultry are slowly simmered in liquid containing large amounts of soy sauce, water or stock, and sherry. The cooking vessel remains covered throughout the simmering process. Because of the dark liquid in which the product is cooked (darkened by the soy sauce), the finished product assumes a dark brown color, which is referred to as "red."

An example of this type of cooking is Soy Sauce Whole Chicken. The liquid in which the chicken is cooked, plus the juices from the cooked fowl, form a flavorful sauce, known as a master sauce, which can and should be used over and over again. A heavy dutch oven or a wok can be used for this type of cooking. Red-cook simmered dishes can be prepared a day or two in advance and either rewarmed in the master sauce or served cold. It is an excellent way to prepare less tender cuts of meat, such as beef rump, brisket, chuck, or short ribs; pork shoulder or butt; and shoulder of veal.

The time required for red-cook simmering varies, depending on the weight of the whole piece of meat and the cut. It should always be cooked until tender, if it is beef, pork, or veal. If it is poultry, it is done when the juices are yellow. Tilt the bird with chopsticks or a wooden spoon until you see juices drip; if they are tinged with pink, it is not ready. (That conforms to American taste, since the Chinese prefer poultry slightly underdone with the juices pink.) Various seasonings can be added to the basic simmering liquid of soy sauce, water, and sherry before the whole piece of meat is added to the cooking vessel. These include five-spice powder or star anise, dried tangerine peel, scallions, or ginger.

The difference between red-cook simmering and braising is that in braising the ingredient is browned first and then slowly simmered in liquid until tender. The browning serves to seal in flavorful juices before the liquid is added.

### Blanching

Blanching means plunging into boiling water. Its purpose is to soften hard vegetables for stir-fried dishes or salads, such as broccoli, carrots, kohlrabi, and string beans. The vegetable is put in boiling water, and after it returns to a boil for about a minute the vegetables are removed and immersed in ice water, which stops the cooking and holds the color. They should then be drained and dried well before stir-frying. This preliminary cooking can be done up to a day in advance; the vegetables should be refrigerated until they are ready to be stir-fried.

### Boning Poultry for Stuffing

The object of boning is to separate a bird's skin and meat from its carcass, with the legs, wings, and tail in place, leaving the shape of the bird intact so it can be stuffed, cooked, and presented whole.

1. With a boning knife, cut away the fold of extra skin extending from the neck on the breast end of the bird (particularly in a duck).

2. Remove both pockets of fat located on either side of the bird's interior at the tail end. Then (particularly in a duck) cut off the two sacs, about the size of a lima bean, located between the skin and the meat at the neck end.

3. Cut through the joint that connects the shoulder to the wing. The purpose of this cut is to sever the wing from the carcass, but be careful to leave the wing attached to the body of the skin. With your thumb, feel for the joint separation, which resembles the space between 2 knuckles. Cut through this with the tip of a boning knife. Then turn the bird around and repeat the procedure on the other side.

4. As you begin to separate the meat from the carcass, be very careful not to pierce or slit the skin. Pull the skin and meat back with your free hand as you scrape away from the carcass with the knife, always taking care not to puncture the skin. Pulling back the skin and meat as you cut away from the bones is as important as the actual cutting; the two should occur simultaneously. You can take some of the cartilage off

the top of the breastbone if necessary, in order to avoid puncturing the skin. Turn the bird around, working the skin and meat away on all sides.

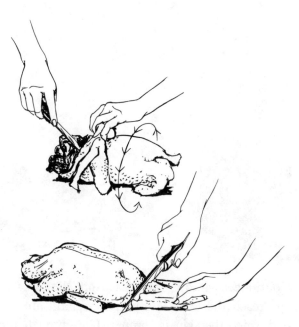

5. When you are a few inches, or about halfway, down the body of the bird, start to pull the skin over the detached wings. Continue turning the bird, working the skin and meat off.

6. To remove the thighbone, it is first necessary to disjoint the leg from the thigh. Start by taking the leg and pushing it up and through the skin, so it appears to be inside out. When you examine the exposed thigh, you will see a seam which marks the connection of the leg to the thigh. Using this seam as a guide, cut through the joint with the tip of your boning knife until the leg is severed from the thigh. Then remove the thigh *bone* with the tip of the boning

knife, leaving the thigh *meat* still attached. When the meat is free from the bone, twist the bone until it comes off.

7. Continue separating the meat from the carcass until you reach the tail. Be especially careful around this end, since the skin is thinner. Cut through the tail with your cleaver; this is the last point of attachment

of the skin and meat to the carcass. At this point you should be able to remove the entire carcass, leaving the skin and meat *inside out*. Remove the pocket of fat near each thigh, being careful not to pierce the skin.

8. Rub a piece of fresh crushed ginger over the surface of the inside-out bird.

9. Turn the mass of skin and meat *right side out*, so the skin is again on the outside. Run your hand over the

interior of the bird to make sure all bones have been removed. Check the skin for slits or punctures; if there are any, sew them up with unwaxed dental floss and a sewing needle.

10. Sew closed the opening at the neck. Stuff the bird; then sew up the opening at the other end. Plump up the sides of the bird with both hands to reproduce the original shape of the bird with bones.

## How to Bone Poultry for Dicing

The object here is to separate the meat from both the skin and the bones, so you can use the white meat from the breasts and the dark meat from the thighs (you do not use the meat from the wings or legs). The large segments of white and dark meat are then ready to be shredded, diced, or minced.

1. Place the bird on a flat working surface, breast side up. With your free hand (not holding the boning knife), pull back the thigh and leg, and feel for the separation at the joint. It should feel like the space between 2 knuckles on your hand. Cut all the way through the joint so the leg is detached from the thigh.

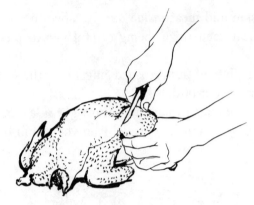

Repeat this procedure with the wings, first feeling for the separation at the joint, then cutting through. Remove the tail with a cleaver.

2. Skin the bird, starting where the lower part of the breast meets the back. Make little nicks with the knife

as you pull back the skin with your free hand. The skin should come away easily, needing gentle assistance from the blade. Remove all the skin, being careful not to make any cuts in the underlying meat.

3. Once you have removed all the skin, start the boning of the breast. Begin at the wishbone and make one long cut, following the upper ridge or contour of the breast bone. Separate the cutlet meat from the underlying bone structure by pulling the meat away with your free hand while you scrape away with the boning knife. Be

sure to get the extra piece of meat near the wing, always omitted by the butcher.

Sever the tendon attached to the shoulder by making an incision with the point of the boning knife. Pull the filet away from the cutlet with your free hand, making nicks with the knife only when necessary. The filet should separate easily, in one smooth piece.

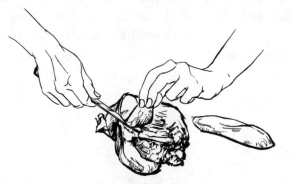

Now you must remove the long white tendon which runs through the filet. Hold the exposed end of the tendon in place with a small piece of paper towel. Put the dull edge of the cleaver on top of that end, with the blade perpendicular to the chopping block.

The cleaver should remain stationary while you pull the tendon toward you, slowly and steadily, with your free hand. Do *not* press down too heavily on the cleaver in order not to break the tendon; it should slide out in one long piece.

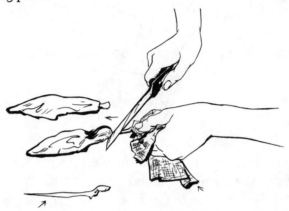

    Repeat this procedure for the other side of the breast; then trim both cutlets of excess fat.

4. Remove the thigh meat by pulling with the free hand and cutting the meat away from the bone, first on one side and then on the other. Twist the thigh bone around in the socket until it comes off. Remove any excess cartilage.

**How to Prepare Shrimp**

1. Start where the head was. Holding the shrimp in one hand, remove the shell and legs from the body. To remove the shell from the tail, cock the tail back until you hear a click. Alternate pulling the two sections of the tail until the shell can be slipped off gently, leaving the tail meat within still attached to the body.

2. Place the shrimp on its side. With a cleaver or knife, remove the intestinal tract, located on the curve that runs along the outside of the body, since it might con-

tain bacteria. This process is inaccurately referred to as "deveining." The vein, which runs along the inside of the body, is left intact.

3. Hold the shrimp in one hand with the outer curve facing the cleaver, and make an incision along the curve, almost but not quite all the way through the body of

the shrimp. When finished, the shrimp should be completely flat or "butterflied."

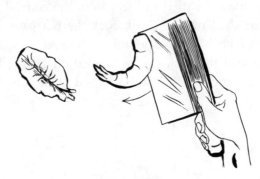

## How to Make a Spring Roll

1. Take a square Spring Roll wrapper and angle it on a flat surface so it faces you as a diamond shape.
2. Take 2 full tablespoons of filling and place them in the lower center of the diamond.
3. Holding the filling firmly with the last 3 fingers of both hands, take the corner of the diamond nearest you and fold it tightly over the filling. Be sure to push the filling toward you while you are folding the corner of the wrapper away from you.
4. Make another fold away from you, doubling over the filling, always pressing in toward the flat working surface.
5. With beaten egg on your fingertips, generously moisten the 3 remaining points of the diamond. (In fact, the diamond has now been folded in half, so the three points are part of the remaining triangle.)
6. Take the 2 side points and fold them in toward the bottom center, folding the left one in first and then the right one. Make sure there is an overlap of at least 1 inch. At this point, the Spring Roll should resemble a bulging envelope.
7. Take the bottom edge of the envelope—the edge near-

est you—and roll it away from you for two complete turns. Again make sure that you press the filling in tightly.

8. Bring the remaining free corner over and seal the moistened tip onto the roll.

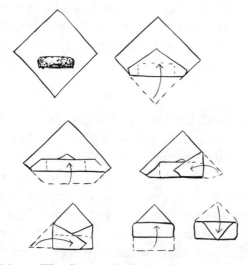

Note: The Spring Roll should be tightly rolled, in order to avoid excessive absorption of oil.

## DEFATTING PAN JUICES AND STOCK

The easiest way to remove fat from pan juices or stock is to pour

liquid into a heat-proof container and place it, uncovered, in the refrigerator until the fat solidifies. That takes several hours. If you do not have enough time, you can use the following method. Remove as much fat as possible with a spoon. To remove the remaining fat, float a small piece of paper towel on the surface. The paper will absorb the top coating. Continue to float pieces of towel until all the fat has been removed. Chicken fat can be refrigerated for one month and used to stir-fry vegetables. It should be noted that chicken fat, while delicious, is extremely high in cholesterol.

### REWARMING

Unfortunately, most Chinese food suffers greatly when it is rewarmed, unless it is a braised dish (such as Braised Gingered Spareribs) or a red-cook dish (such as Soy Sauce Whole Chicken). If absolutely necessary, the best way to rewarm stir-fried dishes is the double-boiler method. Pour 2 inches water in a shallow roasting pan on a burner on top of the stove. Put the loosely covered serving dish in the pan of water and turn the flame to medium. When the water comes to a boil, turn the flame to low and set the timer for 10 minutes. Taste to see if the food is hot before serving. Leftovers can also be rewarmed in a loosely covered serving dish which has been placed in a preheated 325° oven for 10 minutes. Leftover poultry is best eaten cold.

Fried appetizers, such as Shanghai Spring Rolls and Shrimp Toast, are best rewarmed in a preheated 400° oven for 4 to 7 minutes. Place the food on a rack which is resting on a shallow roasting pan to catch the dripping grease. Spareribs and Roast Pork can be rewarmed the same way in a 450° oven for 5 to 10 minutes. Steamed fish is best eaten cold.

### STIRRING LIQUIDS

Always use 2 chopsticks when stirring binders, marinades, and soups. The stirring of liquids such as soups, almond cream, and sweet and sour sauces should be done in a figure-eight motion for thorough mixing and to make sure the center of the pot is reached.

## SERVING DISHES

The Chinese prefer to serve entrées in bowl-shaped serving dishes, since the high sides help retain the heat. I prefer to serve most entrées in flat serving dishes or with shallow sides because it is esthetically pleasing and also because it prevents food from continuing to cook once it is on the table.

To preheat serving dishes, place serving dish in a preheated 200° oven for 10 to 15 minutes.

## BUYING AND PREPARING PORK

Use Boston butt whenever possible. This cut of meat comes from the lean part of the shoulder and weighs about 6 pounds. It is a good choice for most pork dishes since it is well-marbled, tender, and flavorful.

In preparing butt for roast pork, after trimming excess fat, cut as many slices as you will need, going against the grain of the meat, so that the slices cut with the grain will not be too long.

Going with the grain of the meat, cut slices about 1¼ inches thick. Then, with your cleaver, make diagonal crisscross cuts about ½ inch deep on both sides of each slice.

To prepare butt for slicing and shredding (for stir-fried dishes and soups), cut slices the same as above, but omit scoring.

To prepare butt for ground pork (for stir-fried dishes and stuffings), have your butcher trim the outside fat from a whole Boston butt. Have him put the pork through the grinder only *once*, so it will resemble the coarse pork used in China, which is minced by hand.

## SLICING OR SHREDDING MEAT

Freeze meat slightly before cutting in order to make it hard, so it is easier to hold and slice. Room-temperature meat is slippery, which makes it difficult to cut even slices or shreds.

## STORING MEAT

Freeze ground and whole meat in ½-pound quantities to avoid waste.

# INGREDIENTS

### ABALONE

Abalone is a type of mollusk available fresh only on the West Coast. In other places, it is available dried and canned. I prefer the canned variety. Always use the juice from the can in either the same recipe or add it to soup. If you have no immediate use for the juice, freeze it. It is unfortunate that abalone has become so expensive: four dollars or more for a 15-ounce can. If you are willing to spend the money, though, it is well worth it since it is a distinctive and delicious fish. The most important thing to remember about canned abalone is not to overcook it. Once heated, it is ready to eat; if overcooked, it will toughen. If a recipe which calls for abalone in another cookbook says to add it earlier in the cooking procedure, just change the order and add it at the last moment. Abalone can be kept refrigerated in water to cover for one week if the water is changed every day. Naturally, it is better if used immediately. Abalone can be sliced and served cold as an hors d'oeuvre.

### ANISE, STAR

This spice is similar to anise seed, which the Italians use in pastry. It has a licorice flavor and is used sparingly in red-cook simmered and braised dishes, such as Soy Sauce Whole Chicken. It is also one of the spices in five-spice powder. It is sold in cellophane packages but should be transferred to a covered jar, where it will keep on a pantry shelf indefinitely. Do not combine with other ingredients! (Once I stored anise with some dried mushrooms, the mushrooms absorbed the flavor and soon tasted like star anise.) When a recipe indicates the use of 1 whole star anise, it means 8 pods. Frequently most of the stars will be broken, so simply count out eight pods.

### BAMBOO SHOOTS

Bamboo shoots are young sproutings of the bamboo tree, which is an Oriental plant. Unfortunately, only canned bamboo shoots are

available in America. The best are winter bamboo shoots; they are smaller and have a more distinctive flavor, but are about four times as expensive as the spring bamboo shoots. I use both the winter and spring varieties, depending on the recipe.

Storing the winter or spring bamboo shoots is the same. When ready to use, open the can, rinse the shoots in cold water, and empty into a jar or bowl of water. Do not save the liquid from the can since it has preservatives. Refrigerate, and change the water every other day. The same process is used for storing canned water chestnuts. They will last for a month that way.

### BEAN CURD OR FRESH BEAN CURD CAKE

Bean curd (fresh bean curd cake) is made from soy beans which are soaked, boiled, then drained until the curd forms. In China the residue is given to animals. Bean curd is extremely high in protein, low in calories, and very inexpensive. The Chinese call it "meat without bones." Its consistency closely resembles custard. Although it has a bland taste, it has an interesting texture and limitless possibilities. Fresh bean curd is used in soups and in stir-fried, deep-fried, and steamed dishes. Oriental food stores often keep bean curd cakes in a big container of water on a counter. There are two different types of fresh bean curd: Chinese and Japanese. The Chinese is a smaller square and more solid; the Japanese is larger, less solid, and falls apart very easily. They will both keep for one week in the refrigerator when placed in a bowl covered with water which must be changed every other day. After cutting the drained bean curd, liquid will still accumulate in a bowl or plate. Make sure to drain the liquid off before adding the bean curd to the dish you are cooking. Fresh bean curd is also available in a covered plastic container, which will last one month in the refrigerator. Do not open until you are ready to use it.

## BEAN CURD, PRESSED (LIGHT OR DARK)

Pressed bean curd cake is made the same way as the fresh. One type is dark because soy sauce has been added to it. It is pressed by having weights placed on it, which makes it more dense. It can thus be stir-fried easily because it is less fragile. Sealed in plastic wrap or aluminum foil, it will keep for several days in the refrigerator. It may also be frozen, but that will make it spongy.

## BEAN SAUCE

This spicy sauce comes in a can. It contains yellow beans, salt, flour, and vinegar. It also comes in a smoother version, *ground bean sauce*, which consists of the same ingredients, only puréed. When ready to use, open the can and empty the contents into a jar with a cover. Refrigerated, it will keep a year. It has a shelf life of a month. Bean sauce (sometimes referred to as yellow bean sauce or brown flour sauce) is used in many different dishes: as part of a marinade for barbecued or roasted meats or poultry, and in stir-fried and red-cook simmer dishes.

## BEAN SAUCE, HOT (SZECHUAN)

Hot bean sauce is a hot and spicy version of bean sauce. It consists of chili, salt, yellow beans (soy beans), sesame-seed oil, flour, sugar, and spices. This prepared sauce is very hot and is best used along with the regular bean sauce. If a recipe calls for 2 tablespoons bean sauce and you like spicy seasonings, you could add 1 tablespoon bean sauce and 1 tablespoon hot bean sauce.

## BEAN SAUCE, SWEET

Sweet bean sauce is sold in cans. It is made from wheat, flour, soy beans, salt, sugar, and water. It is the authentic dipping sauce for

Peking Duck. It is the sauce most commonly used in China, although in America hoisin sauce is usually substituted.

**BEAN SPROUTS (MUNG, SOY)**
Both mung and soy bean sprouts are low in calories; soy, however, are much higher in protein. The end of the soy bean sprouts are about 6 times as big, and much harder, and need 8 to 10 minutes of cooking time to become tender. Their taste is too strong to be eaten raw or in salads. Mung bean sprouts add an appealing texture to salads (raw) and many stir-fried dishes. When they are added to a stir-fried dish, they need only to be heated through. Further cooking will make them soggy. Once purchased, you should wash and drain them. If you plan to store them (up to 2 days), wrap them in a paper towel, place in a plastic bag, and then refrigerate. If you plan to store them for 7 to 10 days, place them in a bowl of cold water and refrigerate, making sure to change the water every day. While this method of storing in changed water keeps the sprouts white and crunchy, it also unfortunately removes most of the flavor and vitamins. *Never* use canned bean sprouts; they are crunchless and tasteless. If you ever find yourself living in an area where you are unable to purchase bean sprouts, you can easily grow your own from mung or soy beans.

**BEANS, BLACK (SALTED, FERMENTED)**
These are black beans (like those the Spanish use in soup) which are steamed, spiced, and then dried. They are sold in plastic bags and should be transferred to a covered jar and stored in the refrigerator or on the shelf. They will last indefinitely. If they do dry out, soak them in water before using. Refrigeration will retard their drying out. They are very inexpensive, and one package will last six months to two years, depending on how frequently you use them. Black beans are used in Steamed Cantonese Shrimp, Shrimp with Lobster Sauce, Beef with Black Bean Sauce, and several steamed fish dishes. They are sometimes left whole and sometimes minced,

depending on the recipe. They are salty and strong, and should be used sparingly.

## BINDER

A binder consists of water chestnut powder or cornstarch dissolved in liquid (mushroom or chicken stock, sherry, or water). It has several purposes: to thicken soups or sauces; to thicken any natural liquid released by fresh ingredients; and to create a luminous quality. Always keep an emergency binder near the stove in case a sauce does not thicken properly. Remember to restir the binder with a pair of chopsticks before adding it, because the starch separates quickly from the liquid. If you plan to keep a dish with a binder in it warm, use cornstarch instead of water chestnut powder because the latter breaks down and loses its thickening action.

## CORN, BABY

Baby corn is sold in cans. It can be eaten as is or added to stir-fried vegetable dishes for eye as well as taste appeal.

## CURRY PASTE

There are several different brands of curry paste. My favorite is Madras Genuine Sun Brand Curry Paste. It is composed of the following spices: coriander, turmeric, cumin, fennel, pepper, cloves, anise, fenugreek, cinnamon, mustard, garlic, coconut milk, lime juice, curry leaves, and gingili oil. It is available at some department stores, in the specialty food department. Once opened, curry paste will keep in the refrigerator for a year. Curry powder can be used as a substitute, but it is not as flavorful.

## FIVE-SPICE POWDER

This is a marvelous spice which contains star anise, cinnamon, fennel, Szechuan peppercorns, and cloves. It is quite strong and is used sparingly in meat and poultry dishes, never more than ½ teaspoon per pound of meat. The spice keeps for over a year if stored in the refrigerator in a tightly covered jar.

## GINGER ROOT

Fresh ginger is an irregularly shaped root which gives an unusual and appealing flavor to practically all Chinese dishes. It is quite strong, and is used sparingly. When selecting fresh ginger, look for a piece which is light brown with a smooth skin. If it looks shriveled or dry, do not buy it. Mme Chu discovered the best way to store

ginger, which keeps it fresh and saves time. Scrape off the outer skin with a vegetable peeler, rinse it under cold running water, and put it in a jar, covered with dry sherry. You can use the sherry in which the ginger is soaking whenever a recipe calls for sherry; always replenish it with fresh sherry. When stored that way, it will keep for several months, provided that the sherry is changed regularly, about every two weeks. If it is not used for more than a month, the ginger might become moldy. If you find that you are not using the ginger and you want to keep up its freshness, change the sherry. Use the sherry in another dish where sherry or wine is needed, even if the recipe is not Oriental.

## GINGKO NUTS

Although gingko nuts are available in cans, I only use the fresh ones because their taste is better; the canning process robs them of all flavor. They are at the height of their season during the early spring, but available all year. However, you risk getting a high percentage of rotten nuts in seasons other than spring. You can tell they are fresh by the white color of the shell. Cracking the shell is most easily accomplished by hitting each nut separately with a hammer or veal-pounder. If you hit too hard, you will squash the nut. After cracking open the shells, pour boiling water over the nuts and let them stand for five minutes. The inner skin around the nut itself will then be easy to remove, after which it is ready for use. Gingko nuts can be used in stuffiings or stir-fried dishes.

### HAM, SMITHFIELD

Smithfield ham closely resembles the ham used in China. It is very salty, with a strong taste. It is used in small amounts in soups and vegetable dishes. It is possible to purchase it by the slice in China-town and in a few department stores which have specialty food departments. If you buy it raw, prepare as follows:

Wash ham under cold running water with a vegetable brush.
Steam or boil in 1-inch-thick pieces for 20 minutes.
Trim fat and cut in small pieces.

Well-wrapped in aluminum foil, it will keep in the freezer for several months. It will keep in the refrigerator for several weeks. Prosciutto or Westphalian ham can be substituted for Smithfield ham in recipes calling for sliced Smithfield ham. If mincing is required, use baked or boiled ham, since the texture of prosciutto or Westphalian is too soft. In order to minimize waste, ask for a center cut of Smithfield ham when buying; that way you will get the maximum amount of meat and the minimum of fat and bone.

### HOISIN SAUCE

This is one of the most popular of the Chinese prepared sauces. It is sold in a can; once opened, it must be transferred to a tightly covered jar. Under refrigeration it will keep for a year. (You will use it up long before that.) Its shelf life is approximately a month, but I always keep it in the refrigerator when there is room. It is made from yellow beans, sugar, flour, spices, and salt.

There are endless uses for hoisin sauce. It plays perhaps its most important role in roast pork, being one of the strongest ingredients in the flavorful marinade. It is a main ingredient in many barbecue sauces. Some restaurants use it as a dip for Egg or Spring Rolls. Hoisin sauce appears in various quantities in many stir-fried dishes as a minor or major ingredient which influences the flavor of the sauce and meat, poultry, or fish used in the recipe. There is no adequate substitute for hoisin sauce. If an entirely different flavor is desired, however, there are several substitutes for the consistency: oyster sauce, bean sauce, or dark soy sauce.

## Hot Sauce

There are many different hot sauces available on the market. They are used in Szechuan dishes or whenever the cook wants to add spice to a recipe. They can also be used as part of a dipping sauce (such as Soy Sauce–Vinegar Dip, described under Cantonese Fried Chicken). Hot sauces vary in strength depending on the amount of chili pepper added. Usually 1 teaspoon suffices for 1 pound of meat, fish, or poultry. Ingredients vary with each brand of hot sauce. Generally, they include chili peppers, garlic, and sesame-seed oil (the better ones have fresh red pepper).

The following is a list, in order of my personal preference, of some hot sauces currently available.

*Koo's Hot Sauce*, available at The New Frontier, 2394 Broadway, New York City, New York 10024, is one of the best because of its fresh ingredients, such as sweet peppers, which add flavor as well as hotness.

*Chili Paste*, available at the Chinese American Trading Company, 91 Mulberry Street, New York City, New York 10013, is a sauce prepared on a small scale in Chinatown. It adds hotness rather than flavor, and should be used sparingly.

*Chili Paste with Garlic*, available at most Chinese grocery stores, is mass-produced, uses few fresh ingredients, and contributes to the hotness, not the flavor, of a dish. It should also be used sparingly.

*Preserved Horse Beans with Chili,* also available at the Chinese American Trading Company, is another form of a prepared hot sauce which has a base of "horse beans." Chili peppers are added to it, but the taste is quite different from any of the previous hot sauces mentioned. Horse beans are a legume indigenous to China.

All hot sauces will keep for a year in the refrigerator.

### LICHEE FRUIT

Incorrectly referred to as lichee nuts, this fruit can be bought canned or fresh. It is grown in California and Florida as well as China, but is not well known to Americans. That is a shame, because it is a sweet and delicious fruit. Lichees have a limited season, only one month a year (June or July). When fresh, they are sold by the pound. They have a tough reddish-brown outer shell, which must be peeled off before eating. Each person peels his own. When the shell is removed, the fruit inside looks like a large white grape with a hard brown pit in the center. The pit is not eaten. Lichee fruit makes an excellent dessert, since it is delicately flavored and refreshing.

### (TIGER) LILY BUDS (GOLDEN NEEDLES)

Originally for economic reasons, the Chinese tried to utilize a wide range of all edible growing things. The buds of the tiger lily flowers are just one example of a flower included in a recipe. Those buds shoot up straight and turn golden in the sun, hence the name "golden needles." Lily buds are sold dried in cellophane or plastic packages. They should be transferred to a tightly covered jar, and they will keep indefinitely. Before use they must be soaked in warm water for a minimum of 20 minutes, then drained. (This, as well as the water in which tree ears have been soaked, should not be used in cooking, but has a salutary effect on plants.) Each end must be checked for a hard knot (some have it and others do not), which must be cut off. They are then sliced into 2 or 3 pieces widthwise, split in two lengthwise, or knotted. Lily buds are used in soups, Mo

Sho Ro, and red-cook simmered dishes. They have a slightly pungent taste, and a chewy texture.

### MUSHROOMS, CHINESE (DRIED BLACK)

These mushrooms are succulent and have a strong flavor (as opposed to our American cultivated mushrooms). Unfortunately, they are very expensive. In Chinatown they range in price from $7.50 to $13.00 per pound. In other stores they range from $20.00 to $32.00 per pound (in these shops they are sold by the ounce). Every time ¼ cup of Chinese dried mushrooms is called for in a recipe, it amounts to approximately $.50. Mushrooms can be stored in a tightly covered jar for six months to a year.

To prepare these mushrooms, first rinse them briefly in cold running water, then soak them in warm water to cover (¼ cup mushrooms to approximately ½ cup water) for 30 to 60 minutes or until soft. You can soak them up to 4 hours ahead. The amount measured in the dry form should be a full ¼ cup, which will come out to a level ¼ cup after soaking. After soaking, squeeze each mushroom slightly with your hand to extract excess water. Then remove the tough stems (which can be added to the stock pot) and either slice, dice, shred, or mince, as recipe indicates. *Save the water in which the mushrooms were soaked.* This liquid has a marvelous flavor and can be used in many ways: in soup; as a binder; or in place of or in addition to stock (of any kind). If you have any extra, soaked and drained mushrooms will keep for 2 days in the refrigerator. Freeze the mushroom liquid if you have no immediate use for it.

### MUSHROOMS, STRAW

Straw mushrooms are available canned and dried. The canned mushrooms require no preparation.

To prepare dried straw mushrooms, rinse under cold running water, then soak in warm water to cover for 30 to 60 minutes or until soft. Remove the entire outer peeling and leave mushroom whole. Save the liquid in which the mushrooms were soaking for

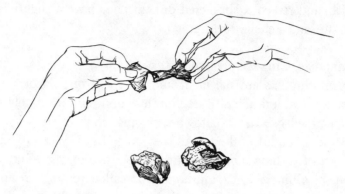

binders, soups, cooking rice, or stock for stir-frying vegetables. The dried mushrooms have a more interesting texture and flavor than the canned.

## NOODLES, CELLOPHANE

These noodles are sold in 1-ounce packages. They are made from mung bean flour and have no taste or aroma, but when soaked they have an interesting texture. Buy them dried, and then soak them for 20 minutes, until they are soft and gelatinous. Drain before using and cut in 3-inch pieces. These noodles are used in soups and stir-fried dishes. They can also be deep-fried and used as a garnish for many different dishes.

For deep-frying instructions, refer to rice noodles.

## NOODLES, EGG

Fresh Chinese egg noodles are made from cornstarch, flour, egg, and water. They are sold by the pound. They can be stored in the refrigerator up to 5 days, if wrapped in aluminum foil and a plastic bag, or in the freezer for a few months, wrapped the same way.

One substitute is dried Chinese or Japanese noodles; another substitute is Italian-style pasta (fettucine or linguine), freshly made or dried. They appear in lo mein dishes; lo mein means soft noodles, chow mein means shallow-fried noodles.

## Noodles, Rice

These are also known as rice sticks and are sold in paper bags. Store in a covered jar or canister for up to one year. They are made from rice flour. To prepare them for use in soups or stir-fried dishes, soak them in warm water for 20 minutes, then cut in 3-inch pieces and stir-fry with meat or boil in soup for a few minutes. They are excellent when deep-fried and used as a garnish for a dish such as Stir-Fried Scallops with Minced Pork. When deep-frying, do *not* soak. Heat oil to 375°. Break rice noodles apart and deep-fry for 1 or 2 seconds or until they puff up. Do not let them turn brown. Drain well on several layers of paper towels. Deep-fry early in the day and set aside.

## Nuts

The Chinese often combine nuts with fish or poultry. The contrast in texture as well as taste has great appeal. Buy almonds, peanuts, cashews, or pine nuts in the raw (blanched, with the outer shell and skin removed).

You can also use walnuts or pecans, but their preparation is more difficult and time-consuming. The procedure for both is as follows. First blanch them, remove the outer casing, then dry them. Heat about 2 cups of oil in wok or deep-fryer to 350°, then fry the nuts for a minute or two until they turn brown. Drain them on several layers of paper towels. They cannot be roasted because of their irregular shape; this shape also makes it difficult to remove the peeling. If the peeling is *not* removed, it will cause a slightly unpleasant sensation in the mouth. Keep them in the freezer in a plastic jar until you are ready to use them.

For all other nuts, the procedure is much simpler. Roast only the amount needed (I always allow a little extra for nibbling, except for cashews, which have 250 calories per ¼ cup). Toss ½ cup of nuts in 1 teaspoon of oil. Spread them out evenly on a shallow roasting pan or cookie sheet. Roast them in a preheated 325° oven for 10 to 15 minutes, shaking the pan once or twice, until the nuts are golden brown. Allow to cool. Roast nuts the same day you plan to use them.

## OIL

In China the most widely used oil is made from soy beans because it is the least expensive. The preferred oil, however, is peanut oil. Store oils in the refrigerator to prevent them from becoming rancid. Remove from refrigerator 15 minutes before using. Other possible oils are corn or safflower oil, the latter being the lowest in saturated fats. Take care not to heat the oil to smoking, since after that point it becomes saturated. Sesame-seed oil and sesame-seed oil with chili are mainly used for flavor, rarely for stir-frying. They should both be stored in the refrigerator, where they will keep for one year. Do not buy this oil unless it indicates on the label that it is 60 percent sesame-seed oil (the other 40 percent is vegetable oil). Both sherry and sesame-seed oil are used to marinate fish because they camouflage any strong odor. They serve the same purpose as lemon in western cuisine.

## OYSTER SAUCE

Oyster sauce is made from oyster extract, water, salt, and acetic acid. For long periods of storing, refrigerate it. It is one of the most commonly used sauces in Chinese cooking, used to season fish, vegetables, or meat. Hop Sing Lung is an excellent brand.

## PEKING DOILIES (MANDARIN PANCAKES)

These are made from boiling water and flour. They can be purchased in Chinatown at United Market, 84 Mulberry Street, or the Chinese American Trading Company, 91 Mulberry Street, both in New York City. They are stored in the same way as the spring roll wrappers. If well wrapped, they should not dry out, and can be prepared directly for steaming by brushing them lightly with sesame-seed oil, restacking them, and then wrapping them flatly in a damp dishtowel. They should be steamed for 5 to 7 minutes.

When you remove them from the steamer, fold each skin in quarters and arrange on a heated platter.

## PEPPER

You should ideally have 3 peppermills handy at all times: one with black, one with white, and one with Szechuan peppercorns.

*Black peppercorns* are used in the northern part of China. Naturally, freshly ground pepper is preferred. Peppercorns grown in India are a first choice.

*White peppercorns* come from the same seed as the black; they are a different color because the outermost skin has been removed. Their flavor is more subtle and delicate than the black, and they are often used in European cooking to make white sauces or clear soups. They can be purchased in most spice stores.

*Szechuan peppercorns* are grown and used in the western part of China. They are not hotter than the black peppercorns; they just have a different taste. An unusual flavor and aroma are released when they are cooked, either in a dry skillet or sautéed in oil. They can be ground in a pepper mill, pulverized in a blender, or crushed with a rolling pin between 2 layers of wax paper. They should be stored in a tightly covered jar. Refrigeration is not necessary.

## PLUM SAUCE

Plum Sauce is a prepared sauce made from plums, chili, ginger, and other spices. It comes in a metal can; once opened, it should be transferred to a covered jar and stored in the refrigerator. It is often used as one of the ingredients in a dip for Spring Rolls, Roast Duck, or Shrimp Toast; in those cases you should remove the chunks of ginger. It is also one of the ingredients in the marinade for Roast Pork.

## RICE, GLUTINOUS

In Chinatown this is known as sweet rice; it is also called sticky rice. It is a short-grain rice that is used in Pearl Balls, Sizzling

Shrimp with Rice Patties, desserts, and poultry stuffings. In a few stores it is sold by the pound, but generally it is sold in 5-pound packages with the words "Sweet Rice" written on the bag.

### RICE FLOUR (RICE POWDER)
Rice flour is made from ground raw rice and is sold in packages. Store it in a canister or covered jar on the shelf for one year. It is used to thicken, as in the case of Almond Cream. It can also be used to coat deep-fried foods.

### SHERRY
Sherry is the American substitute for Chinese Rice Wine. Any good dry sherry will do. Never use cooking sherry that is sold in supermarkets. Bear in mind that if you don't want to drink it, you wouldn't want to eat it either.

### SHRIMP, DRIED
Dried shrimp are sold in ½-pound quantities in cellophane packages. Stored in a covered jar, they will keep on the shelf for one year. They must be rinsed, then soaked in sherry or water for at least an hour in order to reconstitute them. They have an extremely strong flavor, concentrated by the drying process. They are used in very small quantities; one teaspoon per recipe is usually all that is necessary.

### SOY SAUCE
*Dark soy sauce* (black) is used most of the time. It is not really darker in color, as the name implies, but thicker in texture. During the fermentation process, more solids are added, among them molasses, which contributes to its denser consistency.

*Light soy sauce* (thin) is used primarily in salads and for marinating. The Japanese soy sauce can be substituted for Chinese light soy sauce. They both have a shelf life of more than a year.

## Szechuan Preserved Kohlrabi (Szechuan Preserved Vegetable)

Kohlrabi is a member of the cabbage family, a bulb with roots. It is sold in cans; in general all canned food has a shelf life of 6 months. Once opened, rinse the kohlrabi, and store in a covered jar in the refrigerator, for up to three months. It is used in stir-fried dishes to add an unusual, slightly spicy flavor, such as Dry Sautéed String Beans.

## Tea

This is the major beverage in China. Buy only tea that is packaged in a tin. Boxed tea leaves may be spoiled as a result of damp weather during the voyage from China to the United States. The brewing of tea can be done three ways:

1. Rinse a porcelain tea pot with boiling water. Add 1 teaspoon of tea leaves for every cup. Fill pot with the measured boiling water. Cover and let steep for 5 minutes.

2. If you are brewing tea for more people than the capacity of your tea pot, proceed as follows. Assume you want to make tea for 25 people in a pot that has a capacity of 2 to 6 cups. Measure 25 teaspoons of tea leaves in the pot. Cover tea leaves with freshly drawn cold tap water which has been brought to a boil, by about 3 inches. Cover the pot and let it steep for 5 minutes. This liquid can now be called "tea concentrate." While the tea is steeping, bring to boil a large kettle of water. Have all the cups ready. Add a little "tea concentrate" to each cup and then fill the rest of the cup with boiling water. Tea cups are carried in from the kitchen when tea is made this way. Another possibility, if you prefer to serve the tea in front of your guests, would be to use several porcelain or silver tea pots. Use

one for the concentrate and the remaining two for the boiling water.

3. In China, guests consider it an honor if tea is brewed in front of them, which assures them that it is fresh. Each tea cup has its own lid and the tea is brewed in each individual cup. One teaspoon of tea leaves is placed in each cup. Boiling water is poured into each cup just to cover the leaves. The cover is then placed on the tea cup, and the tea is allowed to steep for 5 minutes. After the first cup has been finished, the tea cup is again filled with boiling water, and the tea leaves are allowed to steep another 5 minutes. The second cup of tea, made from the once-used tea leaves, is considered the finest.

## THICKENING AGENTS

*Cornstarch* is a thickening agent that is most commonly used in American-Chinese cooking. In China the amount of corn grown is not sufficient to make by-products of starch or oil. They use tapioca starch or water chestnut powder.

*Water chestnut powder* is made by grinding water chestnuts into a powder. (If you find hard lumps after opening the box, empty entire contents into a blender and blend on a high speed until it returns to a fine powder.) Water chestnut powder has many advantages over cornstarch: it is much lower in calories and carbohydrates; it creates a luminous quality in sauces; and it gives deep-fried dishes an incredible crunchiness that far surpasses any other type of flour or starch. There are two drawbacks: it is expensive— $.95 to $1.35 for a ½-pound box; and, when used as a thickening agent, it breaks down if the dish is kept warm. If this ever happens, just drain the liquid into a pot and rethicken the sauce with a new binder (sherry and water chestnut powder mixed to a smooth paste, ½ tablespoon of water chestnut powder to 1 tablespoon of sherry for every ½ cup of sauce). Heat the sauce over a high flame while stirring with chopsticks in one hand, adding binder with the other hand. Pour rethickened sauce over vegetables or meat.

### Tomato Paste
Use any brand of canned tomato paste. Leftover tomato paste can be frozen up to 6 months.

### Tomato Sauce
Fresh tomato sauce can be made in large quantities and frozen in small containers. One possible recipe is as follows. Sauté chopped onions and crushed garlic in oil. Add canned tomatoes passed through a food mill, or fresh tomatoes, finely chopped, salt and pepper. Simmer, partially covered, for 2 to 3 hours or until thick. Pass through the fine blade of a food mill. If you have to use canned tomato sauce, choose a domestic brand such as Heinz or Del Monte. Do not use prepared Italian tomato sauce, since the herbs will conflict with Chinese seasonings.

### Tree Ears ( Cloud Ears )
Tree ears are fungi that have been dried. They are sold in small cellophane packages. They contain calcium, are inexpensive, and will keep indefinitely if stored in a tightly covered jar. When a recipe calls for 1 or 2 teaspoons, always measure them from the dried state. Then soak them in hot water for 20 minutes or longer. After soaking they must be rinsed thoroughly, as they can be very sandy. Dry with a paper towel or dish cloth. Tree ears are rubbery in consistency, have very little taste, but absorb the flavor of other ingredients used in the same dish. My students have reported to me that the water in which the tree ears are soaked is excellent for plants, and has even revived sick ones. They are used in many stir-fried, braised, and red-cook simmered dishes.

### Vinegar
Red wine vinegar is a good substitute for Chinese rice vinegar; for a sweet and sour sauce I prefer it. It is more interesting to have

several vinegars on hand, though, just as you probably have more than one type for western cooking (wine, tarragon, cider, or white). For a more complete collection, buy Chinese red vinegar (made from rice and water; its color is brown); Japanese rice vinegar (white); and Chenkong (black rice) vinegar. The latter is used in dips, in small quantities to flavor a sweet and sour sauce, or in salads along with sesame-seed oil.

Using a good vinegar can greatly alter the final taste of whatever dish you are preparing. I have had the same bottle of red wine vinegar for many years. If a recipe calls for 4 tablespoons of wine vinegar, I replenish with the same amount of wine. Don't open a good bottle of red wine for this purpose. Use an inexpensive domestic red wine (Savant, California Burgundy, is about two dollars a bottle and quite drinkable). If you have a bottle of dry red wine opened, that too will suffice. If you use a lot of red wine vinegar, then you should have two bottles of vinegar going in order for the fermentation process to take place. If you use this procedure for red wine vinegar, you will notice an incredible difference in your salad dressing.

## WATER CHESTNUTS

The canned variety of water chestnuts is acceptable; they are crunchy, but have very little flavor and even less nutritive value. The advantages of the canned over the fresh are that they are sold in many markets, cost about one-fourth the price, are ready to use once the can is opened (fresh ones have to be peeled), and can be refrigerated for a month (refer to storing instructions for canned bamboo shoots). Canned water chestnuts and bamboo shoots should be rinsed when removed from the can, and the liquid should be discarded. The liquid contains chemical preservatives in it, and thus should not be added to stock or used to cook rice.

The main advantage of the fresh water chestnuts is that they are incredibly sweet and delicious. Many of my students have likened them to raw coconut or apple. They must feel as hard as a potato when pinched and they will keep refrigerated for two weeks.

Peel them, rinse no more than twenty-four hours ahead, and keep them well covered. In addition to the many recipes that call for water chestnuts, ranging from fillings to stir-fried dishes and soups, they also make an excellent snack or hors d'oeuvre.

## WINE YEAST

Wine yeast is sold in plastic packages. It comes in the shape of a round ball about the size of a Ping-Pong ball. It is used to make Wine Rice (refer to Shrimp with Wine Rice). When stored in a covered jar in the refrigerator, it will last for several months.

## WRAPPERS, EGG ROLL

These are sold in 2-pound packages in Chinatown in New York City, and in smaller quantities in the Chinese and Japanese markets north of Chinatown. When you arrive home with them, *immediately* take them out of their wrapper and rewrap in packages of about 10, in 2 layers of aluminum foil. They will keep for 5 to 7 days if they were absolutely fresh when you bought them. Since it is impossible to guarantee their freshness, freeze them after a 3-day period if you have not used them up. For freezing, you wrap them the same way as for storing in the refrigerator, adding a plastic bag to give extra protection. The wrappers will dry out and crack if not properly wrapped. They will freeze well for three to four months. The skins are made from flour and water, and only a trace of egg.

## WRAPPERS, SHANGHAI SPRING ROLL

These wrappers are sold in two forms: square and round. They are much thinner and more fragile. When fried, they are crisper than egg roll wrappers. They are stored the same way and can be used as wrappers (or doilies) for Peking Duck and Mo Sho Ro. While assembling the spring rolls, you must wrap them in a damp towel to keep them from drying out and cracking. My favorite brand is Doll, sold at United Market, 84 Mulberry Street; the Chinese American Trading Company, 91 Mulberry Street; and the New Frontier, 2394

Broadway, all in New York City. To separate these wrappers, start from the middle. If you have 10 wrappers, do *not* begin by pulling off the outermost wrapper first; instead, separate them first into two sections of 5, then 3, then 2, then 1. This method will minimize breaking and cracking. If the wrappers are too dry when you take them out of the package, put them inside a wet towel for 15 to 20 minutes. If you are substituting these wrappers for Peking Doilies, which have to be steamed, follow the instructions on page 66.

### Wrappers, Wonton

These are sold in packages of a hundred, and are very inexpensive. They are stored the same way as egg roll wrappers. The difference between them is not in the ingredients but in size and shape: the wonton wrappers are one-quarter as large, and thinner.

# STAPLES

Keep the following 2 lists of Chinese staples in your cupboard or refrigerator at all times. One is a modified list of absolute essentials; the other is a complete list. With these ingredients on hand, you will be able to prepare Chinese dishes at any time, anywhere in the world.

It is a good idea to write or telephone first, before sending your order. At the writing of this book the addresses are correct, but there is always the possibility that they may move or change their shipping policy.

*New Jersey*
> The Chinese Kitchen
> P.O. Box 218
> Stirling, New Jersey 07980
> Tel: (201) 464-2859
> *(Best current mail order source)*

*New York*

The New Frontier Trading Corporation
2394 Broadway
New York, New York 10024
Tel: (212) 799-9338

Yuet Hing Market
23 Pell Street
New York, New York 10013
Tel: (212) WO 2-7436

*Illinois*

Star Market
3349 North Clark Street
Chicago, Illinois 60699
Tel: (312) GR 2-0599

*Texas*

Oriental Import-Export Company
2009 Plok Street
Houston, Texas 77002
Tel: (713) 233-5621
(Will not fill mail orders under twenty dollars)

*California*

Shing Chong & Company
800 Grand Avenue
San Francisco, California 94108
Tel: (415) YU 2-0949

Kwong On Lung Company
680 North Spring Street
Los Angeles, California 90012
Tel: (213) 628-1069

ESSENTIAL STAPLES LIST
1 can bamboo shoots (whole)
1 can water chestnuts (whole)
1 package Szechuan peppercorns

1 small package chili peppers (dried)
1 bottle dark soy sauce
1 bottle light soy sauce
1 package tree ears
¼-pound package Chinese mushrooms
Raw nuts: cashews, almonds, or peanuts
Water chestnut powder
Hoisin sauce
Bean sauce (whole or ground)
Plum sauce
Oyster sauce
Fermented black beans
Hot sauce
1 package five-spice powder
Ginger root
Glutinous rice (sweet rice)
Lily buds (golden needles)
Sesame-seed oil
Tea

## COMPLETE STAPLES LIST
1 can bamboo shoots (whole, winter)
1 can bamboo shoots (whole, spring)
1 can water chestnuts (whole)
1 can baby corn
Szechuan preserved kohlrabi
1 package tree ears
1 package lily buds (golden needles)
¼ pound Chinese mushrooms (dried)
¼ pound straw mushrooms (dried)
1 can straw mushrooms
Gingko nuts
Raw nuts: cashews, almonds, peanuts, or pine nuts
Dried shrimp
1 can abalone

Smithfield ham
Ginger root (fresh)
Dried egg noodles
Wine yeast
Water chestnut powder
Cornstarch
Rice flour
Glutinous (sweet) rice
Fermented black beans
Bean sauce (whole or ground)
Red bean paste
Hoisin sauce
Oyster sauce
Plum sauce
Hot sauce
Sesame-seed paste
Sesame-seed oil
Sesame-seed oil with chili
1 small package dried chili peppers
Horse beans with chili
Curry paste
Japanese bean paste (soy jam)
Chinese red vinegar
Chenkong vinegar
Tea

# VEGETABLES

**INTRODUCTION**

Choose fresh vegetables with great care. The one general rule to follow is to choose fresh and young vegetables, since they are more sweet and tender. The specific characteristics to look for in each vegetable will be discussed in the following pages. I discuss what qualities to look for, and what to avoid; how to store a vegetable, and for how long; the types of cut appropriate to each vegetable, and for how many minutes each of these cuts should be stir-fried; and what substitutions are possible when a particular vegetable called for in a recipe is unavailable.

There are three general qualities that you should always bear in mind when selecting vegetables: color, crunch, and freshness. To give an example, the choice of asparagus with stir-fried shrimp is quite deliberate, for the following reasons: first, because of the color contrast (the white/pink shrimp with the bright green asparagus); second, because of the texture (the velvety texture of the shrimp contrasts well with the crunchiness of the barely cooked asparagus); third, the freshness (fresh asparagus, when in season, tastes sweet and delicious). A fresh and barely cooked vegetable also is very high in vitamins.

In order for vegetables to retain maximum nutritive value and flavor, they should be picked a few minutes before they are cooked. Unless you have your own garden, however, that suggestion is impractical. Although it is possible to store some vegetables up to 7 days, it is always advisable to buy them the same day or the day before you plan to use them. Try to find a fresh produce market where you can choose your own, individually; avoid buying vegetables that have been bagged in plastic, since they have been stored for a longer period of time, and have already lost a large percentage of vitamins as well as flavor. Plan your menu around vegetables in season, making substitutions wherever necessary in the recipes, but always thinking through the three qualifications of color, crunch, and freshness when substituting a vegetable for one called for in a recipe.

The washing, draining, and drying of vegetables several hours or even days before use is often recommended, since it is an efficient use of time. If it is not convenient for you, then store them in a sealed plastic container until you are ready to prepare them for stir-frying or steaming.

*Blanching Vegetables*: Many vegetables can be cut and immediately stir-fried in a small amount of oil. Others must be blanched or steamed first because they are harder. Some examples of the latter are broccoli, carrots, and string beans.

Over a high flame, bring at least 2 quarts of water to a rolling boil and add 1 pound of prepared vegetables (slant-cut broccoli, for example). When the water returns to a boil, start timing 1 minute. When the 1 minute has elapsed, immediately remove the vegetables from the water with a wire strainer and place them in a bowl of ice water. That will stop the cooking and hold the color. When the vegetables have cooled (about 1 minute), drain them in a colander. They should be dried well before stir-frying. The blanching process can be done 24 hours ahead, if the vegetables are refrigerated and well covered. Since the blanching of vegetables removes 50 percent of their vitamins, it is important to boil down the liquid in which they were blanched until you are left with the amount needed for making rice. Or you can reduce it to half its quantity and freeze it until you are making chicken stock or any other soup base. If you prefer steaming to blanching, you should save the water in the bottom of the steamer.

Since many vegetables are peeled before cooking, after washing them you can save the peelings and boil them down for 15 minutes in water. This vegetable water can be used instead of tap water in making soup or rice; it can also be used instead of chicken stock in sauces.

When very hard vegetables such as broccoli, carrots, and kohlrabi are shredded, for either salad or lo mein, it is not necessary to blanch them. The shredding produces a slice thin enough to have the heat penetrate thoroughly in a short period of time. Blanching is only necessary when you slant or roll-oblique-cut hard vegetables.

*Washing Vegetables*: There is a very effective way of washing all vegetables which removes both sand or dirt and preservatives: soak them in cold water to which white vinegar has been added (1 tablespoon of vinegar for every 2 quarts of water). Then rinse the vegetables under cold water, using a vegetable brush.

*Stir-Frying Vegetables*: If you are stir-frying several kinds of vegetables, the general rule to follow is to add the hardest one first, and the softest last. The time recommended is only approximate. There are so many factors involved that it is impossible to be absolutely precise. These variables include the intensity of the flame you are using; the hardness of the raw vegetables; how thick or thin the slices of the vegetables are; and the amount of vegetables you are stir-frying at one time. Try to cut the vegetables in a uniform size for even cooking. To find out if the vegetables are done, taste a piece; it should be resistant but not raw, and never soggy. When approaching done-ness, the vegetable pieces will begin to look transparent. Eventually you will be able to tell just by looking at them. Once you have mastered the art of stir-frying vegetables, which retains the greatest amount of vitamins and flavor, you won't want to use any other method of preparation. Stir-fried vegetables go well with any type of cuisine.

*General Stir-Fried Vegetable Recipe*: Cut 1 pound of vegetables.

Place wok over high flame for 30 seconds.

Add 1½ tablespoons of oil and heat for 20 to 30 seconds or until oil is hot but not smoking.

Add 1, 2, or 3 of the following—2 chopped scallions, 1 teaspoon minced ginger root, and 1 clove minced garlic—and stir-fry for 15 seconds. The garlic can be crushed instead of minced if you remember to remove it before serving the vegetables. The ginger root can also be sliced instead of minced if removed before serving. Add 1 pound of cut vegetables to wok and stir-fry until they are coated with oil.

Add 1 teaspoon salt, ½ teaspoon sugar, and ¼ teaspoon freshly ground pepper. Mix well and continue to stir-fry for the required amount of time.

Just before the vegetables are done, add a binder, made of 1 teaspoon water chestnut powder dissolved in 1 tablespoon sherry. The binder can also contain 1 tablespoon hoisin sauce and 1 teaspoon hot sauce, or any of the canned prepared sauces that are described in the Ingredients, such as oyster sauce or bean sauce.

Some vegetables contain more water than others, such as those in the Swiss chard and cabbage family. Others contain less water, such as carrots and broccoli. For this reason it is advisable to have ¼ cup stock near the stove, ready to add to the vegetables after they have been tossed and cooked with oil, before adding the binder. That will prevent them from scorching.

This list deals with the vegetables which occur most frequently in Chinese cooking, telling you not only how to select and prepare them, but also how long to stir-fry them, which depends on the softness or hardness of the vegetable. Those which require the longest amount of cooking time include broccoli, carrots, cauliflower, and parsnips, which should be blanched first, unless they have been shredded; they should be added to the wok first. The group of vegetables which require a medium amount of cooking time include bok choy, asparagus, zucchini, snow peas, onions, and peppers; they should be added next. The remaining vegetables, which require the least amount of cooking time (1 to 2 minutes), include bean sprouts, green leaves of bok choy, spinach, and watercress, and should be added last.

### ASPARAGUS

*How to Select*: Asparagus are in season March through June. They should be green all the way to the end, crisp, and thin. Look at the root end for moisture; if it looks dried or moldy, do not buy it. Beads of moisture should form when the stalk is broken.

*How to Store*: Soak asparagus in a vinegar-water solution to remove sand; wash, drain, and dry. You can store asparagus in a plastic bag or covered container for 4 days.

*Equivalents*: Slant-cut 10 ounces is the equivalent of 4 cups, once the stems have been removed.

*How to Cut and Cook*: Slant-cut pieces of 1½ inches (leave the tips whole) require 3 minutes' stir-frying.

*Substitutions*: Snow peas, string beans, or broccoli. The latter two must be blanched first.

### Bean Sprouts (Mung)

*How to Select*: Bean sprouts are in season all year round, because they can be grown indoors as well as outdoors from the dried mung beans, professionally or at home. They should be white and crisp.

*How to Store*: Rinse them in a colander, then drain and dry well. Put them in a plastic bag for no longer than 24 hours. If you wish to keep them for 2 to 3 days, wrap them first in a paper towel or dishcloth, and then in a plastic bag. If you wish to keep them up to 10 days, put them in a bowl of water to cover and refrigerate. Change the water every day. That will keep them white and crunchy, but they soon will lose both vitamins and flavor.

*Equivalents*: 4 ounces in weight is the equivalent of 1 full cup.

*How to Cut and Cook*: Leave bean sprouts whole; stir-fry them for 1 minute.

*Substitutions*: If bean sprouts are unavailable, grow your own.

### Bok Choy (Swiss Chard Family)

*How to Select*: Bok choy is available all year round, reaching its height in spring and summer. Look for white stalks with deep green leaves. If yellow flowers are present, they too are edible. Young bok choy can also be found at certain times. It is sweeter and

more tender; the stalks are thinner and the leaves are a paler green.

*How to Store*: You can store bok choy in a covered plastic container for 4 days. It is sweeter and crunchier if used sooner.

*Equivalents*: 8 ounces is the equivalent of 8 cups.

*How to Cut and Cook*: Remove ½ inch of the tough part of the stem, reserving for stock pot. Discard any brown or yellow leaves. Separate stalks, scrub with a vegetable brush, and soak in vinegar-water solution to remove sand; wash, drain, and dry. Straight- or slant-cut in 1- to 1½-inch pieces, separating the stems from the leafy parts. Stems requires 3 minutes of stir-frying. Leafy parts require 1 to 2 minutes of stir-frying. Shredded bok choy requires 1 to 2 minutes of stir-frying.

*Substitutions*: Young bok choy, hung choy, mustard cabbage, and celery.

## BROCCOLI, AMERICAN

*How to Select*: Broccoli is available all year round, reaching its height in the fall. It should be deep green. The florets and the stems should be crisp. Look at the bottom of the stalk for moisture. It should not show any trace of moldiness or dryness. Shake the whole bunch to see that the florets do not fall off.

*How to Store*: Rinse in cold running water, then drain and dry. You can store broccoli in a plastic bag or covered container for up to 4 days.

*Equivalents*: Slant-cut or shredded, 3 ounces is the equivalent of 1 cup.

*How to Cut and Cook*: To prepare for cooking, cut off 2 inches from the bottom part of stem, remove leaves, then peel 2 inches of remaining part of stems with a vegetable peeler. Slant-cut stems in 1½-inch pieces, blanch them for about 1 minute or until they soften slightly, then stir-fry them for 3 to 4 minutes. Break the florets into small sections, and blanch for about 1 minute before stir-frying for 2 to 3 minutes. You can shred the middle part of the stem, which does not require blanching; it can be stir-fried directly for 2 to 3 minutes.

*Substitutions*: Italian broccoli, Chinese broccoli, snow peas, asparagus, string beans or zucchini.

**BROCCOLI, CHINESE**

*How to Select*: Chinese broccoli is available all year round. It should be young and green, with stems no larger than 1 inch in diameter.

*How to Store*: Same as American broccoli.

*Equivalents*: Same as American broccoli.

*How to Cut and Cook*: Peel 1½ inches off the bottom part of the stem. Remove only the tough outer leaves; then separate the remaining tender leafy parts from the stems. The entire stalk can

be slant-cut. Blanch the stem (not necessary for the leafy parts) and stir-fry for 2 to 3 minutes. It requires less stir-frying time than American broccoli since it is more tender.

*Substitutions*: American broccoli, Italian broccoli, snow peas, asparagus, string beans, zucchini.

**CABBAGE (MUSTARD)**

Follow instructions for Shantung cabbage (below), but increase the stir-frying time by 1 minute.

**CABBAGE (SHANTUNG)**

*How to Select*: Shantung cabbage is available all year round. It should have light green leaves with white stems, which should be crisp and solid. There should be no trace of brown. Sometimes there are brown specks which look like sand embedded in the stems. It is all right to eat this.

*How to Store*: In a sealed plastic container, you can store cabbage for 4 days. It is sweeter when used sooner.

*Equivalents*: Straight-cut or shredded, 8 ounces is the equivalent of 8 cups.

*How to Cut and Cook*: Cut off ½ inch of the stems, as for celery. Remove tough outer leaves, reserving them for the stock pot. Separate stalks; soak them in a vinegar-water solution to remove sand; wash, drain, and dry. Straight-cut or slant-cut the cabbage in 1- to 1½-inch pieces, separating the stems from the leafy parts. The stems require 3 minutes' stir-frying and the leafy parts only 1 to 2 minutes. If shredding, allow less time.

*Substitutions*: American celery, cabbage, celery, bok choy, Shanghai cabbage, young bok choy, hung choy, and mustard cabbage (also called mustard greens).

## CARROTS

*How to Select*: Carrots are in season all year round. Buy them with the greens attached, not already cut and packaged in plastic. (Bagged carrots have been stored longer and have fewer vitamins.) Fresh carrots should be slender and deep orange, with small cores; when peeled, they should be moist. Taste them raw; they should be sweet.

*How to Store*: Remove greens. You can store carrots in a plastic bag or covered container for 1 week.

*Equivalents*: Slant-cut, 16 ounces is the equivalent of 4 cups. Shredded, 2 ounces is the equivalent of 1 cup.

*How to Cut and Cook*: Remove ends with a cleaver. To retain maximum amount of vitamins, do *not* peel; instead, scrub with a vegetable brush, drain, and dry. You can straight-cut or slant-cut them in 1½-inch pieces, blanch them for 1 to 2 minutes until they soften slightly, and then stir-fry them for 3 to 4 minutes. You can roll-oblique-cut them, blanch them for an additional minute, and then stir-fry them for 3 to 4 minutes. You can shred them, in which case blanching is not necessary, and then stir-fry for 2 minutes.

*Substitution*: Parsnips.

## CAULIFLOWER

*How to Select*: Cauliflower is available all year round, reaching its height in the fall. It should be white with no brown spots. Look at the bottom; it should have no traces of mold.

*How to Store*: You can store cauliflower in a plastic bag or covered container for 4 days.

*Equivalents*: 4 ounces of separated florets is the equivalent of 1 cup.

*How to Cut and Cook*: Rinse under cold running water, then soak the cauliflower in a vinegar-water solution to remove sand; drain and dry. Break the whole cauliflower into small florets and stems; then straight-cut the stems. Blanch for 1 to 2 minutes, then stir-fry 2 minutes.

*Substitution*: American broccoli.


## CELERY

*How to Select*: Celery is available all year round. Look for green stems and leaves. It should be very crisp.

*How to Store*: You can store celery in a covered plastic container for 1 week.

*Equivalents*: For slant-cut celery, 3 ounces is the equivalent of 1 cup.

*How to Cut and Cook*: Remove 1 inch of tough stem and leaves, reserving them for the stock pot. Separate stalks, then wash under cold running water with a vegetable brush. Soak in vinegar-water solution, drain, and dry. Slant-cut stalks in 1½-inch pieces require 2 to 3 minutes' stir-frying; shredded stalks require 1 to 2 minutes.


## CHINESE PARSLEY (CORIANDER, CILANTRO)

*How to Select*: Fresh coriander is available all year round. Look for crisp green bunches, with no traces of yellow. It has a strong flavor and is used sparingly.

*How to Store*: Soak desired quantity in vinegar-water solution; drain and dry well in a salad spinner or with paper towels. You can store coriander in a plastic bag or covered container for one week.

*How to Cut and Cook*: Trim the stems, leaving 2 to 3 inches. Leave whole when using as a base or garnish; chop or mince when using over fish or in soup.

*Substitutions*: American parsley or flat Italian parsley.

## KOHLRABI

*How to Select*: Kohlrabi is available all year round, reaching its height in June and July. Select small to medium-size bulbs with fresh tips. They should be pale green with no trace of brown.

*How to Store*: You can store kohlrabi in a plastic bag or covered container for 4 to 7 days.

*Equivalents*: Shredded or sliced, 3 ounces is the equivalent of 1 cup.

*How to Cut and Cook*: Trim stems and leaves; rinse under cold running water and peel. Sliced, it requires 3 to 4 minutes' stir-frying; shredded, it requires 2 to 3 minutes.

## MUSHROOMS (AMERICAN, FRESH; REFER TO INGREDIENTS FOR CHINESE DRIED MUSHROOMS)

*How to Select*: Mushrooms are available all year round. Look for white caps, which are completely closed underneath. There should be no trace of brown.

*How to Store*: You can store mushrooms in a plastic bag or covered container for 2 days.

*Equivalents*: Sliced, 3 ounces is the equivalent of 1 cup.

*How to Cut and Cook*: Rinse under cold running water, drain, and dry well. Trim the stem ends ½ inch. Leave whole if they are small or slice them vertically ¼ inch thick. In either case they require 1½ to 2 minutes' stir-frying.

# ONION FAMILY:

## CHIVES (CHINESE)

*How to Select*: Chives are at the height of their season during the spring and summer and in some places are available all year round. Look for very green, crisp blades. They are about 12 inches long.

*How to Store*: You can store Chinese chives in a plastic bag or covered container for 7 days.

*Equivalents*: The equivalent of 1 bunch is 4 cups, cut in 3-inch pieces.

*How to Cut and Cook*: Remove the stem ends, cut in 3-inch pieces, or chop as you would scallions. Stir-fry them for 1 minute.

## LEEKS

*How to Select*: Leeks are available all year round. They should be white at the root end and deep green on the stalk. They should be firm and crisp, with no traces of wilting, yellow or brown. The size is not as important as the color, but young ones are always a preference.

*How to Store*: Remove root end with a knife. Split down the center, cutting the length of the entire leek. Wash under cold running water to remove all sand. Soak in vinegar-water solution for 5 minutes; remove, drain, and dry. You can store leeks in a covered plastic container for 7 to 10 days.

*Equivalents*: Shredded, the white part of one average leek yields ½ cup. For shredded leeks, 3 ounces are the equivalent of 1 cup. Cut in 1-inch pieces, 1 ounce of leeks is the equivalent of 1 cup.

*How to Cut and Cook*: The green part of the leek is used for soups or braising because it is tough. The white part, straight-cut, requires 4 minutes' stir-frying; shredded, it requires 3 minutes' stir-frying; minced, it requires 2 minutes.

*Substitutions*: Half the amount of scallions; or, in some cases, half the amount of shallots.

## SCALLIONS

*How to Select*: Scallions are available all year round. They should be white at the root end and deep green over the stalk. They should be crisp, with no trace of wilting, yellow or brown. Choose larger ones for shredding, smaller ones for chopping or mincing.

*How to Store*: Wash under cold running water; cut off hairy root with a knife. Remove outermost skin from white root end. Wash, drain, and dry. You can store scallions in a covered plastic container for 7 to 10 days.

*Equivalents*: 2 ounces chopped scallions is the equivalent of 1 cup, or 7 to 10 scallions, depending on their size.

*How to Cut and Cook*: Both the white and green parts of the scallion can be stir-fried. Chopped, slant-cut, shredded, or minced, they require 1 minute of stir-frying.

*Substitutions*: Leeks, white part only, double the amount; shallots, half the amount; in some cases, yellow or pearl onions, same amount.

## SHALLOTS

*How to Select*: Shallots are available all year round. Feel for hard, firm ones with even brown skin. Do not buy if roots are growing out of the end.

*How to Store*: You can store shallots in a plastic bag or covered container up to 2 months.

*Equivalents*: ½ cup of peeled whole shallots is the equivalent of 2 ounces or 10 to 14 shallots, depending on their size.

*How to Cut and Cook*: Cut off root end and peel off outermost layer of dry, brownish skin. Wash under cold running water, drain, and dry. Whole shallots require 3 minutes' stir-frying; chopped require 2 minutes' stir-frying; minced require 1 minute's stir-frying.

*Substitutions*: Same as scallions.

## YELLOW ONIONS, AMERICAN

*How to Select*: Yellow onions are available all year round, reaching their height between February and June. Look and feel for hard firm ones with pale brown skin. Do not purchase if roots are growing out of the end or if there are soft spots.

*How to Store*: You can store onions in a plastic bag or covered container for 1 month.

*Equivalents*: 3 ounces is the equivalent of 1 cup sliced onions.

*How to Cut and Cook*: Cut off root and stem end and peel off first layer of skin. Wash under cold running water, drain, and dry. Sliced and chopped onions require 3 minutes' stir-frying; minced require 2 minutes.

*Substitutions*: Same as scallions.

## PARSNIPS

*How to Select*: Parsnips are available all year round, reaching their height in the fall and winter. They should be cream-colored, firm, and crisp. They should taste sweet when eaten raw.

*How to Store*: You can store parsnips in a sealed plastic container or in the vegetable compartment of the refrigerator for 7 days.

*Equivalents*: 4 ounces of slant-cut parsnips is the equivalent of 1 cup.

*How to Cut and Cook*: Scrub with a vegetable brush under cold running water; drain, dry, and peel. Slant-cut or diced parsnips require 3 to 4 minutes' stir-frying; roll-oblique-cut require 4 minutes.

*Substitution*: Carrots.

## PEAS, AMERICAN

*How to Select*: Peas are available all year round, reaching the height of their season in the spring. Look for green crisp pods containing small peas. They should taste sweet when eaten raw. Only the peas are eaten, since the pod of the American variety is too tough; the pods can be saved for the stock pot.

*How to Store*: You can store peas in a plastic bag or covered container for 3 to 4 days.

*Equivalents*: Weighed with the pod, 4 ounces is the equivalent of 1 ounce shelled peas, or 1 cup.

*How to Cut and Cook*: Shell peas and leave whole; they require 2 minutes' stir-frying.

*Substitutions*: Snow peas, zucchini, broccoli, green pepper.

## PEPPER FAMILY:

### GREEN OR RED BELL PEPPERS (SWEET)

*How to Select*: Peppers are in season all year round, but the red ones are not always available in certain parts of the country. Red pepper comes from the same plant as the green; the difference is

that the red has been allowed to ripen. Red pepper is therefore sweeter; it is always my first choice. Deep crimson peppers are the sweetest. Look for smooth skin with no spots and dark, even color.

*How to Store*: You can store red pepper in the vegetable compartment for 3 to 4 days. You can store green pepper for one week or slightly longer.

*Equivalents*: 3 ounces of triangle-cut pepper is the equivalent of 1 cup.

*How to Cut and Cook*: Scrub with a vegetable brush under cold running water. Cut pepper in half, and remove seeds and membrane. Diced or triangle-cut pepper requires 2 minutes' stir-frying; shredded requires 1 minute.

*Substitution*: Italian peppers (called banana peppers in the South).

### HOT PEPPERS (FRESH—GREEN OR RED)

*How to Select*: Hot peppers are in season all year round but sometimes disappear for several weeks. The larger the pepper, the less spicy it is; the smaller and more pointed its tip, the more spicy it will be.

*How to Store*: Same as sweet peppers.

*Equivalents*: Same as sweet peppers.

*How to Cut and Cook*: Remove seeds and membrane with rubber gloves. Try to avoid touching any part of your face, especially your eyes, after touching the seeds, because they will cause an intense burning sensation. Stir-frying time is the same as for sweet peppers.

*Substitution*: Dried chili peppers, which are available at all Oriental and most Spanish grocery stores.

### SING QUA

*How to Select*: Sing qua is available in all seasons except winter. It reaches its height in late spring. It has a very tough outer skin which should be dark green. It should be young and firm, no larger than 1½ inches in diameter. Do not purchase if it is soft, or has brown spots or mold.

*How to Store*: Same as hairy melon (see page 94).

*Equivalents*: Same as hairy melon.

*How to Cut and Cook*: Remove both ends with cleaver, then remove all of tough green skin with a vegetable peeler. Stir-frying time is the same as for hairy melon. Sing qua is best when roll-oblique-cut.

*Substitutions*: Hairy melon, yellow squash, or zucchini.

## Snow Peas (Pea Pods)

*How to Select*: Snow peas are available all year round. They are cheapest during the summer months. They should be pale green with no trace of yellow or brown; crisp, young, and small pods are best. The whole pod is edible. The peas inside should be tiny and underdeveloped. If they are too large, the pod will be tough. This vegetable is delicious eaten raw as well as slightly cooked.

*How to Store*: Rinse under cold running water; drain and dry. You can store snow peas in a plastic bag or a covered container for 4 to 7 days.

*Equivalents*: 8 ounces slant-cut snow peas is the equivalent of 3 cups.

*How to Cut and Cook*: String each pod by removing the fiber —which runs along the side to which the peas are attached—from both ends. You can leave snow peas whole or slant-cut them in 2 to 3 pieces, depending on their size; that way they require 2 minutes' stir-frying. Shredded, they require 1 to 1½ minutes.

*Substitutions*: Same as American peas.

## Spinach

*How to Select*: Spinach is available all year round. Look for dark green leaves, with no trace of brown or yellow. Buy loose leaves; do not buy it in a plastic bag.

*How to Store*: Trim 1 to 1½ inches off stem. Fill the sink with vinegar-water solution; put spinach in the solution and let soak for 5 minutes. Lift out of sink and place in a colander to drain. Let water and sand drain out of sink. Repeat the process until there is no trace of sand. Dry well on towels or with a salad spin-dryer. You can store spinach in a plastic bag or covered container for 2 days.

*Equivalents*: 5 ounces of whole spinach leaves is the equivalent of 4 cups.

*How to Cut and Cook*: Leave spinach whole or cut in large pieces. If stir-frying alone, do not add stock, since the spinach leaves have enough moisture. Spinach requires 2 minutes' stir-frying.

*Substitutions*: Watercress or the green leaves of bok choy.

## SQUASH FAMILY:

### HAIRY MELON

*How to Select*: Hairy melon is available all year round, reaching its height in the summer. Choose young, small ones, no larger than 2 inches in diameter, with even green coloring, firm and without flaws. There should be no trace of brown marks, mold, or soft spots.

*How to Store*: You can store hairy melon in a covered plastic container for 4 days.

*Equivalents*: 16 ounces, straight- or slant-cut, is the equivalent of 4 cups. 16 ounces, roll-oblique-cut, is the equivalent of 5 cups.

*How to Cut and Cook*: Remove fuzzy skin with vegetable peeler. Wash under cold running water, drain, and dry. Straight- or slant-cut hairy melon requires 2 minutes' stir-frying; roll-oblique-cut requires 3 minutes; shredded requires 1 to 1½ minutes.

*Substitutions*: Zucchini, sing qua, yellow squash.

### YELLOW SQUASH (SUMMER SQUASH)

Same as zucchini, except for the color which should be yellow, and the size which is slightly larger, but no more than 1½ inches in diameter.

### WINTER MELON

*How to Select*: Winter melon (also in the squash family) is available all year round. It should have a green skin, white inner meat, and many seeds. Buy 1- or 2-pound pieces at a time. It has a very bland taste. It can be used for soups as well as in stir-fried dishes.

*How to Store*: You can store winter melon in a plastic bag or covered container for 6 days. A whole melon will last for 2 months if it is kept in a cool dark place.

*Equivalents*: Same as hairy melon after rind has been removed.

*How to Cut and Cook*: Remove rind and seeds. Rinse under cold running water; wash, drain, and dry. Sliced, the stir-frying time is the same as for hairy melon.

*Substitutions*: Zucchini or hairy melon.

## ZUCCHINI

*How to Select*: Zucchini is available all year round, reaching its height during the spring and summer. Choose small zucchini, no larger than ½ inch in diameter. They should be young, firm, and deep green, without flaws. Beads of moisture should form when cut. Do not purchase if it is yellow, has brown marks or is shriveled.

*How to Store*: You can store zucchini in a plastic bag or covered container for 4 days.

*Equivalents*: 16 ounces, straight- or slant-cut, is the equivalent of 4 cups. 16 ounces, roll-oblique-cut, is the equivalent of 5 cups.

*How to Cut and Cook*: Wash under cold running water; scrub lightly with a vegetable brush. Do not scrub too hard or you will remove the outermost green layer. Drain and dry. Stir-frying time is the same as for hairy melon.

*Substitutions*: Hairy melon, yellow squash, or sing qua.

## WATERCRESS

*How to Select*: Watercress is available all year round. Look for crisp, deep green leaves, with no yellow or brown on them.

*How to Store*: You can store watercress in a plastic bag or covered container for 4 days.

*Equivalents*: 1 bunch, with 1½ inches of the stems removed, is the equivalent of 4 ounces or 2 cups.

*How to Cut and Cook*: Remove 1½ inches of the stems. Leave whole for stir-frying or cut for soup in 2-inch pieces before washing to save time. Soak in vinegar-water solution; drain and dry with paper towels or in a salad spin-dryer. Watercress requires 2 minutes' stir-frying.

*Substitutions*: Spinach, or green leaves of bok choy.

### STRING BEANS, AMERICAN

*How to Select*: String beans are available all year round. They should be green and, ideally, no more than ¼ inch in diameter. That is only possible, however, if you live in France or grow your own. Beads of moisture should form when the bean is broken in two. If they are dry, do not buy them.

*How to Store*: Wash the beans under cold running water, drain, and dry. You can store beans in a plastic bag or covered container for up to 4 days.

*Equivalents*: 3 ounces is the equivalent of 1 cup of 1½ inch pieces.

*How to Cut and Cook*: Remove the hard end (attached to the plant) and cut into 1- or 2-inch pieces. Blanch first for 2 minutes, then stir-fry for 1 to 2 minutes.

*Substitutions*: Chinese long beans or wax beans.

# BASIC RECIPES

# ΛPPETIZERS

---

## SHANGHAI SPRING ROLLS
YIELD: 10 SPRING ROLLS

In China, Shanghai Spring Rolls are given as presents on the New Year. In the lunar calendar, it usually comes at the end of January or February, which is the beginning of spring. When fried, Shanghai Spring Rolls resemble golden bars, which symbolize wealth for the New Year.

Once you have made your own Shanghai Spring Rolls, you will be spoiled. The wrappers are crunchy and greaseless, the filling distinguished. Egg rolls are an American variation, made with a thicker skin.

*Filling*

½ pound raw pork shreds
  (should equal 1 cup)
¼ cup Chinese mushrooms
½ cup bamboo shoots
2 cups fresh chives
1 tablespoon sherry
2 tablespoons dark soy sauce
½ teaspoon sugar
1 cup bok choy, shredded
  (white part only)

1 cup mung bean sprouts
2 tablespoons peanut oil
1 tablespoon oyster sauce

**Wrappers**

10 sheets Shanghai Spring
  Roll wrappers
1 egg, beaten

Oil for shallow frying

## PREPARATION

Rinse mushrooms, cover with warm water, and soak for 30 to 60 minutes, or until soft. Save stock for another use.

Slightly freeze pork, and shred.

Shred bamboo shoots, mushrooms, and bok choy. Spread on paper towels to dry well.

Cut chives in 3-inch lengths.

Rinse bean sprouts. Drain and dry well.

Mix together in a bowl, the sherry, soy sauce, and sugar.

## COOKING PROCEDURE

Place wok over high flame for 30 seconds.

Add 2 tablespoons oil and heat for 30 seconds or until oil is very hot but not smoking.

Add pork shreds and stir-fry 3 minutes, or until pork turns white.

Add mushrooms and bamboo shoots. Mix well.

Add sherry, soy sauce, and sugar. Mix well. Continue stir-frying over high flame for 3 minutes.

Add bok choy and chives. Toss for 30 seconds.

Add bean sprouts, and mix well for 15 seconds.

Dish into a strainer set over a bowl to catch drippings.

Allow to cool thoroughly. The filling must be dry and cool; otherwise, it will break the wrappers.

Wrap in Shanghai Spring Roll wrappers as illustrated on page 51, using about 2 tablespoons filling for each roll; use beaten egg to seal them. That should make about 10 rolls.

Using a 10- to 12-inch skillet or wok, pour oil to a depth of 1½ inches. Heat to 350°.

Shallow-fry Shanghai Spring Rolls over a medium-high flame until golden brown for 3 to 4 minutes, turning once after 2 minutes.

Drain well on several layers of paper towels.

Slant-cut in half, and serve immediately with Plum Sauce Dip and Mustard Sauce.

TIMING: The preparation and the stir-frying of the filling can be done early in the day or the day before.

Frying the Shanghai Spring Rolls should ideally be done just before serving. If that is inconvenient, they can be fried and drained a few hours ahead of time and then rewarmed as follows.

Preheat oven to 400° and place Shanghai Spring Rolls on a rack resting on a shallow roasting pan or a cookie sheet. Place Shanghai Spring Rolls in the oven and heat for 8 to 10 minutes. Drain again on paper towels and serve. Although reheating them is possible, it is not recommended, since the wrappers will have a rewarmed flavor.

SUBSTITUTIONS: If Shanghai Spring Roll wrappers are not available, you can substitute egg roll wrappers. The latter are never used in China; they are only made in America. Shanghai Spring Roll wrappers are made from flour and boiling water. The egg roll wrappers, which are American, are made from flour, water, and a trace of egg. They are thicker and therefore must be fried twice in order for them to achieve any degree of crispness. The first frying should take 2 to 3 minutes at 350°. When they turn a light golden brown, remove them from the oil and drain on several layers of paper towels. Allow them to cool for at least 30 minutes. Then refry them in oil heated to 375° until they are golden brown, which will take about another 1 or 2 minutes. Drain them again on paper towels; then cut and serve.

If you are using pork, try to purchase Boston butt. If it is not available, use one pork chop, cut about 1½ inches thick. It will yield about ½ pound, or one cup, of pork. The pork tenderloin is too dry and lacks flavor. Shoulder of veal works very well as a substitute when pork is not a preference.

For the chives, you can substitute 1 full cup of shredded leeks (white part only), or 1 full cup of shredded scallions (both white and green parts). Regular American yellow onions give Shanghai Spring Rolls a common flavor, and I therefore do not recommend them. If using leeks, add them at the same time you add the mushrooms and the bamboo shoots. Scallions are added when the recipe indicates to add the chives.

For the bok choy, you can substitute Shantung cabbage, but use stems only (the leafy parts wilt too quickly). Chinese celery cabbage, an American invention, is a possibility, but not a first choice. It is available in many supermarkets.

If bean sprouts are not available, grow your own! Never use canned bean sprouts—they are tasteless and crunchless.

TIPS: The hardest part of making Shanghai Spring Rolls is to resist eating the filling. One solution is to make the filling and serve it as a hot entrée for lunch or dinner. In that case, do *not* empty the filling into a strainer set over a bowl, because you want to use all the flavorful juices to make a little sauce. Mix 2 teaspoons of water chestnut powder with 1 tablespoon of the mushroom stock and add it to the vegetable-pork mixture along with the bean sprouts. Stir until it has thickened. Place in a heated serving dish and serve immediately. When the filling is served as an entrée, it must be eaten immediately. If kept warm, the vegetables will become soggy.

For handling and storing instructions of wrappers, refer to Ingredients, page 73.

When the filling has cooled, you can use the drippings in the bowl beneath the strainer to stir into rice or to enrich the sauce of stir-fried vegetable dishes. If you have no immediate use for it, it will keep in the freezer for 6 months.

If the Shanghai Spring Roll filling is breaking the wrappers, it is either too hot or too wet. The latter problem is remedied by spreading the filling on paper towels to dry.

## PLUM SAUCE DIP

YIELD: 1 QUART

*This is a variation of Mme Chu's plum sauce, which she adapted to American taste. The Chinese do not use such a heavy or sweet dip with their Shanghai Spring Rolls; they prefer a lighter, soy sauce–based dip such as the one given for Cantonese Fried Chicken, except that they would omit the hot sauce and the mixed pepper relish.*

*You cannot use the Chinese Plum Sauce alone as a dip because it is too strong.*

| | |
|---|---|
| 10 ounces Chinese plum sauce | 4 tablespoons hoisin sauce |
| 10 ounces peach preserves | 2 cloves garlic, minced |
| 10 ounces apricot preserves | 1 tablespoon prepared mustard sauce |
| 20 ounces applesauce | |

### PREPARATION

Mix all above ingredients and use as dip for egg rolls.

N O T E S : Take cubes of ginger out of the plum sauce and save for another use, such as in roast pork marinade.

Sauce will keep for 4 months if refrigerated.

Use sauce for Spring Rolls, spareribs, and any type of roasting meat or poultry, Chinese or American. This sauce is smoother when mixed in a blender for 30 seconds on low speed.

If you wish to keep the plum sauce dip for more than 4 months, omit the applesauce when mixing all ingredients and add it when you are ready to serve the sauce.

## MUSTARD SAUCE

½ cup dry mustard (Col-
   man's or Chinese)
Boiling water

Dry sherry, Noilly Prat vermouth, or dry white wine
¼ cup pommery mustard

### PREPARATION

Put the dry mustard in a bowl.

Add boiling water while stirring with a wooden spoon until it reaches the consistency of thick pancake batter. Add mustard.

Add sherry, vermouth, or wine a tablespoon at a time, until the mustard reaches the desired consistency. The thicker it is, the hotter it will be.

Mustard will keep well for several months, covered in the refrigerator.

**N O T E :** It is the boiling water which releases the flavor of the mustard.

## BARBECUED SPARERIBS

YIELD: 4 TO 6 APPETIZER SERVINGS

1 rack spareribs, 2½ to 3
   pounds
1½ times the marinade for

Roast Pork (see page 208)
3 tablespoons honey

## PREPARATION

Leave rack or racks of spareribs whole, or cut in half once if they are too long for the oven. Trim away any excess fat.

On the thicker end of the rack, make shallow cuts between each rib, going up about 4 inches, but not going all the way through; ½ inch will allow the marinade to penetrate. Marinate the ribs in the same marinade used for Roast Pork, increasing the quantity of the marinade according to the weight of the ribs, for 6 to 8 hours. Turn ribs over in marinade and baste once at midpoint of marination. Keep ribs refrigerated.

Dribble honey over ribs with chopsticks.

## COOKING PROCEDURE

Preheat oven to 350°.

Pierce each half of the sparerib rack with 3 hooks on the less meaty end, and hang hooks over a rung of the oven rack.

Place 4 to 6 cups of water in a pan below to catch the drippings and to keep the ribs moist.

Roast at 350° for 50 minutes and then at 450° for 10 minutes.

Remove ribs from the oven and allow to cool for 5 to 10 minutes.

Cut the ribs apart with a cleaver into single-rib sections and leave whole or cut in 2-inch segments, Chinese style.

Save the pan drippings for stock. (Refer to Tips on Roast Pork.)

Serve plain or with Plum Sauce Dip and Mustard Sauce.

If you are preparing the ribs ahead of time, roast at 450° for 5 minutes. When ready to serve, place ribs on a rack resting on a shallow roasting pan. Preheat oven to 450° and roast for 5 to 7 minutes.

## SHRIMP TOAST

YIELD: 24 PIECES (4 TO 6 SERVINGS IF SERVED ALONE;
8 SERVINGS IF SERVED WITH OTHER APPETIZERS)

*The Shrimp Toast served in restaurants is often so bland it tastes as if a scared shrimp swam quickly through the oil. After you have tried this recipe, you will become a Shrimp Toast devotee.*

½ pound shrimp
4 water chestnuts
1 egg
2 scallions
1 teaspoon ginger root, minced
1 teaspoon salt
½ tablespoon dark soy sauce

½ teaspoon sugar
1 tablespoon water chestnut powder
1 teaspoon sherry
6 slices stale bread
2 to 3 cups peanut oil for deep-frying

### PREPARATION

Shell, devein, wash, drain, dry, and mince shrimp.

Mince water chestnuts, scallions, and ginger.

Dissolve the water chestnut powder in the sherry and soy sauce.

Mix the shrimp together with the water chestnuts, egg, scallions, ginger, salt, soy sauce, sugar, water chestnut powder, and sherry. Refrigerate for at least 1 hour.

Trim the crust off each slice of bread.

Cut each slice into 4 triangles.

Spread about 1 tablespoon shrimp mixture over each triangle.

### COOKING PROCEDURE

Heat oil in wok to 375°.

Holding the triangle in your fingers, gently lower the bread into the oil with the shrimp side down.

After 1 minute, turn over and fry another minute, or until toast has turned golden brown.

Lift Shrimp Toast out of the oil with a wire strainer and let drain well on paper towels.

While Shrimp Toast is draining, blot the tops with paper towel.

Serve immediately.

TIMING: The shrimp mixture can be prepared early in the day.

The bread can be cut up early in the day.

The shrimp mixture can be spread on the bread, placed on a cookie sheet in a single layer, covered with wax paper, and refrigerated up to 2 hours before deep frying. Once the Shrimp Toast is deep-fried and drained well, it must be served immediately.

SUBSTITUTIONS: For the shrimp you can substitute filet of flounder for low-cholesterol or kosher diets.

Use only 6 or 7 ounces flounder to allow for the weight of the shrimp shells.

TIPS: If the bread is too fresh, lay it out on a cookie sheet for an hour or so and then turn it over for another hour.

The bread should be stale so it does not absorb as much oil.

Mince the shrimp with two cleavers.

Do not worry about turning the Shrimp Toast upside down when you lower it into the hot oil. It will not slip off because the mixture of egg and water chestnut powder is quite sticky, and will have solidified under refrigeration.

## PEARL BALLS

YIELD: 4 TO 6 SERVINGS IF SERVED ALONE; 8 TO 12 SERVINGS
IF SERVED WITH OTHER APPETIZERS

1 cup sweet rice
2 scallions (both white and green parts)
1 teaspoon ginger root, minced
1 teaspoon sugar
1 pound ground pork

1 egg, beaten slightly
2½ tablespoons dark soy sauce
2 tablespoons water chestnut powder
2 tablespoons sherry

### PREPARATION

Soak sweet rice in warm water for ½ hour. Drain well in a strainer.

Chop scallions.

Mince ginger root.

Into the pork, mix with chopsticks the egg, soy sauce, scallions, ginger, and sugar.

Dissolve water chestnut powder into sherry and add pork. Mix well.

Wet hands and form into walnut-size balls.

Spread drained rice on a cookie sheet.

Roll pork balls, one at a time, over the rice until each is well coated.

Arrange pork balls in a steamer with ½-inch spaces between each one to allow for expansion of rice.

### COOKING PROCEDURE

Steam for 30 minutes.

Remove Pearl Balls from steamer and arrange on a flat, heated serving dish.

Serve with Soy Sauce–Vinegar Dip, described under Cantonese Fried Chicken, page 145.

TIMING : Pearl Balls can be prepared a day in advance. When preparing ahead, steam for 20 minutes, refrigerate, then steam for 15 minutes just before serving.

Pearl Balls can be kept warm in the steamer for 5 to 10 minutes, with the flame turned off, or on a hot tray. They can be served as an appetizer or as part of a dinner. They are always a favorite with children. Try serving them at the next birthday party instead of hot dogs or hamburgers.

SUBSTITUTIONS : For the ground pork you can substitute ground shoulder of veal.

Minced water chestnuts and Chinese mushrooms (¼ cup each) can be added to the mixture before the balls are formed.

TIPS : Sweet rice is also known as glutinous or sticky rice. (Refer to Ingredients, for information on buying and storing.) If necessary, substitute long-grain rice. The glutinous rice is a significant part of this recipe since, when steamed, it has an opalescent quality which gives the dish its name. If you substitute the long-grain rice, the shape of the ball will be the same but you will lose the pearl-like luster.

Excessive mixing will make the Pearl Balls too dense.

Since Pearl Balls are steamed, they are excellent served in conjunction with other appetizers—most other Chinese appetizers are fried.

If the rice falls off the balls, they have been overcooked.

To allay your fears of undercooking the pork-filled balls, cut into a ball and you will see that the pork has turned white after 30 minutes' steaming.

Leftover Pearl Balls can be steamed the next day for 5 minutes, or deep-fried in oil (preheated to 375°) until brown. Drain well on paper towels.

## SZECHUAN PEPPERCORN CHICKEN

*I have adapted this recipe from Mme Chu's Chinese Cooking School Cookbook. I felt it necessary to include here as well, since it is a recipe that should be in any Chinese cook's repertoire.*

*It is unusual, easy to prepare, and easy to coordinate in a multi-course Chinese dinner. It is also delicious.*

2 whole chicken breasts (12 to 14 ounces each)
2 cups leek tops or scallion greens, cut in 3-inch lengths
2 slices ginger root
4 cups Shantung cabbage, shredded

**Sauce A**

2 tablespoons peanut oil
⅓ cup chopped scallion
1 teaspoon ginger root, minced

½ teaspoon Szechuan peppercorns (*measured after being ground in pepper mill*)
1 *fresh hot chili pepper, chopped*

**Sauce B**

2 *tablespoons dark soy sauce*
1 *tablespoon hoisin sauce*
2 *teaspoons honey*
2 *cloves garlic, minced*
1 *to 2 teaspoons hot sauce*

## PREPARATION

Rinse chicken breasts in water.

Bring 2 quarts of water to a boil in a saucepan with a tight-fitting cover.

Add leek tops and 2 slices of ginger. Bring water back to a boil.

Add whole chicken breasts, cover, and cook over high flame for 15 minutes.

Turn off heat and allow chicken breasts to cool in water for 45 minutes, leaving the cover askew.

Lift chicken breasts out of saucepan and let them drain in a strainer set over a bowl for 20 to 30 minutes.

Refrigerate chicken breasts, well covered, until cold.

Remove skin and bone, then pull chicken meat apart into coarse shreds with fingers.

Refrigerate until ready to use.

Shred Shantung cabbage and refrigerate.

In a small saucepan, mix together ingredients for Sauce A.

In a small bowl, mix together ingredients for Sauce B.

### COOKING PROCEDURE

In a large bowl mix together the chilled cabbage and chicken.

Heat Sauce A until it bubbles, then simmer for 1 minute.

Add Sauce B to Sauce A.

Pour sauces over chicken and cabbage just before serving. Mix well and serve immediately.

TIMING : All the preparations, except the shredding of the cabbage, can be done a day ahead. Make sure the chicken is well wrapped to avoid drying out. The cabbage can be shredded early in the day and then refrigerated. If there is another person in the kitchen, have him or her mix the chicken and cabbage together with Sauces A and B while you are making other preparations. Szechuan Peppercorn Chicken makes an excellent lunch entrée, especially in the summer. I also frequently serve it as an appetizer, either alone or accompanied by Shrimp Toast (which is fried) and Pearl Balls (which are steamed). As most Chinese appetizers are fried, Szechuan Peppercorn Chicken is a welcome relief. The combination of three appetizers using three different cooking techniques creates an interesting contrast of textures, and minimizes last-minute stir-frying hysteria.

Szechuan Peppercorn Chicken is an example of cold mixing. Think of it as a salad, with Sauces A and B as the dressing.

It can also be served as part of a dinner, for it is easy to stir-fry another dish while someone else is mixing the chicken. The sauce should not be mixed in with the chicken and the cabbage until just before serving, lest it become soggy.

SUBSTITUTIONS: Lettuce (iceberg or romaine) can be used instead of the cabbage.

Two dried peppers, seeds removed, can be substituted for the single fresh hot chili pepper. To remove seeds from the dried pepper, cut off the end and shake out the seeds. Mince peppers with cleaver.

TIPS: If possible, every kitchen should be stocked with at least 3 pepper mills: one for black, one for white, and one for Szechuan peppercorns. It takes too much time to change the different peppercorns in the same mill. If there is no extra pepper mill handy, crush the Szechuan peppercorns between 2 sheets of wax paper with a rolling pin.

## PAN-FRIED STUFFED PEPPERS

YIELD: 4 SERVINGS IF SERVED ALONE; 8 SERVINGS IF SERVED
WITH OTHER APPETIZERS; 2 TO 3 SERVINGS IF ENTRÉE

**Stuffing**
½ cup raw shrimp
¼ pound filet of flounder
1 scallion, chopped
1 tablespoon water chestnut
  powder
1 tablespoon sherry
¼ cup ground pork
1 teaspoon salt

½ teaspoon sugar
1 egg white
1 tablespoon light soy sauce

16 hot chili peppers or 8 to 10
  sweet Italian peppers or a
  combination of the 2
  varieties
1 egg, beaten

*Sauce*
1½ *tablespoons fermented*
   *black beans*
2 *teaspoons garlic, minced*
2 *teaspoons ginger root,*
   *minced*
1 *cup chicken stock*
1 *tablespoon light soy sauce*

2 *tablespoons oyster sauce*
½ *teaspoon sugar*

*Binder*
1 *tablespoon water chestnut*
   *powder*
1 *tablespoon sherry*

3 tablespoons peanut oil

## PREPARATION

Mince shrimp and flounder together.

Chop scallion.

Dissolve the water chestnut powder in 1 tablespoon sherry.

Mix all the stuffing ingredients (shrimp, flounder, scallion, water chestnut powder, sherry, pork, salt, sugar, egg white, and soy sauce) together in a bowl.

With a serrated knife, cut a thin slice off the top of each pepper.

Carefully remove the seeds and membrane with a grapefruit knife.

Rinse peppers with water and shake out any remaining seeds.

Fill each pepper with the stuffing, pushing it down with a chopstick.

Brush the top of each pepper with beaten egg.

Mince black beans, garlic, and ginger.

Mix together the stock, soy sauce, oyster sauce, and sugar.

Mix binder ingredients and set aside.

## COOKING PROCEDURE

Place wok over high flame for 30 seconds.

Add 3 tablespoons of oil and heat for 20 seconds or until oil is hot but not smoking.

Add peppers. Cook over medium-low flame for 10 to 12 minutes, turning once at midpoint, until they are well browned.

Remove peppers to a heated serving dish.

Do not wash wok. Add black beans, garlic, and ginger mixture; let sizzle for a few seconds.

Add stock mixture; bring to a boil and cook for one minute.

Restir binder and add with one hand, stirring with the other until sauce thickens.

Pour sauce over peppers and serve immediately.

TIMING : All the preparations can be done early in the day.

You can stuff the peppers several hours ahead, brush them with egg, and refrigerate.

Italian peppers take longer to brown, since their skin is thicker; you will need about 15 minutes.

The peppers can be kept warm, uncovered, on a low setting of a hot tray or in a preheated 200° oven for 5 to 8 minutes.

SUBSTITUTIONS : For the flounder you can substitute any type of white, fresh fish filet.

For the shrimp you can substitute crabmeat or lobster.

TIPS : You can judge how hot a pepper is *not* by its color, but by its size and shape: the smaller and more pointed the pepper is, the hotter it is.

Use a flat serving piece for the peppers, making sure they lie in a single layer.

The technique for frying peppers is sautéing. Check the peppers after 3 or 4 minutes to make sure they are not burning; adjust the flame accordingly.

Use two different woks or sauté pans. Do not crowd the peppers, since that would produce steam. If you do not have two pans, then fry the first batch and keep warm on an *uncovered* heated serving platter in a preheated 200° oven while you fry the second batch. This recipe can be served as a hot appetizer or as part of a multicourse Chinese dinner.

## CANTONESE STUFFED BEAN CURD

YIELD: 2 TO 3 SERVINGS IF SERVED ALONE; 6 SERVINGS
IF SERVED WITH OTHER APPETIZERS

6 pieces fresh bean curd
  (small, Chinese)
1 scallion, shredded

**Stuffing**
*4 dried shrimp*
*2 tablespoons sherry*
*3 ounces filet of flounder*
*6 ounces ground pork*
*1 scallion, chopped*
*1½ tablespoons light soy
  sauce*

*2 teaspoons water chestnut
  powder*

**Sauce**
*⅔ cup chicken stock*
*2 tablespoons oyster sauce*

**Binder**
*2 teaspoons water chestnut
  powder*
*1 tablespoon sherry*

3 tablespoons peanut oil

## PREPARATION

Rinse dried shrimp in water, then soak in sherry for an hour.

Place a terrycloth towel on a flat surface. Place bean curd squares on the towel with a chopping block directly on top of them.

If you do not have a heavy chopping block, put a platter on top of a light one. The weight should be sufficient to squeeze out most of the excess water from the bean curd, which takes 2 to 3 hours. It helps to change towels after an hour.

Mince dried shrimp and flounder.

Mix together the ingredients of the stuffing, including the sherry in which the shrimp was soaking.

Measure out chicken stock and stir oyster sauce into it.

Make a binder with 2 teaspoons of water chestnut powder and 1 tablespoon of sherry.

Cut each piece of bean curd diagonally in half, yielding a total of 12 pieces.

With a grapefruit knife, make as big a pocket in each piece as possible, taking care not to break through the delicate exterior.
Stuff each piece with the fish and pork mixture.

Put the pieces of bean curd on a cookie sheet which is covered with a layer of paper towels, and refrigerate. The recipe can be prepared ahead up to this point.

Remove bean curd from the refrigerator ½ hour before cooking.

## COOKING PROCEDURE
Place wok over high flame for 30 seconds.

Add 3 tablespoons oil and heat for about 30 seconds, until oil is very hot but not smoking.

Add 6 bean curd halves and fry over medium-high flame for 10 minutes, turning pieces onto their bottom, top, and stuffed side in order to brown all sides evenly.

Remove bean curd from wok and let drain on several layers of paper towels for 2 minutes.

Repeat with remaining 6 pieces.

Keep first batch of fried bean curd uncovered in a preheated oven at 250°.

When the second batch of 6 is finished, put all 12 pieces on a heated serving platter.

Pour off any excess oil in wok.

Add stock and oyster sauce mixture to wok and let boil for one minute.

Restir binder and add to mixture, boiling until the sauce thickens (about 1 minute).

Add shredded scallion, pour sauce over bean curd, and serve immediately.

TIMING: The sautéed bean curd can be kept warm for 10 minutes in a preheated 200° oven *uncovered*. Do not add the sauce until right before serving.

The stuffing can be made a day ahead.

The bean curd can be stuffed, placed on a cookie sheet with a layer of paper towels covering the top and the bottom, and refrigerated early in the day.

SUBSTITUTIONS: For the pork you can substitute shoulder or breast of veal.

For the flounder you can substitute any type of white fresh fish filet.

TIPS: Cantonese Stuffed Bean Curd can be served as an appetizer, as a first course, or as part of a multicourse dinner.

Choose a flat serving piece on which to place the bean curd in a single layer.

Refer to Ingredients, page 55 for an explanation of the composition of bean curd and how to store it.

Bean curd is low in cost but very high in nutritive value, which makes this dish economical as well as delicious.

## MINCED SQUAB WITH LETTUCE LEAVES
YIELD: 4 TO 6 SERVINGS IF SERVED ALONE; 6 TO 8 SERVINGS
IF SERVED WITH OTHER APPETIZERS

¼ cup Chinese mushrooms
1 fresh-killed squab (1½
   pounds or 6 ounces boneless chicken meat)
4 ounces chicken liver
1 squab liver
6 ounces ground pork

*Marinade*
*1 tablespoon light soy sauce*
*1 egg yolk*
*2 teaspoons water chestnut*
   *powder*
*½ teaspoon sugar*

⅓ cup shallots, minced
¼ cup water chestnuts,
   minced
¼ cup bamboo shoots,
   minced

*Seasoning Sauce*
*1 tablespoon dark soy sauce*
*1 tablespoon mushroom stock*
*1 tablespoon sherry*
*1 teaspoon water chestnut*
   *powder*
*¼ teaspoon black pepper*
*1 teaspoon sesame-seed oil*

1 head Boston lettuce
3 tablespoons peanut oil

### PREPARATION

Rinse mushrooms, cover with warm water, and soak for 30 to 60 minutes, or until soft. Save the stock.

Skin and bone squab, and cut all meat from breasts and thighs. Dice it small. Reserve legs, wings, giblets and skin for a soup stock. For boning procedure, refer to Cooking Technques, page 45.

Dice livers.

Mix together squab, livers, ground pork, light soy sauce, egg yolk, water chestnut powder and sugar. Marinate for 30 minutes.

Mince shallots, mushrooms, water chestnuts, and bamboo shoots.

Combine all ingredients for seasoning sauce in a bowl.

Separate the lettuce leaves. Wash and dry well. Arrange them on a platter.

## COOKING PROCEDURE

Place wok over high flame for 30 seconds.

Add 1 tablespoon peanut oil and heat for 20 seconds or until oil is hot but not smoking.

Add shallots and cook for 2 minutes over low flame.

Turn the flame to high. Then add mushrooms and cook for 1 minute more.

Add bamboo shoots and water chestnuts and cook 1 minute more.

Empty contents of wok into a heated serving dish.

Heat remaining 2 tablespoons peanut oil in wok over high flame. Restir, then add squab, pork, and liver mixture. Stir-fry for about 3 minutes.

Add seasoning sauce and cook another minute.

Again add shallots, mushrooms, water chestnuts, and bamboo shoots, and cook until well mixed. Serve immediately.

Have each guest take a lettuce leaf and place on it a rounded spoonful of the squab mixture. The lettuce leaf is folded over and eaten with the fingers.

TIMING: All the preparations can be done early in the day. Once stir-fried, this dish must be served immediately.

SUBSTITUTIONS: For the squab you can substitute any type of boneless raw poultry such as Rock Cornish hen, quail, pheasant, duck, or turkey. Use white meat, dark meat, or a combination of the two.

# DEEP-FRIED WONTONS
YIELD: 6 TO 8 SERVINGS IF SERVED ALONE; 10 TO 12
SERVINGS IF SERVED WITH OTHER APPETIZERS

### Wonton Filling

½ pound ground pork
¼ pound shrimp (weighed
   with shells)
¼ pound fresh spinach
¼ cup water chestnuts,
   minced
½ teaspoon ginger root,
   minced fine

½ teaspoon sugar
2 tablespoons sherry
3 tablespoons dark soy sauce

30 wonton wrappers
2 to 3 cups peanut oil (for
   deep-frying)

### PREPARATION

Place ground pork in a bowl.

Shell, devein, wash, drain, dry, and mince shrimp.

Wash and dry spinach. Remove all but 2 inches of the stems, and blanch for 30 seconds. Remove from water and let drain in a colander set over a bowl. Let cool 10 minutes.

Chop spinach.

Mince ginger fine.

Mince water chestnuts.

Add to pork the shrimp, spinach, water chestnuts, ginger, sugar, sherry, and soy sauce. Mix well in one direction with chopsticks.

Make the wontons, as follows:

1. Put one teaspoon of filling in the lower center of a square wonton-wrapper.
2. Moisten the edge farthest from you with water.
3. Fold the unmoistened edge over the filling, away from you, then seal the two sides together.

4. Make a ¼-inch crease upward, on the side away from you, turning the edge up.

5. With thumb and index finger of both hands, take the corners nearest you and pull them together. The corners away from you should be pointing straight up; the

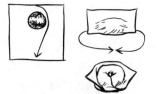

corners nearest you should lie flat. Moisten one of the near corners and place it on top of the other corner, sealing them together. The result should resemble a nun's hat.

Cover with a damp cloth until ready to fry.

Heat 2 to 3 cups oil in a wok or deep fryer until it reaches 350° and fry wontons, 8 at a time, for 2 to 3 minutes, turning once at midpoint. They should be light brown.

Remove the wontons with a wire strainer and let drain on several layers of paper towels. Let cool in a single layer for at least 30 minutes.

Heat oil to 350° and refry wontons, no more than 8 at a time, for one more minute, turning once, until they are golden brown.

Remove wontons from oil with a wire strainer and drain on several layers of paper towels.

Serve immediately with mustard.

 NOTES : A second frying is necessary in order to obtain crispy wontons. The first frying can be done 4 to 5 hours ahead of time.

It is also possible to boil wontons first and then fry them. To do so, bring 4 quarts of water to a boil in a heavy saucepan. Drop in the wontons, either by hand or with a wire strainer. Bring the water to a boil again, and add 1 cup cold water.

Bring to a boil and cook over a medium-high flame for 2 minutes.

Remove wontons with a wire strainer and set aside in a large dish. (The boiling procedure can be done up to a day ahead of the frying.)

To fry the boiled wontons, heat oil 2 inches deep in a wok to 375°. Fry them until they are golden brown, turning them once after 1 minute. Do not fry more than 6 at a time. Remove from oil with a wire strainer and drain well on several layers of paper towels. Serve immediately with mustard.

# SOUPS

---

### CHINESE CHICKEN STOCK

YIELD: ABOUT 4 CUPS

1 four-pound chicken or
   chicken parts or bones
Water to cover chicken
4 to 5 cups leeks

4 slices ginger root
1 tablespoon salt
6 whole black peppercorns

## PREPARATION

Rinse chicken.

Cut leeks in 2-inch pieces. Use both white and green parts.

Slice ginger.

## COOKING PROCEDURE

Place chicken in a large stock-pot and add enough water to cover chicken by at least 4 inches.

Bring to a boil over a high flame.

Remove scum as it rises to the top with a fine mesh strainer. Process takes 5 to 10 minutes.

Add leeks, ginger, salt, and peppercorns.

Cover loosely and turn flame to low.

Simmer 4 to 5 hours, stirring with a wooden spoon every ½ hour or so. Add more water if needed.

Taste for seasoning and add more salt if needed.

If the taste is too bland, remove cover, and simmer until the reduced stock has a strong chicken flavor.

Strain stock through a colander and then through a fine sieve.

**NOTES:** To prevent the chicken stock from becoming cloudy, do not let it boil. Pour stock into a container and refrigerate until the fat solidifies so you can skim it off. If you are freezing the stock, leave the layer of fat on top, which will act as a preservative. The stock will keep for 5 to 7 days in the refrigerator or for 6 months in the freezer. Store it in one large container or smaller containers.

The same procedure can be used for veal, pork, or beef stock.

## HOME-STYLE EGG DROP SOUP

YIELD: 4 TO 6 SERVINGS

4 cups chicken stock
¼ cup Chinese mushrooms
　(reserve stock)
½ cup fresh water chestnuts
¼ cup scallions, chopped
　(white and green parts)

**Binder**
1 tablespoon water chestnut
　powder

2 tablespoons mushroom
　stock

Salt to taste
White pepper, freshly
　ground, to taste
1 egg, slightly beaten
2 teaspoons sesame-seed oil

## PREPARATION

Measure stock in a saucepan.

Rinse mushrooms, cover with warm water, and soak for 30 to 60 minutes or until soft. Save the stock.

Stem and dice mushrooms.

Peel water chestnuts and slice each one in 3 or 4 pieces.

Chop scallions.

Mix binder.

Add any leftover mushroom stock to the measured chicken stock in the saucepan.

## COOKING PROCEDURE

Over a high flame, bring the chicken stock to a boil.

Add mushrooms and boil for 2 minutes, stirring occasionally in a figure-eight motion with a pair of chopsticks.

Restir binder and add gradually with one hand while stirring with the other.

Simmer the soup 1 more minute.

Add scallions and water chestnuts and simmer for another ½ minute.

Add pepper. Test for seasoning; add salt if necessary.

Turn off flame and pour in egg slowly with one hand while stirring with the other.

Add sesame-seed oil and stir again.

Serve immediately.

T I M I N G : All the preparations for the soup can be made early in the day.

Once the soup is cooked, it should be served immediately.

If the soup is rewarmed, the scallions will wilt and the water chestnuts will lose their sweet flavor.

TIPS: If you use College Inn chicken broth, little or no salt will be required.

If you like a spicier soup, substitute 1 teaspoon sesame-seed oil with chili for the plain sesame-seed oil.

## SEASONAL VEGETABLE SOUP WITH BEAN CURD

YIELD: 4 TO 6 SERVINGS

1 fresh bean curd cake
½ cup snow peas, shredded
1 cup bok choy, shredded (both stems and leafy parts)
½ cup carrots, shredded
½ cup American broccoli, shredded (middle part of stem)
1 cup leeks, shredded (white part only)

*Binder*
*1 teaspoon water chestnut powder*
*1 tablespoon sherry*

4 cups chicken stock
1½ tablespoons light soy sauce
Salt to taste
¼ teaspoon freshly ground white pepper
1 teaspoon sesame-seed oil

### PREPARATION

Shred bean curd and all vegetables.

Mix binder.

### COOKING PROCEDURE

Bring chicken stock to a boil and add leeks, broccoli, carrots, and pepper.

Simmer for 2 minutes.

Restir binder and add with one hand while stirring with chopsticks with the other hand.

When soup returns to a boil, add bok choy stems, snow peas, and bean curd.

When soup returns to a boil, add bok choy leaves.

Return soup to a boil and add soy sauce.

Taste for salt.

Add sesame-seed oil, stir briefly, pour soup into a soup tureen, and serve immediately.

TIMING : All preparations can be made early in the day or the day before.

Once cooked, this soup must be served immediately; otherwise, the vegetables will become soggy.

SUBSTITUTIONS : Choose any vegetable combination you prefer, according to the season. Other possibilities include zucchini, American peas, kohlrabi, spinach, fresh mushrooms, or any of the choy family vegetables.

TIPS : Fresh home-made stock is always preferable when making soups.

Chicken, beef, veal, or pork stock would all be appropriate for this recipe. If using canned stock, College Inn is the preferred brand.

Place stock in the refrigerator a day in advance to facilitate the removal of fat.

# HOT AND SOUR SOUP

YIELD: 6 SERVINGS IF SERVED AS FIRST COURSE;

3 SERVINGS IF ENTRÉE

½ cup raw pork shreds (¼ pound)

¼ cup Chinese mushrooms, soaked

12 lily buds, soaked

1 tablespoon dry tree ears, rinsed and soaked

1 cake fresh bean curd

¼ cup bamboo shoots

½ teaspoon sugar

1½ tablespoons light soy sauce

1 tablespoon black rice vinegar

2 to 3 tablespoons wine vinegar (red)

1 egg

2 tablespoons scallions, chopped (white and green parts)

*Binder*

*2 tablespoons water chestnut powder*

*About ¼ cup mushroom stock (reserved from water in which dried mushrooms were soaking)*

4 cups chicken broth

¼ teaspoon black pepper, ground fresh

1 teaspoon sesame-seed oil with chili

## PREPARATION

Partially freeze pork, then shred.

Rinse mushrooms, cover with warm water, and soak for 30 to 60 minutes or until soft, then shred. Reserve stock.

Soak lily buds, remove hard end, and cut in half.

Soak tree ears, and shred.

Shred bean curd and bamboo shoots.

Mix together in a bowl the sugar, light soy sauce, and vinegars.

Beat egg.

Chop scallions.

Dissolve 2 tablespoons water chestnut powder in the mushroom stock.

## COOKING PROCEDURE

Bring chicken stock to a boil.

Add pork shreds and stir immediately. Bring to boil again, and remove scum.

Add mushrooms, tree ears, lily buds, and bamboo shoots. Return to boil.

Cook for 3 minutes, over a medium flame. (Dish can be prepared ahead up to this point.)

Bring soup back to a boil.

Drain bean curd, and add to soup.

Add sugar, soy sauce, vinegars, and pepper. Bring to boil.

Restir binder and add with one hand while stirring gently with the other.

Simmer soup until it thickens (about 1 minute).

Add sesame-seed oil with chili.

Sprinkle with chopped scallion. Stir briefly with chopsticks.

Turn off flame.

Slowly pour in egg, while stirring with chopsticks.

Serve immediately.

TIMING: The preparation of all the ingredients can be done early in the day.

The soup can be cooked early in the day, up to the addition of the vegetables (mushrooms, tree ears, lily buds, and bamboo shoots).

The remainder of the recipe requires only a few minutes.

SUBSTITUTIONS: For the pork you can substitute shoulder of veal.

If using pork, use Boston butt or loin.

If fresh bean curd is not available, omit it. A possible substitute would be one cup of cooked lo mein noodles.

If Chenkong vinegar is not available, use 3 to 4 tablespoons wine vinegar.

TIPS: Make sure the flame is off before you add the egg.

If you wish to make the soup more sour, add more vinegar. If you wish to make it hotter, increase the pepper and the sesame-seed oil with chili to taste.

When you add the binder and the egg, stir with one hand while you pour with the other.

Use College Inn chicken broth if fresh stock is not available.

Refer to Ingredients, for information on all the dried ingredients.

## FRESH SPINACH SOUP WITH HAM
## AND SHRIMP DUMPLINGS

YIELD: 6 SERVINGS IF SERVED AS FIRST COURSE;

3 SERVINGS IF ENTRÉE

*Dumplings*
½ *pound shrimp*
¼ *cup ham, minced*
1 *scallion, chopped (white and green parts)*
1 *egg, slightly beaten*
2 *tablespoons water chestnut powder*
½ *teaspoon salt*
1 *teaspoon sugar*
2 *teaspoons dark soy sauce*

*Soup*
6 *cups chicken stock*
⅓ *cup Chinese mushrooms*
½ *chicken breast*
½ *egg white, slightly beaten*
1 *pound fresh spinach*
⅓ *cup water chestnuts*
¼ *teaspoon white pepper, ground fresh*
*Salt to taste*

## PREPARATION

Shell, devein, wash, drain, dry, and mince shrimp.

Mince ham.

Chop scallion.

Blend together thoroughly the egg, water chestnut powder, salt, sugar, and soy sauce.

Combine with minced ham, shrimp, and chopped scallion.

Bring chicken stock to a boil, then turn flame to low.

Drop dumpling mixture, one full teaspoon at a time, into the simmering chicken stock. The dumplings will float when they are done, but continue to let them simmer for one more minute to avoid any taste of the water chestnut powder.

Remove the dumplings from the soup with a wire strainer and set aside.

Rinse mushrooms, cover with warm water, and soak for 30 to 60 minutes or until soft. Stem and dice.

Add mushroom stock to chicken stock.

Bone chicken breast and freeze until partially frozen.

Cut chicken breast into slices 1 inch × 1 inch × ¼ inch.

Mix the chicken slices with the egg white.

Wash spinach and cut into 1½-inch pieces.

Peel water chestnuts (if using fresh ones) and slice each one in 3 or 4 pieces.

## COOKING PROCEDURE

Bring chicken stock to a boil over a high flame in a saucepan. Add mushroom pieces and boil for 2 minutes.

Add spinach and stir with chopsticks.

When stock returns to a boil, add chicken pieces and mix well in a figure-eight motion to prevent chicken pieces from sticking together.

When stock returns to a boil, add water chestnuts, dumplings, and pepper. Taste, and add salt if necessary. When soup returns to a boil again, turn off flame. Pour into a soup tureen ad serve immediately.

TIMING : The dumplings can be prepared and cooked a day in advance. Remove them from the chicken stock, and refrigerate the dumplings and the stock separately.

All the remaining preparations can be done a day in advance or early in the morning.

Once the soup is made, it should be served immediately.

Never cover the soup, because the spinach greens would wilt.

If possible, use an enamel or copper pot, so you can make and serve the soup in it.

Although this soup appears light and delicate, it contains nourishing and balanced ingredients, and it can be served as an entire meal for three to four people.

SUBSTITUTIONS : Filet of flounder can be substituted for the shrimp.

For low-cholesterol diets, eliminate the ham and the egg yolk, and add an extra egg white to the dumplings.

One bunch watercress can be substituted for the spinach. If using watercress, remove about 1½ inches of the stems and discard. Cut the remaining bunch of watercress in 1½-inch pieces, put the pieces in a colander, rinse with cold water, and drain. By cutting the whole bunch of watercress first before washing you can save time. Another possibility is the green leaves of bok choy, cut in 1½-inch pieces. Proceed as with spinach.

TIPS : Drop about half the total amount of dumpling mixture by spoonfuls into the stock and stir gently with chopsticks in a figure-eight motion to avoid their sticking to the bottom of the pot.

As soon as they float, start to time them. If the dumplings are overcooked, they will become rubbery.

If there are any leftovers, strain the soup through a sieve or colander.

Refrigerate the soup, the vegetables, and the dumplings separately.

The stock may be frozen, but the dumplings and vegetables will suffer if frozen.

## VEGETABLE WONTON SOUP

YIELD: 10 SERVINGS IF SERVED AS FIRST COURSE;

6 SERVINGS IF ENTRÉE

**Filling**
½ pound ground pork
¼ pound shrimp (weighed
    with shells)
¼ pound fresh spinach
½ teaspoon ginger root,
    minced fine
¼ cup water chestnuts,
    minced
½ teaspoon sugar
2 tablespoons sherry
3 tablespoons dark soy sauce

Salt to taste
6 cups chicken stock
30 wonton wrappers

**4 cups shredded vegetables**
Choose 2 or more of the following:
Fresh spinach (½ to 1
    pound)
Green part of bok choy leaves
Stems of bok choy
Shantung cabbage
Fresh mustard greens

## PREPARATION

Place ground pork in a bowl.

Shell, devein, wash, drain, dry, and mince shrimp.

Wash and dry spinach. Remove all but 2 inches of the stems, and blanch in the chicken stock for 30 seconds. Remove from stock and let drain in a colander set over a bowl to catch the dripping stock. Let cool 10 minutes. Pour any liquid from the drained spinach back into the chicken stock in which it was blanched.

Chop spinach.

Mince ginger very fine.

Mince water chestnuts.

Add to pork the shrimp, spinach, water chestnuts, ginger, sugar, sherry, and soy sauce. Mix well in one direction with chopsticks, but be careful not to overmix the filling ingredients, lest the mixture does become too dense.

Using about 1 full teaspoon of filling, wrap wontons as illustrated on page 121.
Cover with a damp cloth until ready to boil. (At this point you can freeze them.)

Shred 4 cups of vegetables and place in a bowl.

## COOKING PROCEDURE

Boil 4 quarts water in a heavy saucepan and drop in wontons, either by hand or with a wire strainer. Bring to boil again, and add 1 cup cold water.

Bring to boil and cook over a medium-high flame for 2 minutes. Remove wontons from the boiling water with a wire strainer and place in a large soup tureen or paella dish.

While wontons are boiling, bring the chicken stock to a boil and blanch the shredded vegetables for 1 minute. Remove vegetables from broth with a wire strainer and place in a bowl.

Taste for seasoning, and add salt if needed.

TIMING: Wontons can be boiled early in the day, then drained and placed on a greased cookie sheet with a plastic cover. To rewarm, place in simmering soup for no more than 1 minute. If the wontons are overcooked, the filling will fall out.

Wontons made from freshly ground pork can be frozen *before* being cooked. Put them in a square or rectangular aluminum or stainless steel pan with 2-inch sides (typical brownie pan). Put down one layer of wontons, cover it with plastic wrap, then add another layer. Wrap the entire pan in aluminum foil, then put in a plastic bag. They will last 1 month, frozen.

For storing wonton wrappers, refer to the Ingredients, page 74.

When boiling frozen wontons, it is *not* necessary to defrost them or adjust the cooking time; just allow more time for the water to return to a boil.

Pour boiling chicken stock over the wontons and garnish with shredded vegetables. Serve immediately.

SUBSTITUTIONS : For the pork, you can substitute shoulder of veal.

For the shrimp, you can substitute crab or lobster.

For the spinach and water chestnuts, you can substitute 1 cup mustard greens or 1 bunch blanched watercress.

For the 2 cups shredded vegetables, you can substitute 1 cup of shredded roast pork and ½ pound fresh spinach leaves, cut in large pieces.

TIPS : Wontons can be deep-fried or pan-fried after boiling. Be sure to drain and dry them well on several layers of paper towels before frying. For frying procedure, see Notes under Deep-Fried Wontons, page 121.

## SEVEN-INGREDIENT WINTER MELON SOUP

¼ cup Chinese mushrooms

1 cup abalone liquid (from can)

1 pound winter melon (weighed with rind)

⅓ cup peanuts

2 tablespoons minced Smithfield ham

½ cup leeks, chopped (white part only)

½ cup fresh water chestnuts

*Binder*

*1½ tablespoons water chestnut powder*

*2 tablespoons mushroom stock*

¾ cup abalone

5 cups chicken stock

Salt to taste

White pepper to taste

### PREPARATION

Rinse mushrooms, cover with warm water, and soak for 30 to 60 minutes or until soft.

Dice, adding mushroom stock to abalone stock.

Rinse winter melon in cold running water; remove seeds and rind; dice.

Roast peanuts (refer to Ingredients, page 65).

Mince ham.

Chop leeks.

Slice water chestnuts.

Mix binder.

Slice Abalone.

### COOKING PROCEDURE

Bring chicken stock (to which abalone-mushroom stock has been added) to a simmer.

Add mushrooms, winter melon, and leeks. Simmer uncovered for 5 minutes.

Remix the binder and add gradually, pouring the binder with one hand while stirring with chopsticks with the other hand in a figure-eight motion. Simmer for 1 minute more.

Add water chestnuts and peanuts and bring to a simmer again.

Check seasoning; add salt and pepper if needed.

Add abalone and mix.

Pour into a tureen or individual soup bowls.

Sprinkle with minced ham. Serve immediately.

TIMING : All the preparations can be made early in the day. The soup should be cooked immediately before serving.

SUBSTITUTIONS : For the abalone, you can substitute ¾ cup canned clams. Add to soup at the same time you would the abalone.

For the abalone, you could also substitute approximately 16 fresh clams or mussels. Scrub well with a vegetable brush and boil in water to cover until the shells open. Strain stock through a sieve lined with cheese cloth. Reduce stock to 1 cup, and add to the chicken stock instead of canned abalone liquid. Add clams or mussels in the shell to the soup at the same time you would the abalone.

Another abalone substitute is ¾ cup or ¼ pound fresh bay scallops. Add to the soup before adding binder.

For the winter melon, you can substitute ½ pound zucchini.

For the leeks, you can substitute ¼ cup shallots, minced.

For the Smithfield ham, you can substitute baked Virginia ham.

TIPS : For information on choosing and storing winter melon, refer to Vegetables, page 94.

# POULTRY

---

## CHICKEN WITH BEAN SAUCE AND NUTS

YIELD: 3 TO 4 SERVINGS IF SERVED ALONE; 6 TO 8 SERVINGS
IF SERVED WITH OTHER ENTRÉES

2 whole chicken breasts, 12 to 14 ounces each

### Marinade
½ egg white, beaten slightly
2 teaspoons water chestnut powder
1 tablespoon sherry

¼ cup Chinese mushrooms
½ cup water chestnuts
½ cup sweet red pepper or ½ cup snow peas (2 ounces)
1 or 2 fresh hot peppers or 4 to 6 dried hot peppers

3 to 4 scallions (white and green parts)
¼ cup bamboo shoots

### Seasoning Sauce
1½ tablespoons bean sauce
2 tablespoons hoisin sauce
1 tablesoon dark soy sauce
1 tablespoon sherry

¼ cup nuts (almonds, cashews, or peanuts)
3½ tablespoons peanut oil
½ teaspoon salt

## PREPARATION

Skin and bone chicken breasts as illustrated.

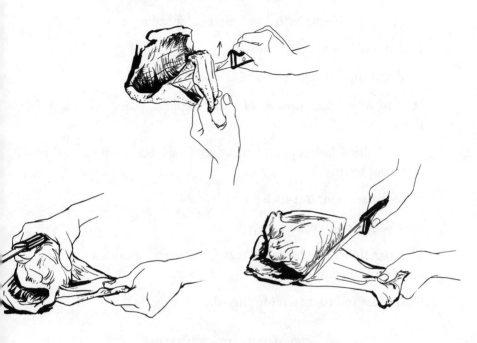

Dice the breasts large, about ¾-inch pieces.

Marinate chicken pieces in egg white, water chestnut powder, and sherry.

Refrigerate at least ½ hour, up to 12 hours.

Rinse mushrooms, cover with warm water, and soak for 30 to 60 minutes or until soft.

Cut each mushroom into 4 to 6 pieces, depending on size.

Peel and slice water chestnuts.

Seed and triangle-cut sweet and hot peppers.

If using snow peas instead of sweet peppers, string and slant-cut them.

If using dried hot peppers instead of fresh, cut off wide end and shake out seeds.

Slant-cut scallions in 1-inch pieces.

Slice bamboo shoots in 1-inch pieces.

Mix together ingredients of seasoning sauce: bean sauce, hoisin sauce, soy sauce, and sherry.

Roast nuts and cool (refer to Ingredients, page 65).

## COOKING PROCEDURE

Place wok over high flame for 30 seconds.

Add 1 tablespoon oil and heat for 20 seconds or until oil is hot but not smoking.

Add mushrooms and stir-fry for 1 minute.

Add scallions, and sweet and hot peppers, and stir-fry 30 seconds.

Add bamboo shoots and water chestnuts, and stir-fry for another minute.

Add salt, mix well, then empty contents of wok into a heated serving dish.

Do not wash wok.

Stir chicken pieces in marinade with chopsticks.

Heat 2½ tablespoons oil over high flame for 30 seconds.

Add chicken pieces and stir-fry for 2 to 3 minutes or until the chicken turns opaque (white).

Add seasoning-sauce mixture and mix well for a few seconds.

Add vegetables again and stir-fry 1 more minute or until the vegetables, chicken, and seasoning sauce are thoroughly mixed and very hot.

Empty contents of wok into a heated serving dish and sprinkle with nuts.

Serve immediately.

TIMING: Do not keep this dish warm in the oven or on a hot tray. The chicken pieces will dry out and the vegetables will become soggy.

SUBSTITUTIONS: For the chicken breasts you can substitute ¾-pound white and dark boneless poultry, such as the breast and thigh from a 2½-to-3-pound chicken, or any other type of raw poultry available. For the chicken you can also substitute the following cuts of meat: veal (shoulder or leg, cut in 1-inch × ¼-inch slices); beef (flank or skirt—diaphram—steak) or pork (Boston butt or loin).

Excluding the scallions, the recipe calls for a total of 1½ cups of vegetables. Possible substitutions for the peppers, water chestnuts, and bamboo shoots are zucchini and carrots (the carrots should be slant-cut and blanched first). Others include asparagus, green pepper, and American peas.

TIPS: Instead of the combined bean sauce and hoisin sauce you can substitute 3 tablespoons of hoisin sauce or 2 tablespoons of oyster sauce.

Remember you are working with boneless, skinless chicken breasts that cook in a few minutes. Overcooking them by 1 minute will dry them out.

This marinade affects the texture, not the taste, of the chicken breasts: it gives them a velvety texture. Be sure to measure the water chestnut powder carefully, leveling off the teaspoon with a chopstick. There are several reasons for such careful measurement: first, too much will cause the chicken pieces to stick to the wok; second, there will be too obvious a coating on the pieces; third, the sauce will become too lumpy or thick.

Let the oil heat for at least 30 seconds in the wok before adding the chicken breasts; otherwise, they will stick.

To double the recipe: bone and marinate 4 whole chicken breasts. Complete all other preparations, doubling all ingredients. Stir-fry ½ the amount of chicken in 2½ tablespoons oil. Empty chicken into a serving dish. Deglaze wok (see Cooking Techniques). Wash and dry wok well. Using 2 tablespoons of oil, stir-fry double the amount of vegetables in the same wok. Empty vegetables into the same serving dish as the chicken. Do not wash wok. Heat 2½ tablespoons of oil in the same wok and stir-fry the remaining ½ chicken until the pieces turn opaque. Add seasoning-sauce mixture and mix well for a few seconds. Add vegetables again and stir-fry 1 more minute or until the vegetables, chicken, and seasoning sauce are thoroughly mixed and very hot. Empty contents of wok into a heated serving dish and sprinkle with nuts.

Do not attempt to stir-fry more than 2 whole chicken breasts at a time, because they will start to steam instead of fry.

Steaming will also occur if you try to make more than twice this recipe in one wok. To avoid steaming, use 2 woks and stir-fry the same ingredients simultaneously. That method is not recommended for the beginner.

## CANTONESE FRIED CHICKEN

*This recipe is an excellent entrée as well as appetizer. When served alone as an appetizer, allow 1 pound of chicken for 2 people. When served in conjunction with other appetizers, allow 1 pound of chicken for 4 people. When served alone as an entrée with an accompanying vegetable dish, allow ¾ pound of chicken per person.*

1 fresh-killed chicken

**Marinade**
1 one-inch piece of ginger root for every pound of chicken
1 scallion (white and green parts) for every pound of chicken
2 tablespoons light soy sauce for every pound of chicken
1 tablespoon sherry for every pound of chicken
1 teaspoon sesame-seed oil for every pound of chicken
½ teaspoon sugar for every pound of chicken
¼ teaspoon pepper for every pound of chicken

Water chestnut powder for dredging
3 cups oil for deep-frying

## PREPARATION

With a heavy cleaver and rubber mallet, cut chicken into small serving pieces, about 1½ inches × 1½ inches.

Crush ginger with the side of the cleaver or put through a garlic press.

Cut scallion in 1-inch lengths.

Mix together—in a bowl large enough to hold chicken—ginger, scallion, soy sauce, sherry, sesame-seed oil, sugar, and pepper.

Add chicken to bowl, mixing well, and let marinate for at least 2 hours.

Refrigerate if marinating longer (up to 4 hours), turning once every hour.

Remove chicken pieces from marinade, drain, then dredge in water chestnut powder 1 piece at a time, massaging briefly. If skin has separated from chicken, replace skin before coming in contact with water chestnut powder.

## COOKING PROCEDURE

In a wok or deep-fryer, heat oil to 325° and add chicken pieces, not more than 1 pound at a time (about 8 to 10 pieces). The chicken should fry between 300° and 325°. Keep checking the oil temperature with a Taylor deep-fat-frying thermometer. Cook, turning pieces in the oil with chopsticks, for about 5 minutes.

Remove the chicken with a wire strainer and drain well on several sheets of paper towels.

Return oil temperature to 325°. That should take no more than 1 minute.

Add another batch of chicken and repeat frying process until all the chicken pieces have been fried once, and drained on paper towels.

Let chicken and oil cool at least 30 minutes (up to 4 hours).

Strain oil, and put back in wok.

Reheat oil to 375°.

Add chicken pieces, no more than 6 at a time, and fry another 1 minute.

Drain again on paper towels. Bring temperature of oil back to 375° before adding next 6 pieces of chicken and repeat the frying process, until all chicken pieces have been fried for the second time.

Serve on a flat platter, taking care not to pile chicken pieces on top of each other, so they will remain crisp. Garnish with American or Chinese parsley or with watercress.

Cantonese Fried Chicken has its own distinctive character, but if desired, it can be accompanied by different dips, such as:

### I. Szechuan Peppercorn Powder
Place a wok or heavy skillet over a medium flame for about 30 seconds.

Do *not* add oil.

Add ¼ cup Szechuan peppercorns and 2 teaspoons coarse salt. Dry-cook for 3 to 5 minutes, stirring slowly but constantly, until the mixture turns dark brown. The peppercorns will start to smoke before they turn dark brown.

Let the mixture cool.

Place the mixture in a blender and blend until it becomes a powder.

A variation on this powder would be to add 1 teaspoon five-spice powder after the mixture has been blended. Or, add ½ teaspoon to ½ the mixture and serve ½ the powder with five-spice powder and ½ without.

Another interesting dip (a liquid as opposed to a dry one) could be used:

## II. Soy Sauce–Vinegar Dip
Combine the following ingredients:

2 tablespoons Chenkong vinegar

2 teaspoons wine vinegar

1 to 2 teaspoons hot sauce

2 teaspoons mixed pepper relish

1 teaspoon garlic, minced

2 tablespoons light soy sauce

1 teaspoon sesame-seed oil

1 tablespoon sherry (sherry in which ginger has been soaking)

1 teaspoon ginger root, minced

Mix this dip the day before. It will keep for 6 months if refrigerated.

All these dips can be used for deep-fried chicken, duck, shrimp, wontons, Shrimp Toast, and so on.

TIMING: Cutting up the chicken is the hardest part of the recipe. You can have the butcher cut the chicken in joints, as if preparing for a fricassee. Then you can make the final cut with a heavy cleaver and a rubber mallet so that each piece is 1½ inches long. That can be done a day ahead. The marinade can be mixed the day ahead, but the chicken pieces should not marinate for more than 4 hours before the first frying, since that would make them too salty. The first frying can be done up to 4 hours ahead and allowed to drain and cool on paper towels, in a single layer.

*Never* rewarm this dish, since the chicken would dry out. The rewarmed flavor completely ruins the dish. If you are serving it as an appetizer, do not keep on a hot tray.

Cantonese Fried Chicken can be served hot, warm, or cold. When you are serving it as part of a meal, complete the second frying before you cook the stir-fried dishes.

s u b s t i t u t i o n s : Any type of poultry can be substituted for the chicken.

If using duck, increase the frying time to 8 minutes on the first frying.

t i p s : Use fresh-killed poultry whenever possible. The cost is about twice the supermarket price, but the flavor is at least 4 times as good. Fresh-killed poultry is available at kosher markets and in Chinatown.

Twice-frying is necessary in order to have a moist piece of chicken on the inside with a very crusty exterior. When prepared this way, the chicken will remain crisp even when cooled.

Select a large, flat serving piece to serve chicken.

The pieces should be arranged in a single layer, because if the pieces are piled on top of each other when hot, they will continue to steam and become soggy.

Garnish with American or Chinese parsley, watercress, or any interesting greens you may have on hand.

The chicken pieces should be light brown after the first frying and a dark golden brown after the second frying.

Never crowd chicken pieces in the wok or deep fryer, since they create too much steam and stick together. Crowding also causes the oil temperature to cool down too rapidly.

Keep checking the oil temperature after the addition of each new batch of chicken and remember to bring the oil back to the required heat in both the first and second frying.

If the oil temperature is too low, the water chestnut powder will start to come off. If the oil temperature is too high, the chicken pieces will stick together and become dried out.

## SOY SAUCE WHOLE CHICKEN
YIELD: 4 TO 6 SERVINGS IF SERVED WITH A VEGETABLE;
8 TO 12 SERVINGS IF SERVED WITH 3 OTHER DISHES

*Master Sauce*
1½ *cup dark soy sauce*
1 *cup chicken stock*
½ *cup sherry*
2 *tablespoons sugar*
1 *teaspoon five-spice powder*
  *or 1 whole star anise (8*
  *pods)*

1 whole chicken, 5 to 5½
  pounds
Shantung cabbage leaves or
  fresh coriander leaves
  (base and garnish)

### PREPARATION
Combine ingredients for master sauce—soy sauce, chicken stock, sherry, sugar, and five-spice powder—in a 14-inch wok.

Remove giblets; clean and dry chicken (leave whole).

Separate, wash, and dry Shantung cabbage leaves or fresh coriander.

### COOKING PROCEDURE
Heat master-sauce mixture in wok.

Add chicken (breast facing up), and bring to boil.

Turn flame to very low; cover loosely and cook for 2 to 2¼ hours, turning and basting chicken every 15 minutes. (For the last ½ hour, the chicken should be breast-side up, and the cover should be removed.)

Lift chicken out of liquid by inserting a wooden spoon into the cavity.

Place chicken in rack resting on a plate to catch drippings.

When chicken is at room temperature, cut into bite-size pieces, with skin and bone.

Arrange cabbage leaves on platter; reassemble chicken pieces over cabbage to look like a whole bird flattened out.

Sprinkle with 2 to 3 tablespoons master sauce.

TIMING : Do not cut up the chicken more than 1 hour before serving. If you are serving it the same day, plan to cook the chicken approximately 5 hours before serving (say at two or three in the afternoon), and do not refrigerate. Let cool at room temperature. This is good served cold, so can be prepared the day ahead.

TIPS : The sauce in which the chicken is cooked is your master sauce. It may, and *should,* be used over and over again. There is a restaurant in China that boasts of a master sauce more than 150 years old. I plan to will mine to my son, Todd! If you are serving the chicken the next day, wait until it has cooled thoroughly, and then refrigerate (whole).

Save some of the master sauce for future use. Put it in a plastic jar suitable for freezing, leaving a good layer of fat (which acts as a preservative). It can be refrigerated for a week without freezing, or frozen indefinitely. When you want to use the master sauce again, remove the layer of fat and measure the liquid to see if you still have 3 cups. If not, add a bit more sherry, soy sauce, and stock (in proper proportions—refer back to recipe), to bring it back up to 3 cups. The more you use your master sauce, the better it becomes. You can cook any 5-to-6-pound bird in this manner, except turkey and capon, which are too large. Cooking time would be as follows:

| | |
|---|---|
| Chicken (3 to 4 pounds) | 1¼ to 1½ hours |
| Chicken (5 to 6 pounds) | 2 to 2¼ hours |
| Duck (5 pounds) | 2 to 2¼ hours |
| Rock Cornish Hen | ¾ hour |
| Squab | ¾ hour |

There are other uses for master sauce. I use it in lo mein instead of soy sauce. A couple of tablespoons will improve the flavor of braised dishes as well as stir-fried vegetables.

If you want to avoid cutting up the chicken, which is the only difficult part of the recipe, you may serve it hot and carve it as you would a freshly roasted chicken. Cutting through the skin and bone is the authentic Chinese way of serving Soy Sauce Whole Chicken. It is best done with a heavy meat cleaver and a rubber mallet. If that seems too difficult, poultry shears can be used.

I cannot emphasize enough the importance of buying a fresh-killed chicken for this recipe. The finished chicken should have a dark brown glaze, similar to the color of a roasted chicken, only darker and more even. If possible, buy your chicken in Chinatown; if not, buy it at a kosher butcher shop. The chickens in China-town are fresh-killed, coming from farms where they are specially fed, and their flavor is superior to any I have tasted.

## SZECHUAN DICED CHICKEN

YIELD: 2 TO 3 SERVINGS IF SERVED ALONE;
4 TO 6 SERVINGS IF SERVED WITH 3 OTHER DISHES

¾ pound boneless chicken
(2 chicken breasts weighing 12 ounces each, or a chicken weighing 2–3 pounds, boned, excluding legs and wing meat)

*Marinade*
½ *egg white*
1 *tablespoon sherry*
1 *tablespoon light soy sauce*
2 *teaspoons water chestnut powder*

½ teaspoon Szechuan peppercorns, ground (measured after grinding)
1 teaspoon ginger root, minced

3 scallions (white and green parts)
1 fresh hot chili pepper or 3 dried chili peppers

*Seasoning Sauce*
1 *tablespoon dark soy sauce*
1 *tablespoon sherry*
1 *teaspoon sesame-seed oil*
1 *teaspoon sugar*
1 *tablespoon stock (chicken or mushroom)*
1 *tablespoon Chinese red vinegar*
1 *teaspoon water chestnut powder*

2 cups peanut oil

## PREPARATION

Bone chicken, dice, and marinate in egg white, sherry, light soy sauce, and water chestnut powder.

Refrigerate for at least ½ hour (up to 12 hours).

Grind Szechuan peppercorns in a pepper mill.

Mince ginger.

Slant-cut scallions in 1-inch pieces.

Triangle-cut hot pepper. If using dried peppers, cut off ends and shake out seeds.

Put ginger, scallions, and peppers in a bowl.

Combine ingredients of the seasoning sauce in a bowl.

## COOKING PROCEDURE

Pour 2 cups oil in wok and heat to 325°.

Restir chicken in marinade, add to wok, and stir gently with chopsticks, cooking chicken over high flame for about 2 minutes.

Remove chicken from oil with wire strainer. Empty chicken into another strainer placed over a bowl to drain.

Empty oil into another pan or bowl, leaving 1 tablespoon oil. Do not wash wok.

Heat the remaining tablespoon oil over medium flame.

Add Szechuan peppercorns and brown for about 1 minute.

Add scallions, peppers, ginger; stir-fry 1 minute.

Add chicken and seasoning sauce, and stir-fry over high flame for another minute or two.

Empty contents of wok into a heated serving dish and serve immediately.

Do not keep warm.

TIMING: This recipe is best served immediately, but if necessary it can be kept warm on the low setting of a hot plate, or uncovered in a preheated 200° oven for 3 to 5 minutes. If you are planning to keep it warm, deep-fry the diced chicken for 1½ minutes in the oil heated to 325°.

All the preparations can be made early in the day.

The sliced chicken can be fried up to 4 hours ahead, drained, allowed to cool, then covered. If doubling the recipe, do not pile the chicken pieces on top of each other. They will continue to cook in their own steam and become soggy. Use two different strainers or colanders if necessary.

SUBSTITUTIONS : For the chicken you can use any other type of fresh-killed, boned, raw poultry, including white and dark meat, such as duck, turkey, or any type of wild or domestic bird in season.

Instead of the scallions, you can use 6 to 8 whole shallots, peeled.

The shallots need an additional minute of cooking time.

TIPS : If you prefer to make this dish spicier, increase the Szechuan peppercorns from ½ to 1 teaspoon.

It is important that the oil temperature be correct. If it is too hot, the chicken pieces will stick together. If it is too cool, they will sink to the bottom of the wok and absorb too much oil. Use a Taylor or mercury deep-fat-frying thermometer to accurately judge the temperature of the oil. The technique of deep-frying the chicken first (before subsequent stir-frying) is called *passing through*. It is described in detail under Cooking Techniques. It is crucial that the chicken pieces are *not* overcooked. Remember you are working with skinless, boneless chicken pieces which cook through in a few minutes. They are done when they turn opaque (white). If overcooked, the chicken pieces will be dry, instead of moist and juicy.

*To double the recipe*, do not attempt to fry more than ¾ pound chicken at a time. The oil temperature will cool down too rapidly. Marinate double the amount of chicken (1½ pounds) in the same bowl. Fry ½, remove from oil, then fry the second ½. You can add double the amount of vegetables to the wok at the same time, since they require slightly less intense heat. Do *not* attempt to triple this recipe in one wok, even if you have fried only ¾ pound of chicken at a time. The chicken and vegetables would steam instead of fry, which would result in an inferior tasting dish.

# LEMON CHICKEN

YIELD: 4 TO 6 SERVINGS IF SERVED ALONE; 8 TO 12
SERVINGS IF SERVED WITH 3 OTHER DISHES

*Lemon Chicken has become a very popular dish with Americans, even though it is not based on an authentic Chinese recipe. It was developed by a Chinese chef who was working in a restaurant in New York, with the American palate in mind. It is considered to be an adaptation of the classic sweet-and-sour sauce, and is a good example of the new hybrid: a Chinese-American dish which is inauthentic but delicious.*

4 whole chicken breasts
(12 to 14 ounces)

**Marinade**
2½ tablespoons light soy
sauce
1 teaspoon sesame-seed oil
1 tablespoon gin or vodka

2 small carrots
3 scallions (white and green
parts)
1 cup snow peas or 1 small
green pepper

**Sauce**
½ cup white rice vinegar
½ scant cup sugar (½ cup
less 2 tablespoons)
6 ounces chicken stock

6½ tablespoons fresh lemon
juice
1 teaspoon grated lemon rind
(zest—outermost yellow
skin—only)

**Binder**
2 tablespoons water chestnut powder
4 tablespoons chicken stock

3 egg whites
2 cups peanut oil for deep-
frying
¾ cup water chestnut
powder for dredging
1 cup shredded Shantung
cabbage

## PREPARATION
Bone chicken breasts, separating the filet from the cutlet. That will yield a total of 16 pieces.

Place chicken pieces in a bowl or dish.

Combine ingredients for the marinade—soy sauce, sesame-seed oil, and gin—and pour over the chicken pieces.

Toss to coat and let stand 30 minutes. If marinating longer, then refrigerate.

Shred carrots and place in bowl.

Shred scallions and snow peas, and place in a bowl.

Grate lemon rind.

Squeeze lemon juice.

Mix binder.

Mix the vinegar, sugar, remaining chicken stock, lemon juice, and grated lemon rind in a saucepan.

Beat egg whites slightly.

## COOKING PROCEDURE
Heat oil in wok to 325°.

While oil is heating, drain the chicken and discard the marinade.

Dip the chicken in beaten egg whites, one piece at a time.

Coat chicken in water chestnut powder; shake off excess.

Fry the chicken (not more than 2 whole breasts at a time in a 14-inch wok) for 4 to 5 minutes, turning with chopsticks once after 2 minutes. The chicken should fry in the oil at a temperature somewhere between 280° and 300°.

Remove first batch of chicken from oil with a wire strainer or chopsticks, and drain on several sheets of paper towels.

Reheat oil to 325° and repeat frying and draining process. The entire preparation up to this point can be done ahead 4 hours.

The chicken breasts must cool at least 30 minutes before they are fried a second time.

Strain oil through a sieve lined with cheesecloth.

Reheat oil to 375°.

While oil is reheating, place saucepan with lemon sauce over a medium-high flame and bring to a boil. Remix binder and add to sauce by pouring with one hand while stirring in a figure-eight motion with the other. When sauce has thickened, turn flame to low and let simmer. Refry cooled chicken breasts, no more than 3 pieces at a time, for about 30 seconds on each side. Remove them and drain. Be sure to bring oil temperature back to 375° before adding the next 3 pieces, until all the chicken has been fried for the second time.

Drain well on paper towels for one minute. While draining, bring lemon sauce back to a rapid boil.

Add carrots and boil one minute.

Add scallions and snow peas; cook 30 seconds. Immediately remove saucepan from heat.

Slice chicken breasts crosswise and place over shredded Shantung cabbage.

With a perforated spoon, place vegetables and some of the sauce over chicken.

Serve extra sauce in a separate bowl.

TIMING: The chicken breasts can be boned and marinated up to 12 hours ahead.

The vegetables can be shredded early in the day or the day before if wrapped well.

The sauce can be prepared a day in advance.

The first frying of the chicken can be done 4 hours ahead; it is then drained on paper towels and allowed to cool in a single layer. When cool, cover with wax paper.

After the oil has cooled, strain it, wash out the wok, and then pour the oil back into the wok.

The second frying of the chicken and the heating of the sauce should be the last thing you do when serving Lemon Chicken as part of a dinner, because it must be served immediately.

SUBSTITUTIONS: For the chicken breasts you can substitute veal scallops, filet of sole, or flounder.

When using fish, reduce the first frying time to 3 minutes.

Fresh lime juice can be used instead of lemon juice.

Shredded iceberg lettuce can be substituted for the cabbage.

Cornstarch or flour can be used instead of water chestnut powder, but the chicken will not be as crisp.

TIPS: The most difficult part of preparing Lemon Chicken is the timing at the end of the recipe. Read the recipe over several times before you complete the final part, which is the second frying of the chicken and the thickening of the sauce. When trying it for the first time, plan a very simple meal with a soup, appetizer, and Lemon Chicken as your only entrée. It serves four to six people.

Choose a flat serving piece so the chicken pieces are placed in a single layer and do not continue to steam when put on the table.

If the butcher has boned the breasts for you, separate the cutlets from the filets.

Lemon Chicken can also be served as an appetizer. In that case, omit the vegetables from the recipe and serve the lemon sauce in a bowl placed on a platter with the chicken pieces surrounding it. Each person dips a piece of chicken into the sauce.

When doubling the recipe, use two woks or deep fryers, and double all the ingredients.

## BARBECUED ROAST DUCK

YIELD: 3 SERVINGS IF SERVED WITH 1 ACCOMPANYING
VEGETABLE DISH; 6 TO 8 SERVINGS IF SERVED
WITH 3 OTHER DISHES

*This recipe is adapted from Mme Chu. It is an excellent method of preparing duck, and it rivals Peking Duck. It is good served alone (with rice and stir-fried vegetable), in conjunction with other entrées, or cold on a picnic.*

1 Long Island duckling

**Marinade**
1½ tablespoons bean sauce
　　sauce
1½ tablespoons hoisin sauce

1 tablespoon dark soy sauce
2 tablespoons sherry
1 teaspoon five-spice powder

1 leek

### PREPARATION

Thaw duck if frozen.

Submerge duck in boiling water for 30 to 60 seconds to remove some of the fat.

Drain.

Hang duck by the neck in a cool place overnight or for a minimum of 6 hours. If neck is too short, loop string around both wings.

Mix ingredients of marinade in a small bowl.

Massage duck with the marinade inside and out.

Place leek inside cavity of duck.

Place duck on a rack in a shallow roasting pan, and refrigerate for 3 to 5 hours, breast side up.

### COOKING PROCEDURE

Preheat oven to 325°.

Take duck out of refrigerator, and fill roasting pan containing duck with water to a depth of ½ inch.

Roast duck at 325° (breast side up) for 70 minutes.

Prick with a trussing needle along the sides, thighs, and back, after 35 minutes, to allow some of the fat to escape.

Prick again after 35 minutes. Every time you prick the duck, which should be done every 30 to 35 minutes throughout the entire cooking time, check water in bottom of pan.

Turn duck over at the end of the 70 minutes (back side up) and roast for another hour at 325°; then prick duck and check water.

Turn duck over again (breast side up), prick again, reduce oven to 300°, and roast for another 30 minutes. To avoid burning pan drippings which will be used in sauce, transfer duck to new roasting pan.

Prick duck again, raise oven temperature to 375°, and cook for a final 10 to 15 minutes. (Total cooking time is between 2 hours 45 minutes and 2 hours 55 minutes).

Remove from oven, place duck (still on rack) over a plate or cookie sheet, and let cool for 10 to 15 minutes.

Defat pan juices, and boil down to a scant ½ cup for sauce.

Cut up duck, and reshape on platter (as for Soy Sauce Whole Chicken).

Serve sauce separately.

TIMING: The duck can be defrosted the day before and hung to drain overnight. The purpose of hanging the duck is to dry out the skin. That will make the skin crisper and keep it crisper, even after it has cooled slightly.

It can then be marinated in the refrigerator and removed 3 hours (at least ½ hour) before roasting.

While the duck is cooling on a rack, you will have time to stir-fry 2 dishes, one of which can be kept warm, and the other of which is last-minute.

SUBSTITUTIONS: For the duck you can substitute chicken. The timing is then changed to 20 minutes per pound; the total time will depend on the weight of the chicken.

TIPS: Keep checking to see that there is ½ inch water in the roasting pan every time you prick the duck, so the pan drippings do not burn.

Use a frozen duck for this recipe, since it will be less fatty. The skin will be crisper, and there will be no layer of fat between the skin and the duck meat. If you do have a layer of fat, it can be easily removed with a boning knife after the duck has been split in half with the cleaver.

Submerging the duck in boiling water (blanching) before hanging affects both the skin and the subcutaneous fat.

When pricking duck, do *not* prick the breast.

When substituting chicken, choose a fresh-killed chicken whenever possible.

. If sauce from the pan drippings is not used, save it for Roast Pork Lo Mein, using it in place of ½ cup chicken stock. The sauce will keep for 6 months in the freezer.

If you buy a fresh duck (from Chinatown), be sure to remove the oil sacs near the tail. All frozen ducks have had them removed.

Leftover duck is best eaten cold or shredded for Fried Rice or Banquet Lo Mein.

# BONELESS STUFFED DUCK, CANTON STYLE

YIELD: 3 TO 4 SERVINGS IF SERVED ALONE; 8 PORTIONS
IF SERVED WITH OTHER DISHES

1 five-pound Long Island
duck

**Stuffing**
½ cup Chinese mushrooms
1¼ cups rice
1¾ cups duck stock
16 to 18 gingko nuts or
⅓ cup fresh chestnuts,
parboiled and chopped
¼ cup Smithfield ham

2 scallions (white and green
parts)
Duck gizzard, heart, and
liver
½ cup ground pork
2 tablespoons dark soy sauce

1 slice ginger root, ½ inch
thick
1 teaspoon salt

## PREPARATION

Bone duck as illustrated, pages 42 through 45.

Rinse mushrooms, cover with warm water, and soak for 30 to 60 minutes or until soft.

Cook 1¼ cups of rice in 1¾ cups of duck stock.

Cook rice for 15 minutes. Let rice remain in pot with cover on for 20 minutes. This is called relaxing the rice. Uncover rice and cool while preparing stuffing ingredients.

Shell gingko nuts by pouring boiling water over them to cover. Let stand 10 minutes. Remove brown skin.

Dice ham and mushrooms.

Chop scallions.

Mince giblets removing outer casing of gizzard first.

Stir into rice the scallions, giblets, mushrooms, ham, ground pork, gingko nuts, and soy sauce.

Rub the inside of the duck with ginger which has been put through a garlic press.

Turn skin right side out and truss one end.

Stuff with the prepared stuffing. Be careful not to overstuff.

Truss the other end (fasten with poultry skewers or sew with un-waxed dental floss).

## COOKING PROCEDURE

Place duck on a cake rack, and put this directly on the rungs of the oven rack. Place a roasting pan with ½ inch of water in it underneath the duck, on the floor of the oven, to catch the drippings.

Roast in a preheated 300° oven for 1½ hours.

Turn oven to 375° and roast for ½ hour.

Check the water in the pan underneath, adding more if too much has evaporated.

Take duck out of oven and transfer it to a serving platter.

Sprinkle the top with 1 teaspoon salt.

Cut at the table with a knife. First cut down the center length-wise, then cut across in fourths, so the duck will be in 8 parts.

TIMING: If you are using a frozen duck, thaw it in the refrigerator the day before.

Make duck stock from the carcass, neck, and giblets in the morning.

Make the stuffing in the morning.

Stuff the duck just before roasting, to avoid the possibility of dangerous toxins forming (due to bacterial growth) which are not destroyed during the roasting.

Bone the duck early in the day or just before stuffing.

SUBSTITUTIONS: For the duck you can substitute a 5-pound fresh-killed chicken, which should roast at 300° for 1 hour, and 375° an additional ½ hour.

For the gingko nuts, you can substitute ½ cup Italian chest-nuts, diced and parboiled.

TIPS: Use a fresh-killed duck for this recipe if possible.

To prevent the stuffing from leaking out, use skewers and un-waxed dental floss to close the cavity before roasting.

Refer to illustration for boning of duck. The first time you bone a duck, it will take about 30 minutes. As you become more familiar with the anatomy of the duck, it will take less time; you can get it down to about 10 minutes. Try to avoid cutting the duck skin. If you do pierce the skin, it can be sewn with a needle and unwaxed dental floss after it has been stuffed. Time your dinner for 2 hours after you have placed the duck in the oven.

## PEKING DUCK

YIELD: 3 TO 4 SERVINGS IF SERVED ALONE; 6 TO 8 SERVINGS
IF SERVED WITH 3 OTHER DISHES

1 five-pound Long Island duck
2 tablespoons honey
2 cups sherry
14 scallions (white part only)

10 Peking Doilies (See page 284)

*Dipping Sauce*
*4 tablespoons hoisin sauce*
*1 teaspoon sesame-seed oil*

### PREPARATION

Thaw duck if frozen.

Wash duck under cold water; pat dry inside and out with paper.

Tie one end of a cord around the skin of the neck. If skin has been cut away, loop the cord under both wings.

Combine 6 cups water and 2 tablespoons honey in casserole or saucepan (large enough to hold duck) and bring to a boil over high flame.

Holding duck by the string, lower it into the boiling liquid. With the string in one hand and a spoon in the other, turn the duck from side to side until all the skin and the cavity are moistened with the liquid.

Remove the duck and hang it in a cool place for at least 8 hours (preferably overnight).

Place duck in a rectangular pan and pour 2 cups sherry over it.

Marinate for an hour; turn and marinate for another hour.

Hang up again until there is no more dripping (3 to 4 hours).

Prepare scallions: using white portion only (2½- to 3-inch lengths), make 2 horizontal cuts, each 1 inch deep. (See illustration.)

Rotate scallion 90° and make 2 more cuts, so the splayed end resembles a brush. Put scallions in a bowl of ice water for 30 minutes.

## COOKING PROCEDURE

Roast duck on a rack in a roasting pan with ¼ inch water in it as follows: 375° for 30 minutes, breast side up; 300° for 1 hour, breast side down.

Remove duck from oven. Transfer to a clean rack and roasting pan, with water covering the bottom of the pan.

Return duck to the oven and cook at 375° for 30 minutes, breast side up.

Check the duck every ½ hour, to make sure there is enough water to cover the bottom of the pan.

Wrap doilies in a damp dishcloth and steam for 5 to 7 minutes.

While they are steaming, remove duck from the oven and transfer to a clean rack set over a pan.

Allow it to cool for 5 minutes.

TIMING: Peking Duck must be served immediately. It is normally served as part of a banquet. In China the skin is served first and then the meat, since the skin is considered the most delectable part.

TIPS: To present Peking Duck, proceed as follows:

With a sharp boning knife, remove legs and wings. Remove all skin, and cut it into 1-inch × 2-inch rectangular pieces. Then remove the duck meat from the carcass, and cut it into similarly sized pieces. Arrange a platter with the legs and wings on the outside, then the skin, with the meat in the center. Serve the scallions and sauce in separate bowls. Have each person spread a doily on a plate. Take a scallion, dip it in the sauce and brush the doily with it. Place the scallion in the middle of the doily; then put a piece of duck skin and a piece of meat on top. Roll up the doily and eat with fingers.

Another dipping sauce, more authentically Chinese, would be 4 tablespoons sweet bean sauce, 1 teaspoon sesame-seed oil, and 1 tablespoon sherry.

Do not make Peking Duck in the summertime.

There are several possible arrangements for hanging the duck. If your bathroom has a window in it, which provides the necessary ventilation, you can hang it from the shower-curtain rod. Or you can hang it on an opened wire hanger from a drawer in the kitchen with an open window nearby. You could also hang the duck from an iron pot-rack. The purpose of hanging is to dry out the skin so that it will remain crisp after the duck has been cooked and begins to cool.

Use a frozen duck for this recipe because it will be less fatty and the skin will be crisper. It does not have as thick a layer of fat between the skin and the meat as does a fresh-killed duck.

Hang the duck the night before you intend to cook it. Start to marinate it in the morning.

To remove wings, first make an incision around the joint, and pull the wing away from the breast with your free hand. When the joint begins to separate, use the knife blade to sever it from the shoulder. Follow the same procedure with the legs.

To remove skin, with a sharp boning knife make a cut midway, all around the side of the duck, dividing it into upper and lower halves. Starting on the upper half, gently separate the breast skin from the meat; you should try to remove this piece of skin intact, in one piece. There should *not* be a layer of fat adhering to the skin, but if there is, gently scrape it away. Then turn the duck over, breast side down, and remove the skin from the back and thighs, also in one piece. Make one cut down the center of each of these large pieces of skin, lengthwise; then make 4 to 6 cuts across.

To remove meat from carcass, first make a lengthwise cut along the breast bone; then make 5 or 6 cuts across, on each side of the breast. With the knife and your fingers, pull the breast meat away from the carcass. Turn the duck over and remove the meat from the back and thighs, in similarly sized pieces. Save the carcass for stock.

Since carving the duck requires some skill, many people avoid making Peking Duck at home. That is a shame, because it is a sensational method of roasting duck. An alternate suggestion would be to serve Peking Duck as you would a French or German roast duck: quarter it with poultry shears, and serve it with applesauce, wild rice, and a stir-fried vegetable. Served Chinese style, it is enough for eight people as part of a banquet. Cut in quarters, it will serve two to four people, depending on their appetites and the accompaniments.

Changing roasting pans will keep fat from spattering; it will also prevent the pan drippings from burning so they can be used later, such as for the stock of lo mein.

# SEAFOOD

---

## STIR-FRIED SHRIMP WITH ASPARAGUS

YIELD: 3 TO 4 SERVINGS IF SERVED ALONE; 6 TO 8 SERVINGS
IF SERVED WITH 3 OTHER DISHES

1 pound shrimp (raw,
   weighed with the shell)

*Marinade*
*½ egg white, slightly beaten*
*2 teaspoons water chestnut*
   *powder*
*1 tablespoon sherry*
*1 teaspoon salt*

3 cups slant-cut asparagus
   (about 1¼ pounds)
4 scallions (white and green
   parts)

2 cloves garlic
2 teaspoons ginger root,
   minced
¼ cup almonds

*Binder*
*2 teaspoons water chestnut*
   *powder*
*1 to 2 teaspoons hot sauce*
*1 tablespoon sherry*

3½ tablespoons peanut oil
½ teaspoon salt
⅓ cup chicken stock

## PREPARATION

Shell, devein, split, wash, drain, and dry shrimp.

Marinate shrimp in egg white, 2 teaspoons water chestnut powder, 1 tablespoon sherry, and 1 teaspoon salt.

Refrigerate for at least ½ hour, up to 12 hours.

Slant-cut asparagus in 1½-inch pieces.

Chop scallions.

Mince garlic and ginger.

Roast almonds (refer to Ingredients, page 65).

Mix binder.

## COOKING PROCEDURE

Place wok over high flame for 30 seconds.

Add 1 tablespoon oil and heat for 20 seconds or until oil is very hot but not smoking.

Add asparagus and stir-fry for 2 to 3 minutes.

Add ½ teaspoon salt and mix well.

Empty asparagus into a heated serving dish. Do not wash wok.

Heat remaining 2½ tablespoons of oil in wok over high flame.

Add scallions, garlic, and ginger; stir-fry ½ minute.

Restir marinated shrimp with chopsticks; then add to wok and stir-fry for 2 to 3 minutes or until pink.

Again add asparagus, pour in stock, and bring to a boil.

Restir binder and add with one hand while stir-frying with the other, until sauce has thickened.

Empty contents of wok into a heated serving dish, sprinkle with almonds, and serve immediately.

**TIMING :** This dish requires last-minute attention and must be served immediately.

The shrimp can be marinated up to 12 hours ahead of time.

The vegetables can be cut early in the day or a day ahead if refrigerated and wrapped well.

The garlic loses its flavor if minced more than 1 hour before stir-frying.

If desired, the shrimp, garlic, scallions, and ginger can be stir-fried up to 4 hours ahead of time, emptied into a serving dish, allowed to cool, then covered and refrigerated. Remove from the refrigerator 15 minutes before completing the stir-frying of the asparagus. This is helpful if you are preparing a multicourse meal or if you are doubling the recipe and must stir-fry one pound of shrimp at a time, which requires you to deglaze the wok after the first pound of shrimp has been stir-fried (refer to Cooking Techniques, page 31).

**SUBSTITUTIONS :** For the shrimp you can substitute scallops (only 14 ounces, to allow for the weight of the shrimp shells) or 1 pound of boneless poultry, diced—white meat, dark meat, or both.

Veal possibilities are 1 pound of boneless veal from the shoulder sliced thinly against the grain, like flank steak, or 1 pound of veal from the leg, first cut into scallops and then diced into 1-inch pieces. When substituting boneless poultry or veal, add 1 tablespoon dark soy sauce to the binder.

For the asparagus you can substitute snow peas, bok choy, or American peas which can be stir-fried directly. You could also use broccoli or string beans, both of which must be blanched first.

Use the water in which they were blanched to cook rice or add it to stock.

**TIPS :** Buy fresh gray shrimp from Florida or Carolina whenever possible.

To determine the tender portion of the asparagus, hold the bottom of each individual stalk in left hand, in a gently closed fist. With right hand, palm open, slap the green stalk so it breaks cleanly.

The bottom portion of the asparagus stalks can be boiled in water for 15 minutes.

Boil down the stock and use it to cook rice or in soup stock.

For doubling the recipe, refer to notes on Chicken with Bean Sauce and Nuts.

## STEAMED CANTONESE SHRIMP

YIELD: 3 TO 4 SERVINGS IF SERVED ALONE; 6 TO 8 SERVINGS
IF SERVED WITH 3 OTHER DISHES

1 pound shrimp (raw, weighed with the shell)

*Marinade*
*¾ tablespoon light soy sauce*

2 teaspoons fermented black beans
1 clove garlic
2 slices ginger root
6 water chestnuts
3 scallions (white and green parts)

½ teaspoon sugar
6 ounces ground pork
1 teaspoon sesame-seed oil
1 egg, slightly beaten
1 tablespoon light soy sauce
1 teaspoon dark soy sauce

*Binder*
*1 tablespoon water chestnut powder*
*1 tablespoon sherry*

## PREPARATION

Shell, devein, split, wash, drain, and dry shrimp.

Marinate shrimp in ¾ tablespoon light soy sauce for 30 minutes.

Mince black beans, garlic, ginger, and water chestnuts.

Chop 2 of the scallions.

Mince 1 scallion (for garnish).

Mix binder.

Mix together in a bowl the black beans, garlic, ginger, water chestnuts, 2 chopped scallions, binder, sugar, ground pork, sesame-seed oil, egg, and light and dark soy sauces.

## COOKING PROCEDURE

Spread the pork mixture in the center of the steaming dish.

Place dish in the steamer and steam for 20 minutes.

Remove dish from the steamer. Closely pack the shrimp, tails pointing outward, around the edges of the steaming dish, saving 7 shrimp to place on top of the pork mixture.

Return dish to the steamer and steam for 3 to 5 minutes depending on size of shrimp.

Remove dish from steamer and sprinkle with the minced scallion.

Serve immediately.

TIMING: All preparations except the shrimp can be done early in the morning.

The center filling—consisting of black beans, garlic, ginger, water chestnuts, 2 scallions, binder, sugar, ground pork, sesame-seed oil, egg, and light and dark soy sauces—can be put in the dish early in the day, and then refrigerated. Remove it 15 minutes before steaming.

Do not marinate the shrimp more than 2 hours, because they will get too salty.

Refrigerate them if you marinate them more than 30 minutes ahead.

TIPS : Select large shrimp. Choose a serving dish that will fit into the steaming arrangement you have set up. I always use the roasting-pan arrangement described in Cooking Techniques under Steaming, because a rectangular or oval dish does not fit into a traditional, rounded steamer. A porcelain dish is a good choice for this recipe, since you can both steam and serve in it.

A deep oval dish is preferable to a rectangular one. It should be no larger than 4 inches × 8 inches × 2 inches.

## SIZZLING SHRIMP WITH RICE PATTIES

YIELD: 3 TO 4 SERVINGS IF SERVED ALONE; 6 TO 8 SERVINGS
IF SERVED WITH 3 OTHER DISHES

1 pound shrimp (raw, weighed with the shell)

Deep-fried Rice Patties (See page 174.)

*Marinade*
1 tablespoon sherry
2 teaspoons water chestnut powder
1 teaspoon salt
½ egg white

¼ cup Chinese mushrooms
2 teaspoons ginger root, minced
1 clove garlic
2 scallions (white and green parts)
¼ cup water chestnuts, diced
½ cup snow peas, slant-cut
3 tablespoons peanut oil

*Sauce*
5 tablespoons tomato sauce
1 tablespoon tomato paste
⅔ cup chicken stock
1 teaspoon sugar
1 teaspoon salt
1 tablespoon dark soy sauce
1 teaspoon Chenkong vinegar
1 to 2 teaspoons hot sauce

*Binder*
2 tablespoons water chestnut powder
4 tablespoons chicken stock

## PREPARATION

Follow recipe for rice patties through the breaking of the baked patties into squares.

Shell, devein, split, drain, and dry shrimp.

Mix shrimp with marinade ingredients: sherry, water chestnut powder, salt, and egg white.

Marinate shrimp in refrigerator for at least ½ hour, up to 12 hours.

Rinse mushrooms, cover with warm water, and soak for 30 to 60 minutes or until soft.

Mix binder. Dissolve 2 tablespoons of water chestnut powder in 4 tablespoons chicken stock.

In a bowl, combine sauce ingredients: tomato sauce, tomato paste, chicken stock, sugar, salt, soy sauce, Chenkong vinegar, and hot sauce.

Mince ginger and garlic.

Chop scallions.

Dice mushrooms.

Slice water chestnuts.

String snow peas, then slant-cut in 2 or 3 pieces.

## COOKING PROCEDURE

Deep-fry rice patties according to recipe on page 174, drain, and keep warm in a 300° oven.

Place wok over high flame for 30 seconds. Add 3 tablespoons oil and stir-fry garlic, scallion, and ginger for 15 seconds.

Add shrimp and stir-fry until pink (2 to 3 minutes). Empty contents of wok but do not wash.

Add sauce mixture and bring to a boil.

Restir binder, then add to sauce, stirring with a wire whisk and boiling for one minute.

Add mushrooms, snow peas, and water chestnuts.

Bring to a boil again.

Add shrimp, mixing all ingredients thoroughly.

Pour over Sizzling Rice Patties and serve immediately.

T I M I N G : This dish requires last-minute attention and must be served immediately.

The shrimp can be marinated up to 12 hours ahead of time.

The sauce can be mixed the day ahead.

The cutting of the vegetables can be done early in the day or a day ahead if refrigerated and wrapped well.

The garlic loses its flavor if minced more than 1 hour before stir-frying.

If desired, the shrimp can be stir-fried up to 4 hours ahead of time, emptied into a serving dish, allowed to cool, then covered and refrigerated. Remove from the refrigerator 15 minutes before completing the stir-frying of the vegetables. This step is helpful if you are preparing a multicourse meal, or if you are doubling the recipe and must stir-fry one pound of shrimp at a time, which requires deglazing the wok after the first pound of shrimp has been stir-fried (refer to Cooking Techniques, page 31).

The rice patties can be baked and broken the day ahead, but the frying of the patties must be done at the last minute.

Put the metal platter on which you are presenting the dish in a preheated oven at 300° for at least 20 minutes before serving time.

After the rice patties have been fried and drained on paper towels, put them on the preheated platter.

It is the boiling sauce (in which the shrimp are cooked) which will create the sizzle when poured on the very hot platter. An aluminum steak platter, or a metal paella pan, is ideal for this dish.

SUBSTITUTIONS: For the shrimp you can substitute scallops, which are marinated in the same way.

For the snow peas you can substitute American peas.

Canned water chestnuts are passable in this dish, since they are disguised by the spicy sauce.

TIPS: This dish can be made spicier by increasing the amounts of hot sauce and ginger.

Buy fresh gray shrimp from Florida or Carolina whenever possible.

Add binder to sauce with one hand and stir in a circular motion with a wire whisk to avoid lumps in the sauce.

To save time, bring sauce to a boil in a small saucepan before adding it to the wok. It will take a shorter time to return to a boil again.

Undercook the shrimp slightly when you are stir-frying them, since they will be added to the wok a second time to be heated and mixed with the vegetables and sauce.

If the shrimp are overcooked, they will toughen.

Do not attempt to cook more than double this recipe in 1 wok, since the shrimp and sauce will create too much steam. If you wish to prepare more than 2 pounds of sizzling shrimp, you will need 2 different woks or 1 wok and 1 saucepan with high sides. That is not recommended for the beginner. Always try a dish the first time as the recipe indicates before you try to double the quantity.

## RICE PATTIES

1 cup glutinous (sweet) rice     2 cups peanut oil
1¼ cups cold water

### PREPARATION

Rinse rice in cold water.

Place rice in square aluminum or stainless steel pan, 9 × 9

inches, and add 1¼ cups cold water. Spread the rice evenly over the bottom of the pan.

Cover with foil.

## COOKING PROCEDURE

Bake in oven at 375° for 30 minutes.

Remove foil and bake at 300° for 30 to 45 minutes or until dry enough to remove from the pan with a spatula.

With your hands, break into 1½- × 1½-inch squares.

Deep-fry rice squares in oil at 375° over high flame for 1 minute, turning once, until light brown and crisp.

Drain on paper towels and place in serving dish; keep warm uncovered in a 300° oven.

## SHRIMP WITH LOBSTER SAUCE

YIELD: 3 TO 4 SERVINGS IF SERVED ALONE; 6 TO 8 SERVINGS
IF SERVED WITH 3 OTHER DISHES

1 pound shrimp (raw, weighed with the shell)

2 scallions (white and green parts)

*Marinade*
½ *egg white*
¼ *teaspoon salt*
1 *teaspoon water chestnut powder*
1 *tablespoon sherry*
¼ *teaspoon sugar*

2 eggs
2 cloves garlic
2 teaspoons fermented black beans
2 slices fresh ginger root

*Binder*
½ *tablespoon water chestnut powder*
2 *tablespoons chicken stock*

1 tablespoon sherry
1 teaspoon dark soy sauce
½ teaspoon sugar
½ cup chicken stock
½ cup (¼ pound) ground pork
2 tablespoons peanut oil

## PREPARATION

Shell, devein, split, wash, drain, and dry shrimp.

Mix shrimp with the ½ egg white, ¼ teaspoon salt, 1 teaspoon water chestnut powder, 1 tablespoon sherry, and ¼ teaspoon sugar.

Refrigerate for at least ½ hour, up to 12 hours.

Beat the 2 eggs lightly.

Mince the garlic, black beans, and ginger.

Cut the scallions into 2-inch pieces.

Dissolve ½ tablespoon water chestnut powder in 2 tablespoons chicken stock.

Into a small bowl put 1 tablespoon sherry, 1 teaspoon soy sauce, and ½ teaspoon sugar.

Measure into another bowl ½ cup stock.

Set aside ½ cup ground pork.

## COOKING PROCEDURE

Place wok over high flame for 30 seconds.

Add 2 tablespoons oil and heat for 20 seconds or until oil is very hot but not smoking.

Add the black beans, garlic, and ginger. Stir-fry 15 seconds.

Add pork and continue stirring until the pork turns white (3 minutes).

Restir shrimp in marinade with chopsticks; then add to wok and stir-fry until they turn pink (2 to 3 minutes).

Add 1 tablespoon sherry, 1 teaspoon soy sauce, and ½ teaspoon sugar. Mix well.

Add scallions. Mix again.

Add ½ cup stock. Bring to a boil.

Cover and cook over a medium flame for 2 to 3 minutes.

Remix binder and add, pouring with one hand while you stir with the other until the liquid thickens.

Stir in the eggs, turning off the flame immediately.

Empty contents of wok into a heated serving dish. Serve immediately.

TIMING: This, as all other fish and seafood dishes, would suffer if kept warm or rewarmed, and should therefore be served immediately.

SUBSTITUTIONS: For the shrimp you can substitute a 1¼-pound lobster. Cut it in serving pieces, omit the marinade, and proceed as recipe indicates.

You can substitute 14 ounces scallops. If you use bay scallops, leave them whole; if you use sea scallops, cut each one into 3 slices across as you would a water chestnut. Marinate both as you would shrimp.

Or you can substitute 1 pound of soft-shell crabs. Coat in flour and shake off excess, then add when recipe indicates to add shrimp. Sauté for 2 minutes on each side. Proceed with recipe as indicated.

TIPS: It is important that the flame be turned off immediately after the eggs are added to achieve a smooth, flowing sauce.

Most Americans are used to eating this dish with an abundance of sauce because many of the Chinese-American restaurants serve it this way. The recipe given here is a more authentic version. If you prefer more sauce, increase the stock from ½ to ¾ cup, and the binder from ½ to 1 tablespoon water chestnut powder.

## SHRIMP WITH WINE RICE
### YIELD: 3 TO 4 SERVINGS IF SERVED ALONE; 6 TO 8 SERVINGS
### IF SERVED WITH 3 OTHER DISHES

1 pound shrimp (raw, weighed with the shell)

**Marinade**
1 teaspoon water chestnut powder
½ egg white
1 tablespoon sherry

6 tablespoons wine rice, measured with its liquid (See page 180.)

**Seasoning Sauce**
4 tablespoons tomato sauce

2 teaspoons hot sauce
1½ teaspoons dark soy sauce
2 teaspoons hoisin sauce
2 tablespoons chicken stock
1 teaspoon water chestnut powder

2 teaspoons garlic, minced
2 teaspoons ginger root, minced
½ cup scallions, chopped (white and green parts)
3 tablespoons peanut oil

### PREPARATION

Shell, devein, split, wash, drain, and dry shrimp.

Mix shrimp in marinade.

Refrigerate for at least ½ hour, up to 12 hours.

Mix wine rice with seasoning-sauce ingredients in a bowl.

Mince garlic and ginger.

Chop scallions.

### COOKING PROCEDURE

Place wok over high flame for 30 seconds.

Add 2½ tablespoons oil, and heat for 20 seconds or until oil is hot but not smoking.

Add shrimp and stir-fry for 3 to 4 minutes. Empty contents of wok.

Using the same wok, add ½ tablespoon oil and let the garlic, ginger, and scallions sizzle for a minute.

Add the wine rice and seasoning-sauce mixture.

When mixture boils and starts to thicken, return the shrimp to the wok and mix with the sauce.

Cook over high flame for a minute.

Serve immediately.

TIMING : Always cook the fish course last, since fish deteriorates quickly if kept warm. You can marinate the shrimp up to 12 hours ahead and stir-fry it up to 4 hours ahead. After stir-frying, empty shrimp into the serving dish, allow to cool for 30 minutes, and then cover and refrigerate. If stir-frying the shrimp ahead, undercook it slightly. Leave the wok on the stove and do not wash it. The garlic, scallions, and ginger will be stir-fried in the same wok just before serving. The seasoning sauce can be prepared a day ahead. The garlic should not be minced more than 1 hour before stir-frying. The wine rice is best made about a week in advance.
many other types of fish.

SUBSTITUTIONS : For the shrimp you can substitute
One shellfish possibility is lobster. Have fish market cut up a live lobster in serving pieces as for Lobster with Black Bean Sauce. Dry lobster pieces with paper towel and do not marinate. Stir-fry until shells turn bright red (about 3 minutes).

Another possibility is soft-shell crabs: cut in half crosswise, dry with paper towel, and do not marinate. Sauté until shells turn red (about 2 or 3 minutes on each side).

If you use scallops, marinate them as you would the shrimp, and then stir-fry about 3 minutes. If using bay scallops, leave them whole; if using sea scallops, cut each scallop in three slices as you would a large water chestnut.

You can also use a whole fish such as red snapper, sea trout, sea bass or striped bass. Have the fish market clean the fish and trim the tail. It should weigh about 1½ pounds. Make three diagonal cuts, ½ inch deep, on each side of the whole fish.

Dry fish with paper towel and coat with water chestnut powder.

Heat 4 cups of oil in a 14-inch wok to 375°.

Gently lower the fish into the oil and deep-fry over medium-high flame for 6 minutes on each side. The oil temperature should be between 335° and 350° while the fish is frying.

Turn the fish with 2 spatulas.

With a ladle, baste the part of the fish which is not covered by oil the entire time it is frying.

Increase the timing by 2 minutes for a 2-pound fish.

Lift the whole fish out of the wok with a wire strainer, and let drain on several layers of paper towels.

Place fish in upright swimming position on a flat serving platter.

Pour sauce over fish and serve immediately.

TIPS : This dish can be made spicier by increasing the amount of hot sauce to 1 tablespoon.

Mix the wine rice with the seasoning sauce in a small saucepan several hours before dinner. Bring it to a boil before adding it to the wok. That is important if you are doubling the recipe, since it will significantly reduce the amount of time needed to boil the sauce, and it will boil down more quickly. Use a wire whisk to stir the seasoning sauce after adding it to the wok, to prevent lumping. The sauce should be very thick before you add the shrimp again. When the sauce comes to a boil again, after the shrimp has been added, it is done. Do not continue to boil, since that would over-cook and ruin the shrimp.

## WINE RICE

YIELD: APPROXIMATELY 3 CUPS

2 cups glutinous (sweet) rice
1 teaspoon wine yeast,

crushed to a fine powder
1 teaspoon flour

## PREPARATION

Soak rice in 3 cups cold water for 4 hours. Drain.

Steam rice in a steamer over a piece of cheesecloth or a *white* paper towel for ½ hour.

Discard cheesecloth and place rice in a colander.

Rinse in warm water for 2 to 3 minutes. Drain. *Rice should still be warm!*

Mix the wine yeast with the flour.

Sprinkle the mixture of wine yeast and flour over the rice. Mix well.

Smooth down the mixture with a moistened hand.

Make an indented circle in the rice with a chopstick, about the size of a quarter. You should be able to see the bottom of the casserole.

Cover casserole with aluminum foil secured with a rubber band; then cover with a towel and leave in warm place for 36 to 48 hours or until the well is filled with liquid.

Place rice with all the liquid in a covered glass jar. (It can be kept in the refrigerator for 2 months.)

NOTES: Wine yeast comes in the form of a round ball, about the size of a Ping-Pong ball. It can be stored for several months in a covered jar in the refrigerator.

You can crush wine yeast with a rolling pin, placing it between two layers of wax paper.

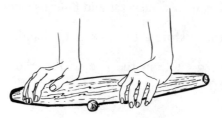

Once you have made a jar of wine rice, it is necessary to open the jar every few days to release gas. If you want to make a new batch, save about ½ cup of the old batch and add it to each quart of the fresh wine rice, after the new batch has fermented.

*To double the recipe*, never stir-fry more than 1 pound of shrimp at a time in the wok unless you have an extremely high flame. After stir-frying the first pound of shrimp, empty it into a serving dish, deglaze, wash, and dry the wok. Then stir-fry the second pound of shrimp and empty the second pound into the serving dish. Do not wash wok. Proceed with the recipe as indicated, remembering to heat the seasoning sauce–wine rice mixture in a small saucepan before adding it to the wok.

Do not attempt to triple this recipe. Even though you have stir-fried 3 pounds of shrimp, a pound at a time, when you mix together the shrimp and seasoning sauce, too much steam will be created and the dish will not be successful. If you wish to make 3 or 4 pounds of shrimp with wine rice, then plan to use 2 woks simultaneously, or 1 wok and 1 sauté pan with high sides.

## SWEET AND SOUR SHRIMP
YIELD: 3 TO 4 SERVINGS IF SERVED ALONE; 6 TO 8 SERVINGS IF SERVED WITH 3 OTHER DISHES

1 pound shrimp (raw, weighed with the shell)

**Marinade**
½ egg white
1 tablespoon sherry
2 teaspoons water chestnut powder

¼ pound snow peas
1 medium-size sweet red pepper
2 scallions (white and green parts)
½ cup water chestnuts, fresh if possible
¼ cup bamboo shoots
½ cup fresh mango or pineapple

**Sweet and Sour Sauce**
¾ cup chicken stock
3 tablespoons honey
3 tablespoons wine vinegar
1 tablespoon Chinese red vinegar
1 tablespoon Chenkong vinegar
1 tablespoon dark soy sauce
1 tablespoon American chili sauce
1 clove garlic, minced

**Binder**
¼ cup pineapple juice
1½ tablespoons water chestnut powder

¼ cup pine nuts
2½ tablespoons peanut oil
1 teaspoon salt

## PREPARATION

Shell, devein, split, wash, drain, and dry shrimp.

Marinate shrimp in egg white, sherry, and water chestnut powder.

Stir well with chopsticks and refrigerate for at least ½ hour or up to 12 hours.

String snow peas and slant-cut each snow pea in 2 or 3 pieces depending on size.

Seed and triangle-cut red pepper.

Slant-cut scallions in 1-inch pieces.

Peel and slice water chestnuts.

Roll-oblique-cut bamboo shoots.

Peel, then roll-oblique-cut mango, or cut pineapple in chunks.

Mix ingredients for sweet and sour sauce in a bowl: chicken stock, honey, vinegars, soy sauce, chili sauce, and garlic.

Mix binder.

Roast nuts (refer to Ingredients, page 65).

## COOKING PROCEDURE

Place wok over high flame for 20 seconds.

Add 2½ tablespoons oil and heat for 20 seconds or until oil is very hot but not smoking.

Restir marinated shrimp with chopsticks. Add shrimp to wok, stir-frying them for 2 to 3 minutes or until they turn pink.

Add 1 teaspoon salt. Mix well, then empty shrimp into a heated serving dish.

Do not wash wok. In the same wok, add the sweet and sour sauce. Bring to a rapid boil over a high flame.

Restir binder. Add binder slowly and stir vigorously with a wire whisk until the sauce thickens.

Add bamboo shoots, red pepper, scallions, and mango. Continue to cook sauce, stirring with a wooden spoon or chopsticks for ½ minute.

Add snow peas and water chestnuts.

Allow the sauce to come to a boil again, then add the shrimp again.

Mix well until the shrimp are hot and the flavors have blended— about ½ minute.

Empty contents of wok into a heated serving dish. Sprinkle with roasted pine nuts.

Serve immediately.

TIMING: This dish requires last-minute attention and must be served immediately.

The shrimp can be marinated up to 12 hours ahead.

The sauce can be mixed the day ahead. If it is made more than one day ahead, freeze it, omitting the garlic. Add the garlic after the sauce has defrosted.

Cut the vegetables early in the day, or a day ahead if you then refrigerate them and wrap them well.

If desired, the shrimp can be stir-fried up to 4 hours ahead, emptied into a serving dish, allow to cool, then covered and re-frigerated. Remove from the refrigerator 15 minutes before thickening the sauce and adding the vegetables. It is a great help to cook the shrimp earlier in the day if you are preparing a multi-course meal or if you are doubling the recipe and must stir-fry one pound of shrimp at a time—which requires deglazing the wok after the first pound of shrimp has been stir-fried.

SUBSTITUTIONS: For the snow peas, you can substitute roll-oblique-cut zucchini, or triangle-cut green pepper.

For the red pepper, you can substitute roll-oblique-cut carrots.

TIPS : Some variations are listed as separate recipes; two abridged recipes follow.

For sweet and sour roast pork, slice roast pork in pieces ½ inch thick and 1½ inches long (refer to Roast Pork recipe). Heat sweet and sour sauce, thicken with binder, add vegetables, then add the roast pork slices. Empty contents of wok onto a heated serving dish and sprinkle with pine nuts.

For sweet and sour chicken, substitute 2 whole chicken breasts, weighing between 12 and 14 ounces each, for the 1 pound shrimp. Follow the recipe for Sweet and Sour Shrimp.

Add binder to the sauce with one hand and stir in a circular motion with a wire whisk to avoid lumps in the sauce.

To save time, bring the sauce to a boil in a small saucepan before adding it to the wok. It will take a shorter time to return to a boil again.

Undercook the shrimp slightly when you are stir-frying it, since it will continue to cook when added to the wok the second time.

For chili sauce, use an American brand such as Heinz or Del Monte; do not use a spicy one, or one with garlic.

If shrimp is overcooked, it becomes tough.

Do not cook more than twice this recipe in one wok, because the shrimp and sauce will create too much steam. If you wish to prepare more than 2 pounds of Sweet and Sour Shrimp, you will need 2 different woks or 1 wok and 1 high-sided saucepan.

Doubling is not recommended for the beginner. The first time you try this recipe, follow the proportions indicated.

# SWEET AND SOUR STEAMED FLOUNDER BALLS (LOW-CHOLESTEROL)

YIELD: 3 TO 4 SERVINGS IF SERVED ALONE; 6 TO 8 SERVINGS IF SERVED WITH 3 OTHER DISHES

**Fish Balls**
1 pound filet of flounder
2 scallions (white and green parts)
1 teaspoon ginger root, minced
1 tablespoon light soy sauce
1 tablespoon sherry
1 tablespoon water chestnut powder
1 egg, slightly beaten
1 teaspoon salt
¼ teaspoon white pepper, ground fresh

**Vegetables for Sauce**
¼ pound snow peas
1 medium-size sweet pepper (red)
2 scallions (white and green parts)

¼ cup fresh water chestnuts
¼ cup bamboo shoots
½ cup fresh mango or pineapple

**Sweet and Sour Sauce**
¾ cup chicken stock
3 tablespoons honey
3 tablespoons wine vinegar
1 tablespoon Chinese red vinegar
1 tablespoon dark soy sauce
1 tablespoon chili sauce
1 clove garlic, minced

**Binder**
¼ cup pineapple juice
1½ tablespoons water chestnut powder
¼ cup pine nuts

## PREPARATION

Mince flounder with 2 cleavers.

Chop scallions.

Mince ginger.

Mix together the light soy sauce, sherry, and water chestnut powder.

In a bowl mix together the ingredients for the fish balls: flounder, scallions, ginger, egg, salt, pepper, soy sauce, sherry, and water chestnut powder.

Wet hands and roll mixture into walnut-size balls.

Steam flounder balls over a medium-high flame for 10 minutes (refer to Cooking Techniques, page 38).

String snow peas and slant-cut each snow pea in 2 or 3 pieces, depending on size.

Seed and triangle-cut pepper.

Slant-cut scallions in 1-inch pieces.

Slice water chestnuts in 3 to 4 pieces.

Roll-oblique-cut bamboo shoots.

Peel, then roll-oblique-cut mango or cut pineapple in chunks.

Mix ingredients for sweet and sour sauce in a bowl: chicken stock, honey, vinegars, dark soy sauce, chili sauce, and garlic.

Mix binder.

Roast nuts (refer to Ingredients, page 65).

### COOKING PROCEDURE

In 1½- to 2-quart saucepan or wok, bring the sweet and sour sauce to a boil over a high flame.

Turn flame to low.

Restir binder. Add binder with one hand and stir vigorously with a wire whisk with the other hand, until the sauce thickens.

Add fish balls and return sauce to a boil.

Add bamboo shoots, red pepper, scallions, and mango. Continue to cook sauce, stirring with a wooden spoon or chopsticks for ½ minute.

Add snow peas and water chestnuts.

Bring to a boil again.

Empty contents of wok into a heated serving dish.

Sprinkle with roasted nuts.

Serve immediately.

See also Timing, Substitutions, and Tips on Sweet and Sour Shrimp.

TIMING: Flounder balls can be steamed early in the day or the day before if wrapped well and refrigerated.

SUBSTITUTIONS: Any white fish filet can be substituted for flounder.

TIPS: For low-cholesterol diets, use 2 egg whites and omit the egg yolk.

Fish balls may be deep-fried and served as an appetizer.

If you wish to deep-fry them, follow this procedure. Heat 3 to 4 cups oil in a wok to 375°. While oil is heating, wet hands and form fish balls. With a spoon, lower one ball at a time into the oil, never exceeding six. Fry fish balls 2 to 3 minutes, turning them with a chopstick in either hand to brown evenly and to avoid them sticking together. Remove balls with a wire strainer and drain on several layers of paper towels. Serve immediately.

While the first 6 are draining, keep them warm on a cookie sheet or shallow roasting pan lined with paper towels in a preheated 200° oven.

Serve alone or with Plum Sauce Dip or Soy Sauce–Vinegar Dip.

One pound 2 ounces shrimp, weighed with the shells, can be substituted for the flounder.

If fish store grinds fish for you, be sure to drain well in a sieve. That will get rid of excess water from the ice with which the fish is ground.

# FLOUNDER WITH LOBSTER SAUCE
## (LOW-CHOLESTEROL)

YIELD: 3 TO 4 SERVINGS IF SERVED ALONE; 8
SERVINGS IF SERVED WITH 3 OTHER DISHES

*I created this dish for those who, due to religious or health reasons, are not allowed to eat shrimp or lobster dishes. It closely approximates Lobster Cantonese because of the ingredients in the sauce.*

1 pound filet of flounder

**Marinade**

1 *egg white, slightly beaten*
1 *tablespoon water chestnut powder*
1 *tablespoon sherry*
1 *teaspoon salt*

4 egg whites, slightly beaten
1 tablespoon fermented black beans
2 cloves garlic, minced
2 teaspoons ginger root, minced

3 scallions (white and green parts)
1 tablespoon sherry
2 teaspoons dark soy sauce
½ teaspoon sugar
¼ pound ground veal
½ cup chicken stock

**Binder**

½ *tablespoon water chestnut powder*
1 *tablespoon sherry*

3 cups safflower oil for deep frying

## PREPARATION

Rinse and dry flounder.

Cut in 1- by 1½-inch pieces.

Marinate the flounder pieces in egg white, 1 tablespoon water chestnut powder, 1 tablespoon sherry, and 1 teaspoon salt.

Refrigerate for at least ½ hour, up to 12 hours.

Beat 4 egg whites slightly.

Mince black beans, garlic, and ginger. Place in a cup.

Slant-cut scallions in 1-inch pieces.

Put 1 tablespoon sherry, 2 teaspoons dark soy sauce, and ½ teaspoon sugar in a cup.

Put ¼ pound veal aside in a cup.

Measure stock.

Mix binder.

## COOKING PROCEDURE

Heat oil in wok until it reaches 325°.

Stir marinated flounder with chopsticks and add to wok.

Over a high flame, stir flounder gently with chopsticks for 2 to 3 minutes, or until the flounder turns white.

Carefully lift flounder pieces out of oil with a wire strainer and drain on several layers of paper towels.

Pour all but 1 tablespoon of oil out of wok into a heat-proof container and reserve for another use.

Do not wash wok.

In the same wok, over a high flame, add black beans, garlic, and ginger, and stir-fry 15 seconds.

Add veal and continue to stir-fry another 2 minutes or until veal turns white.

Add scallions, 1 tablespoon sherry, 2 teaspoons dark soy sauce, and ½ teaspoon sugar, and mix well.

Add chicken stock and bring to a rapid boil.

Add binder and stir until sauce begins to thicken.

Again add flounder and stir-fry gently until it is heated through, about ½ minute.

Turn off flame and stir in egg whites.

Empty contents of wok into a heated serving dish and serve immediately.

**TIMING :** This, like all other fish and seafood dishes, will suffer when kept warm or rewarmed, and should therefore be served immediately.

**SUBSTITUTIONS :** For the flounder you can substitute filet of sea trout (weakfish), striped or sea bass, halibut, or hake.

**TIPS :** Turn off flame immediately after the eggs are added to avoid scrambling the eggs.

When doubling the recipe, increase stock to ¾ cup.

## LOBSTER WITH BLACK BEAN SAUCE
YIELD: 2 SERVINGS IF SERVED ALONE; 4 TO 6
SERVINGS IF SERVED WITH 3 OTHER DISHES

1 lobster (1¼ to 1½ pounds)
2 scallions (white and green parts)
2 tablespoons fermented black beans
1 teaspoon ginger root, minced
1 clove garlic

*Binder*
*2 tablespoons sherry*
*2 teaspoons dark soy sauce*
*2 teaspoons water chestnut powder*

3 tablespoons peanut oil
⅔ cup chicken stock

## PREPARATION
Have the fish market chop the body of the lobster into 2-inch sections, and chop the claws in half. Dry lobster pieces with paper towels.

Shred scallions.

Mince black beans, ginger, and garlic.

Mix binder.

## COOKING PROCEDURE

Place wok over high flame for 30 seconds.

Add 3 tablespoons oil, and heat for 20 seconds or until oil is very hot but not smoking.

Add lobster pieces, and stir-fry for 2 minutes.

Add black beans, ginger, and garlic, and stir-fry for 30 seconds.

Add scallions, and stir-fry for 5 seconds.

Add stock around the sides of the wok and bring to a boil.

Cover and cook for 3 minutes over a medium-high flame.

Uncover; restir binder and add it with one hand as you stir-fry with the other. Continue until the sauce has thickened, the lobster shells are bright red, and the meat is white.

Empty contents of wok into a heated serving dish. Serve immediately.

TIMING: As is the case with all fish and seafood dishes, this dish should be served immediately. It will deteriorate if kept warm.

The lobster can be cut up and refrigerated early in the day. Put the lobster pieces in a bowl with paper towels on the bottom of the bowl and plastic wrap on top.

The remaining preparations can all be done early in the day.

Do not mince garlic more than 1 hour before stir-frying.

SUBSTITUTIONS: For the lobster you can substitute shrimp, scallops, or soft-shell crabs. Specific breakdowns of the basic recipe for each of these substitutions are as follows:

### I. Shrimp with Black Bean Sauce

Marinate 1 pound of shrimp (weighed with shell) in ½ egg white, 2 teaspoons water chestnut powder, and 1 tablespoon sherry. Refrigerate for ½ hour or up to 12 hours.
Follow the previous recipe, adding the shrimp when the lobster is called for.

When the recipe indicates to cover, cook the shrimp for only 1 minute, unless you are using very large shrimp, which should be cooked for 2 minutes.

### II. Scallops with Black Bean Sauce

Marinate 14 ounces scallops in the same marinade as the shrimp. Leave the scallops whole. If you are using bay scallops, do not cover the wok and omit the 3 minutes of cooking that the lobster requires. If you are using sea scallops, cover for 1 minute, then follow the same timing as for the shrimp.

### III. Soft Shell Crabs with Black Bean Sauce

Have the fish market kill the crabs and leave whole if they are very small, or cut in half once crosswise. Dry well with paper towels. Dredge each crab in flour and shake off excess.

Fry crabs over medium-high flame for 2 minutes on each side, or slightly longer if crabs are large.

Continue as recipe indicates, covering for 2 minutes after the stock has been added.

TIPS : Have a little chicken stock ready to pour around the sides of the wok if the sauce becomes too thick.

Choose a flat serving piece in which to serve the lobster. Arrange the cut segments in the shape of the whole lobster.

## SPICED FILET OF SEA TROUT WITH BROCCOLI
### YIELD: 2 TO 3 SERVINGS IF SERVED ALONE; 4 TO 6 SERVINGS IF SERVED WITH 3 OTHER DISHES

¾ pound sea trout filet

**Marinade**
1 egg white
½ teaspoon salt
1 tablespoon sherry

2 teaspoons water chestnut powder

¾ pound Chinese broccoli
4 Chinese mushrooms
¼ cup bamboo shoots, sliced

3 scallions (white and green parts)

1 teaspoon ginger root, minced

1 teaspoon water chestnut powder

1 teaspoon sesame-seed oil with chili

**Seasoning Sauce**

1½ to 2 teaspoons hot sauce
½ teaspoon sugar
1½ tablespoons sherry
2 tablespoons mushroom stock
1 tablespoon dark soy sauce

**Broccoli Seasoning**

1 teaspoon sherry
1 teaspoon salt
½ teaspoon sugar

2 cups peanut oil (for deep-frying)

## PREPARATION

Have fish market bone and skin sea trout. Cut filet into 1-inch cubes.

Marinate the fish cubes in egg white, salt, sherry, and water chestnut powder for at least ½ hour (up to 12 hours) in the refrigerator.

Slant-cut broccoli and blanch (cook in boiling water) for 2 minutes.

Remove broccoli from boiling water and plunge into a bowl of ice water.

Drain broccoli well, then dry with paper towels. The preparation up to this point can be done up to 24 hours before. Refrigerate all prepared ingredients until ready to stir-fry.

Rinse mushrooms, cover with warm water, and soak for 30 to 60 minutes or until soft. Save mushroom stock.

Cut each mushroom in 4 to 6 pieces.

Slice bamboo shoots.

Slant-cut scallions in 1-inch pieces.

Mince ginger.

Mix seasoning-sauce ingredients in a bowl: hot sauce, sugar, sherry, mushroom stock, soy sauce, water chestnut powder, and sesame-seed oil with chili.

Put broccoli seasoning (sherry, salt, and sugar) in a small cup.

## COOKING PROCEDURE

Heat 2 cups peanut oil in a wok until it reaches 325° on a deep-fat-frying themometer.

While the oil is heating, place another wok over high flame for 3 seconds. Add 1 tablespoon oil, and heat for 20 seconds or until oil is very hot but not smoking.

Then add broccoli and stir-fry for 1 minute.

Add the broccoli seasoning and stir-fry for one more minute.

Remove the broccoli and place on a heated serving dish.

Keep the broccoli warm in preheated 200° oven.

When the two cups of oil in the first wok register 325°, gently lower the marinated sea trout cubes into the oil and stir carefully with chopsticks for about 2 minutes.

Remove fish from oil with a wire strainer and drain on several layers of paper towels.

Pour off the oil into a pot or bowl, leaving about 1 tablespoon oil in the wok.

Do *not* wash wok.

Turn the flame to high and add scallions, ginger, mushrooms, and bamboo shoots.

Stir-fry for 1 minute.

Restir the seasoning sauce.

Add fish cubes and seasoning sauce. Mix thoroughly for about 1 more minute.

Empty the contents of the wok (the sea trout) over the middle of the broccoli, which had been placed on a heated serving platter a few minutes before.

Serve immediately.

TIMING: The sea trout can be marinated up to 12 hours in advance.

The broccoli can be blanched 24 hours in advance.

The vegetables and the seasoning sauce can be prepared early in the day or the day before.

The recipe must be served immediately, since the fish will deteriorate when kept warm.

SUBSTITUTIONS: For the sea trout you can substitute red snapper, sea bass, or striped bass.

You can use American broccoli or asparagus instead of the Chinese broccoli.

TIPS: Choose a flat serving piece so the contrasting colors of the dish can be seen. The broccoli should form a green bed and border for the white fish cubes, which are placed in the center.

When doubling this recipe, do not fry more than ¾ pound fish at a time, since that will cause the oil temperature to cool down too rapidly.

If you want to make this dish spicier, increase the amount of hot sauce by 1 teaspoon.

This frying technique, *passing through*, is described under Cooking Techniques, page 36.

## STEAMED FISH WITH HOISIN SAUCE
### YIELD: 2 SERVINGS IF SERVED ALONE; 4 TO 6 SERVINGS
### IF SERVED WITH 3 OTHER DISHES

*Steaming is a light and delicate method of preparing fish. It is low in calories and easy to coordinate in a meal plan, since it takes care of itself while you are madly stir-frying the last-minute dish.*

Sea bass totaling 1½ pounds

**Seasoning Sauce**
1 *tablespoon dry sherry*
1 *tablespoon dark soy sauce*
2 *tablespoons hoisin sauce*
1 *teaspoon hot sauce*

2 *teaspoons sesame-seed oil*

1 teaspoon fermented black beans
1 scallion, shredded
1 tablespoon ginger root, shredded

### PREPARATION
Wash and clean sea bass, both inside and out, leaving whole.

Dry inside and out with paper towels.

Place whole bass on a dish or platter that will fit into the steamer, remembering that it will be served in the same dish.

Spoon the seasoning sauce over the fish, then sprinkle fermented black beans on top.

Place scallion and ginger shreds over the top of the fish in a decorative fashion.

Cover, refrigerate, and let the fish marinate for 1 to 2 hours.

### COOKING PROCEDURE
Heat water in bottom of steamer (water should be 2 to 3 inches deep) to boil.

Set dish with bass in it in steamer and cover.

Cook over high flame for about 15 minutes.

Turn off flame. Do not remove cover; fish will hold for 2 to 3 minutes.

Serve bass on same dish in which it was steamed.

TIMING: The seasoning sauce can be mixed early in the day. Pour it over the fish placed on the dish in which it will be steamed (and served) several hours ahead. Put the fish in the refrigerator, covered with wax paper.

While the fish is steaming you will have time to stir-fry two more dishes.

If the timer goes off before you have finished any last-minute preparations, turn off the flame and leave the cover on the steamer. It will keep for 5 minutes.

SUBSTITUTIONS: For the bass you can substitute red snapper, striped bass, whiting, carp, sea trout (weakfish), and butterfish. They are all good choices for steaming, because of their firmness. A flounder, for example, would not be a good choice for steaming because it is too soft.

TIPS: Alternate seasonings for the hoisin sauce would be: bean sauce, spicy bean sauce, or oyster sauce.

A 1½-pound fish (or two smaller ones equaling 1½ pounds) absorbs more of the seasoning sauce than a larger fish. If you need 3 pounds of fish, try to buy twin 1½-pounders, and place them alongside of each other. If only large fish are available, make 3 to 4 diagonal cuts on both sides of the fish, about ½ inch deep, and increase the steaming time slightly, depending on how thick the fish is. A 2- to 2½-pound fish would only need 2 to 3 additional minutes' cooking time. A 3-pound fish would require 4 to 5 additional minutes. When the eye bulges from the socket, it is done. The cheeks are considered the most delicate part of the fish, and they are usually served to the guest of honor.

In steaming, you place the item *above* the water, and it is cooked by the steam from the boiling water below. A French fish-poacher, therefore, *cannot* be used for steaming unless you have a rack that will elevate the fish above the water, as well as a cover that fits securely. A roasting pan or a dutch oven is easily converted to a steamer by placing an empty can (approximately 3

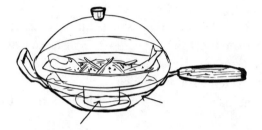

inches high $\times$ 4 inches wide), with its top and bottom removed to form a cylinder, in the bottom of the pan. Fill the pan with water to a depth of 2 to 3 inches. Place the dish in which you will cook and serve the fish on top of the can. (The fish is on the dish, with sauce and garnish over it.) Cover with the top part of the roasting pan (or dutch oven). When preboiling water, the cover should be on so that some steam builds up.

Steaming in a wok is another possibility. Place a rack in the bottom of the wok, fill with water to just below rack, and place dish on top of rack.

If you plan to buy a Chinese steamer, there are two kinds from which to choose: bamboo or aluminum. The bamboo steamer will fit into a 14-inch wok which has been filled with 2 to 3 cups of water. A bowl is about the only shape of serving dish you can use, however, because of the round shape of the steamer. I prefer to use the aluminum steamer: it is easier to clean and lasts longer. Fill the lower part of the steamer with water, then place the layers on top (usually 2, sometimes 3). If the fish is too long, and the pieces do not fit side by side when cut in half, place the thickest half in the bottom layer, the other half in the second layer. If this is done, both halves will cook in the same time, since the thickest portion is closest to the source of steam.

I have used Pyrex, my best china, aluminum, and plastic dishes for steaming; they all work. If you have an appropriate dish for serving the fish, make sure that it fits in the steamer in such a way as to allow the steam to circulate all through the steamer, in order for the fish to cook properly.

To filet fish at the table, start just below the head and make a horizontal cut running down the backbone to the tail. With two large spoons, lift off pieces of fish, first from one side and then from the other. Then lift out the entire backbone, which frees the bottom of the fish.

## STUFFED RED SNAPPER

YIELD: 2 TO 3 SERVINGS WHEN SERVED ALONE; 4 TO 6
SERVINGS WHEN SERVED WITH 3 OTHER DISHES

1 two-pound red snapper

**Stuffing**
2 Chinese mushrooms
   (medium size)
½ cup minced leeks (white
   part only)
1 teaspoon ginger root,
   minced
½ pound shrimp
¼ pound ground pork
1½ tablespoons light soy
   sauce

**Binder for Stuffing**
1 teaspoon water chestnut
   powder
1 tablespoon sherry
1 tablespoon peanut oil

Unwaxed dental floss (for
   sewing)
3 slices ginger root
3 scallions (white and green
   parts)

**Seasoning Sauce**
1 tablespoon bean sauce
2 teaspoons hoisin paste
1 to 2 teaspoons hot sauce
1 tablespoon dark soy sauce
2 tablespoons sherry
1 teaspoon brown sugar

4 tablespoons peanut oil
½ cup chicken stock
flour for dredging

## PREPARATION

Have fish market remove the backbone of the red snapper but leave the fish whole with the head and tail intact. (The fish will look as if it were butterflied.)

To prepare stuffing:

Rinse mushrooms, cover with warm water, and soak for 30 to 60 minutes or until soft.

Mince mushrooms, leeks, and ginger.

Peel, devein, wash, drain, and dry shrimp.

Dice shrimp small.

Set aside ¼ pound ground pork.

Mix binder.

To cook stuffing:

Heat wok over high flame for 30 seconds.

Add 1 tablespoon of oil and heat for 20 seconds or until oil is hot but not smoking.

Add pork and stir-fry for 2 to 3 minutes or until it turns white.

Add mushrooms, leeks, and ginger, and stir-fry for 1 more minute.

Add soy sauce and mix briefly.

Add shrimp and cook for 30 seconds.

Restir binder and add to wok with one hand while stirring with the other for another 30 seconds.

Empty contents of wok onto a plate and allow the stuffing to cool (about ½ hour).

Stuff fish from head to tail. Do not overstuff.

Sew both the dorsal and ventral sides closed with unwaxed dental floss. Taking separate pieces of floss, tie the fish at the head and at least 3 other places along the body.

Slice ginger root.

Slant-cut scallions in 1-inch pieces.

Mix ingredients for the seasoning sauce in a bowl and set aside.

## COOKING PROCEDURE

Dredge fish in flour and brush off excess.

Heat wok over high heat for 30 seconds.

Add 4 tablespoons of oil and turn flame to medium. When oil is hot but not smoking, gently lower the fish into the wok, using both hands.

Sauté fish for 4 to 5 minutes, shaking the wok every minute or so to prevent the fish from sticking.

Using two spatulas, turn the fish over and cook for another 3 minutes.

Turn off flame.

Remove excess oil with basting syringe or spoon.

Turn flame to medium-low and pour the seasoning sauce directly over the fish. Place scallions and ginger on top of the seasoning sauce.

Pour the ½ cup stock around the sides of the wok.

Cover the wok and cook fish for another 10 minutes, shaking the wok every 2 minutes to prevent it from sticking. After 5 minutes, lift the cover to make sure that there is enough liquid in the wok, and to check the flame. The fish should cook at a fast simmer.

Remove the fish from the wok and place it on an oval or rectangular serving platter. The finished dish should have about ½ cup sauce.

Pull the floss gently (it should slip out easily) and serve immediately.

TIMING: Once cooked, this dish must be served immediately.

The stuffing can be cooked, allowed to cool, and then refrigerated a day in advance. The fish can be stuffed, sewed, and refrigerated 2 hours ahead.

SUBSTITUTIONS: For the red snapper you can use sea bass or striped bass.

TIPS: This is a very special recipe and quite delicate. It makes a lovely meal when served with a stir-fried vegetable dish and white rice. It can be made without the stuffing; the timing would remain the same, but it is not necessary to remove the back.

Be sure to sew the fish on both sides, even though it is only split on one side, since it will open up when sautéed.

When serving fish, alert your guests that there may be a few bones remaining.

You can also use an oval sauté pan to prepare this recipe.

Hoisin paste comes in a 4-ounce jar and is available in Chinese grocery stores. It is made from sugar, soy sauce, bean paste, white vinegar, yellow bean powder, and garlic. It is richer than hoisin sauce and is used in much smaller quantities. If hoisin paste is unavailable, use 1 full tablespoon of hoisin sauce.

# STIR-FRIED SCALLOPS WITH MINCED PORK

YIELD: 2 TO 3 SERVINGS IF SERVED ALONE; 6 TO 8
SERVINGS IF SERVED WITH 3 OTHER DISHES

½ pound scallops (1 cup)

*Marinade*
*½ egg white*
*1 teaspoon water chestnut*
  *powder*
*1 teaspoon sherry*

¼ cup Chinese mushrooms
1 cup ground pork
1 clove garlic
2 slices ginger root
¼ cup water chestnuts,
  minced
½ cup bamboo shoots,
  minced
2 scallions, chopped (white
  and green parts)

1 tablespoon sherry
2 tablespoons oyster sauce
¼ cup mushroom stock
  (liquid in which dried
  mushrooms were soaking)
½ cup chicken stock

*Binder*
*1 tablespoon water chestnut*
  *powder*
*1 teaspoon sugar*
*1 tablespoon dark soy sauce*
*½ teaspoon sesame-seed oil*
*1 tablespoon sherry*

2 tablespoons peanut oil

## PREPARATION

Rinse scallops; drain and dry well. If using sea scallops, slice in thirds, keeping round shape; if using bay scallops, leave whole. Mix with ½ egg white, 1 teaspoon water chestnut powder, and 1 teaspoon sherry; then marinate and refrigerate for at least ½ hour.

Rinse mushrooms, cover with warm water, and soak for 30 to 60 minutes or until soft. Save stock.

Set aside 1 cup ground pork.

Mince garlic, ginger, mushrooms, water chestnuts, and bamboo shoots. Chop scallions.

Combine in a cup 1 tablespoon of sherry, oyster sauce, mushroom stock, and chicken stock.

In another cup, mix binder until you have a smooth paste.

### COOKING PROCEDURE

Place wok over high flame for 30 seconds.

Add 2 tablespoons oil, and heat for 20 seconds or until oil is very hot but not smoking.

Add garlic, ginger, and scallions and let sizzle for 15 seconds.

Add ground pork and stir-fry until it loses its redness (about 3 minutes).

Restir scallops in marinade, then add to wok; stir-fry for 2 minutes.

Add minced vegetables—mushrooms, water chestnuts, and bamboo shoots—and stir-fry for ½ minute.

Add sherry–oyster sauce mixture and stir-fry on the highest flame possible for ½ minute.

Restir binder and add with one hand while stirring with the other.

Turn flame to high and cook until sauce thickens, about another ½ minute.

Empty contents of wok into a heated serving dish and serve immediately.

T I M I N G : All the preparations can be done early in the day or the day before. This dish can be kept warm on a hot tray (low setting) or in the oven for 5 minutes.

S U B S T I T U T I O N S : For the pork you can substitute shoulder or breast of veal. For the scallops, you can substitute abalone. Slice in 1-inch square pieces, about ¼-inch thick. Be sure it is the last ingredient added (after the sherry–oyster sauce mixture and before the binder); it should be cooked for no longer than ½ minute, lest it become tough. The best canned-abalone brand is Calmex. Save the liquid from the can and use in place of chicken stock.

TIPS : Rice noodles are excellent as a garnish, since they are crunchy and contrast well with the softer texture of the scallops and pork. Refer to Ingredients, page 65 for instructions on how to deep-fry rice noodles.

# PORK

---

## ROAST PORK

YIELD: 6 TO 8 SERVINGS IF SERVED ALONE AS APPETIZER,
10 TO 12 SERVINGS IF SERVED WITH OTHER APPETIZERS;
4 SERVINGS IF SERVED ALONE AS ENTRÉE

*In China, most homes have no ovens. Roast pork, duck, chicken, whole pig, and their accompanying innards are sold at stores, fully cooked. They are prepared in central ovens, which are as big as closets. You can see them in Chinatown if you make friends with a grocery store clerk. The meat or fowl is marinated first, and then hung in the oven to roast.*

*Mme Chu devised a way of cooking Roast Pork in the following manner, which is adaptable to any American stove. It is a remarkable way of roasting, far superior to the rack-roasting pan method. The heat circulates all around the meat; the end result is a moist piece of meat on the inside with a crusty exterior.*

*Roast Pork can be served as an entrée, as a garnish for wonton soup, stir-fried with vegetables, as an appetizer (hot or cold), shredded in lo mein, diced in fried rice, or converted to sweet and sour. When Roast Pork is called for in a recipe, I will always specify Roast Pork. (When raw pork is called for, as in Hot and Sour Soup, I will simply call for pork.)*

2 pounds lean part of Boston butt

**Marinade**
*4 slices ginger root*
*2 scallions, cut in 2-inch lengths (white and green parts)*
*2 tablespoons dark soy sauce*
*4 tablespoons hoisin sauce*

2 tablespoons American chili sauce
*¼ teaspoon pepper*
*1 tablespoon plum sauce*
*1 tablespoon bean sauce*
*2 cloves garlic, crushed*
*4 tablespoons sherry*
2 tablespoons honey

## PREPARATION
Cut pork into strips, 5 inches × 3 inches × 1½ inches.

Score each strip at intervals of about 1½ inches.

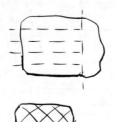

Mix together ingredients of marinade.

Marinate for 2 to 8 hours, turning over once at midpoint of marination.

Refrigerate if marinating longer than 2 hours. Save 2 to 3 tablespoons marinade to add to sauce later on.

Dribble honey over pork.

### COOKING PROCEDURE

Preheat oven to 350°.

Pierce each strip with metal hook and hang each hook over a rung
of the oven rack.

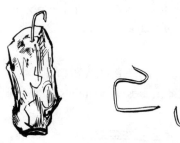

Place water to a depth of 1 inch in a pan below to catch the drippings and to keep the pork moist.

Roast for 40 minutes at 350° and 15 minutes at 450°.

Remove pork from oven. Cool pork for 5 minutes on a rack resting on a plate.

Slice and serve.

TIMING: Roast Pork can be made a day or two in advance, then rewarmed before serving.

When rewarming, in order to prevent pork from becoming overcooked and too dry, reduce timing to 10 minutes instead of 15 minutes at 450°. When ready to serve, preheat oven to 450°, put pork on a rack, and place the rack in a roasting pan to catch drippings; then roast for an additional 5 to 7 minutes.

Roast Pork and all the following variations can be refrigerated for up to 4 days and will stay fresh. It can be frozen if wrapped well in freezer paper or aluminum foil and then in a plastic bag, and will keep for one month.

SUBSTITUTIONS: There are many cuts of meat which can use this marinade; the most familiar is spareribs, which is listed as a separate recipe in the Appetizer section.

Lamb cut in chunks (from the leg) prepared in this marinade, as for shish kebab, is delicious. To the marinade add chopped parsley or cilantro (fresh coriander), and 2 tablespoons of lemon juice. Omit the 2 tablespoons sherry. Barbecue the lamb chunks on an outdoor grill, or run them under the broiler for 3 to 4 minutes on each side. (Cut one chunk of meat to test for done-ness: it should be pink inside.) Serve the lamb with either the traditional accompaniment of onions, tomatoes, and peppers, or a Chinese-style accompaniment of Stir-Fried Zucchini with Yellow Summer Squash.

Roast loin of pork, or shoulder or loin of veal, when prepared with this marinade each makes a great family or company dinner. Place meat in a plastic bag with marinade for 8 hours. Place a rack in a shallow roasting pan with 1 inch of water and place the meat on top of rack and above water, fat side up. Roast at 325° for 30 minutes to the pound or until meat reaches the internal temperature of 170°.

In addition to the cuts I have mentioned, try marinating your own favorite beef, pork, or veal cut and see what favorable reactions your guests and family have. The Roast Pork goes well with apple sauce, baked acorn, squash, broccoli, or brussels sprouts. It is another great way to add some excitement to an otherwise traditional American meal.

TIPS : The Taylor Instant meat thermometer, which works on the same principle as a fever thermometer, is the most accurate. Approximate the cooking time of the roast and, when it is almost done, remove the roast from the oven and take its temperature, being careful to insert the thermometer in the center where it is free of bone or gristle. People usually panic and overcook pork, which is a shame, because then it becomes tough and dry. If your thermometer is accurate, the pork will be white on the inside at 170°.

Always wash your hands, the cleaver, and the chopping block after finishing with them. It *is* possible to contract trichinosis from raw pork, although it is not common. I say this not to scare but to caution you.

If a natural sauce is desired, skim fat from pork drippings and boil down to ¾ cup. Add 2 tablespoons measured marinade and boil again for 1 more minute. Serve on the side, or pour over Roast Pork. Sauce can be thickened, if necessary, with 2 teaspoons water chestnut powder dissolved in 1 tablespoon sherry. Add after the marinade has cooked for 1 minute in the sauce. If the sauce is not used or if there is any left over, it can be frozen and used instead of chicken stock for Roast Pork Lo Mein.

Do not marinate pork longer than 8 hours, since it will toughen the meat.

Chili sauce is not a hot sauce. Use an American brand such as Heinz or Del Monte.

The hooks used to hang the pork while roasting can be made by cutting wire coat-hangers into 3- or 4-inch pieces, bending them to form an S shape, boiling them in water for 10 minutes, scrubbing them with a steel wool pad until all the paint is removed, then filing the ends until they are smooth. If that sounds like a lot of work, it is. Other possibilities are drapery or shower curtain hooks, and poultry skewers which can be bent in the appropriate shape.

If you are making the hooks yourself, do them at least a day before you roast the pork; otherwise, it will take all the fun out of the cooking.

## ROAST PORK WITH MIXED VEGETABLES

YIELD: 3 TO 4 SERVINGS IF SERVED ALONE; 8
SERVINGS IF SERVED WITH 3 OTHER DISHES

1 pound roast pork

2 cloves garlic

*Vegetables*

*Binder*

*¼ pound snow peas*

2 teaspoons water chestnut

*¼ pound bok choy*

   powder

*¼ pound fresh water*

1 tablespoon sherry

   *chestnuts*

1 tablespoon dark soy sauce

*¼ pound mung bean sprouts*

¼ cup almonds, for garnish

4 scallions (white and green

1½ tablespoons peanut oil

   parts)

⅓ cup stock

2 teaspoons ginger root,
   minced

## PREPARATION

Slice roast pork in ½- × 1-inch pieces.

String and slant-cut snow peas in 2 or 3 pieces.

Slant-cut bok choy in 1-inch pieces. Separate leafy parts from the stems.

Peel and slice water chestnuts in 3 to 4 pieces.

Wash and drain bean sprouts.

Slant-cut scallions in 1-inch pieces.

Mince ginger and garlic.

Mix binder.

Roast almonds (refer to Ingredients, page 65).

## COOKING PROCEDURE

Place wok over medium-high flame for 30 seconds.

Add 1½ tablespoons oil and heat for 20 seconds or until oil is hot but not smoking.

Add garlic, scallions, and ginger, and let sizzle for 15 seconds.

Add bok choy stems and stir-fry for 2 minutes.

Add snow peas and stir-fry 1 minute.

Add water chestnuts and bean sprouts, and stir-fry ½ minute.

Add stock around the sides of the wok, turn flame to high, and bring stock to a rapid boil.

Restir binder and add to wok with one hand while you stir-fry with the other, until sauce begins to thicken.

Add roast pork slices and stir-fry until they are thoroughly heated.

Empty contents of wok into a heated serving dish and sprinkle with roast almonds.

Serve immediately.

TIMING: Roast pork can be made the day ahead or up to one month ahead, then wrapped well and frozen (refer to Roast Pork).

The vegetables can be prepared early in the day or the day ahead, if wrapped well and refrigerated. The garlic should not be minced more than 1 hour before stir-frying.

The nuts can be roasted early in the day.

This dish cannot be kept warm, since the vegetables would become soggy.

SUBSTITUTIONS : The recipe calls for 1 pound vegetables. They can be American or Oriental or both.

Pick any combination you like, always bearing in mind color, crunch, and freshness.

You may prefer to use 2 vegetables instead of 4. Choose vegetables in season.

An example of 4 vegetables is fresh mushrooms, sweet pepper, leeks, and asparagus. Examples of 2 vegetables are broccoli and water chestnuts, or zucchini and carrots. Refer to Vegetables, pages 77–96 for how long to cook each vegetable.

Instead of scallions you can substitute 1 cup of leeks, cut in 1-inch pieces, white part only, or ¼ cup minced shallots.

TIPS : If the vegetables start to scorch, turn down the flame under the wok.

To double the recipe, follow the recipe exactly, using twice the amount of all ingredients except the oil. 2½ tablespoons oil is sufficient. The purpose of the oil in stir-frying is only to coat the wok.

The stock that is called for in the recipe should ideally come from the defatted pan juices which remain when you roast your own pork. That will enhance the whole flavor of the dish. If it is not possible, try to use a stock made from deglazed roast drippings.

A last choice for this particular recipe would be College Inn chicken stock.

## MO SHO RO

YIELD: 3 TO 4 SERVINGS IF SERVED ALONE AS APPETIZER;
8 SERVINGS IF SERVED WITH OTHER APPETIZERS;
2 SERVINGS IF SERVED ALONE AS ENTRÉE

½ pound boneless pork
  (Boston butt)
¼ cup Chinese mushrooms
12 dried lily buds, soaked
½ cup bamboo shoots
1 cup bok choy
2 cups Chinese chives or
  1 cup leeks, shredded,
  (white part)

3 eggs
2 tablespoons dark soy sauce
1 tablespoon sherry
½ teaspoon sugar
Peking Doilies (2 per person;
  refer to page 284.)
½ cup bean sprouts
3 tablespoons peanut oil

### PREPARATION

Partially freeze pork.

Slice pork thin, then shred it.

Rinse mushrooms, cover with warm water, and soak for 30 to 60 minutes or until soft. Save stock.

Soak lily buds in warm water for 30 minutes. Remove hard end and cut in half.

Shred bamboo shoots, mushrooms, and bok choy.

Cut chives in 2-inch lengths or shred leeks, white part only.

Scramble 3 eggs in 1 tablespoon oil. Set aside.

Measure soy sauce, sherry, and sugar in a small bowl.

### COOKING PROCEDURE

Wrap Peking Doilies in a damp dishtowel and steam for about 5 minutes while stir-frying other ingredients.

Place wok over high flame for 30 seconds.

Add 2 tablespoons of oil, and heat for 20 seconds or until oil is very hot but not smoking.

Add the pork shreds and stir-fry for about 3 minutes.

Add soy sauce, sherry, and sugar. Mix well.

Add mushrooms, lily buds, and bamboo shoots; stir-fry another 2 minutes.

Add bean sprouts and chives; mix briefly.

Add eggs, breaking into small pieces. Mix all ingredients well and empty contents of wok into serving dish.

Serve with Peking Doilies.

T I M I N G : This dish cannot be kept warm, since the vegetables are shredded fine and would become soggy.

All the preparations can be made early in the day.

Mo Sho Ro is usually served as an appetizer but could also be part of a dinner, accompanied by Peking Doilies or with rice.

S U B S T I T U T I O N S : For the boneless butt you can substitute loin of pork, or the following cuts of veal: shoulder, rib, loin, or leg (scallops).

For the bok choy, you can substitute Shantung cabbage or celery.

For the leeks or Chinese chives, you can substitute 1 cup sliced American yellow onions, or 1 cup scallions, shredded (white and green parts).

T I P S : The doilies are served separately. Guests should fill doilies themselves.

There should be no liquid in the finished dish if you are serving it with Peking Doilies because the moisture will break through the wrapper.

Reserve mushroom stock for another recipe, freezing it if you have no immediate use for it.

Refer to Ingredients for treatment of tree ears, page 71, and lily buds, page 62.

Peking Doilies or Mandarin Pancakes can be made at home or purchased at Oriental grocery markets. Ask for Peking Doilies, or Mandarin Pancakes, which are the same thing; you could also use Shanghai Spring Roll wrappers. Refer to Ingredients, page 73 for storing information.

To steam doilies, separate them by pulling apart with hands. Brush each one *lightly* with sesame-seed oil, then wrap well in a damp dishtowel and steam for 5 minutes. Fold each doily to ¼ its size and place all doilies on a plate.

When using leeks or yellow onions, add with mushrooms, lily buds, and bamboo shoots.

When using scallions, add at the time the recipe indicates for adding chives.

## PORK CURRY

YIELD: 3 TO 4 SERVINGS IF SERVED ALONE; 6 TO 8 SERVINGS IF SERVED WITH OTHER DISHES

*Although curry is a combination of spices indigenous to India, the Chinese developed a taste for it and use curry in several dishes. This particular recipe is an excellent illustration of how the Chinese combine a foreign spice with a native cooking technique, stir-frying.*

1 pound fresh pork (Boston butt or loin)

**Marinade**
1 tablespoon water chestnut powder
1 tablespoon sherry
1 egg white, beaten slightly

1 medium-size green pepper
1 medium-size red pepper

1 medium (4-ounce) Spanish onion
2 cloves garlic
1 teaspoon salt
3 tablespoons curry paste
1 tablespoon tomato paste
1 tablespoon sherry, plus ¼ cup at end for deglazing
1 tablespoon dark soy sauce
1 teaspoon sugar
3 tablespoons peanut oil

## PREPARATION

Freeze pork slightly and slice into ⅜-inch-thick slices, removing any excess fat.

Put pork slices in a bowl and add 1 tablespoon water chestnut powder, sherry, and egg white.

Stir well in one direction with chopsticks until egg white and water chestnut powder coat meat thoroughly. Refrigerate for at least ½ hour, up to 12 hours.

Triangle-cut peppers.

Quarter onion, then separate each quarter into its natural layer divisions; if pieces are too large, cut layer divisions into 1-inch pieces.

Mince garlic.

## COOKING PROCEDURE

Place wok over high flame for 30 seconds.

Add 1 tablespoon of oil, and heat for 20 seconds or until oil is very hot but not smoking.

Add garlic and let sizzle a few seconds.

Add onion and stir-fry for 2 minutes.

Add salt.

Add peppers and stir-fry for another minute or two. Empty contents of wok, but do not wash wok.

Add 2 tablespoons oil in the same wok and heat over a high flame until oil is very hot.

Restir pork in marinade with chopsticks, then add to wok and stir-fry for 1 minute.

Add curry paste and stir-fry for 3 more minutes.

Add tomato paste and stir-fry for another minute.

Add sherry, soy sauce, and sugar. Mix well.

Return vegetables to wok and stir-fry until thoroughly mixed.

Empty contents of wok into a serving dish.

Deglaze wok with sherry; pour deglazing liquid over pork curry and serve.

TIMING : This dish is best served immediately, but if necessary, it can be kept warm in a preheated 200° oven *uncovered* for 3 to 5 minutes. If you plan to keep it warm, use red and green peppers and slightly undercook them. Snow peas will not keep well warmed.

All the preparations can be made early in the day, except for the garlic, which should not be minced more than 1 hour before cooking. You can stir-fry the pork up to 4 hours ahead. Empty it into a serving dish and deglaze the wok. (See Deglazing, page 31.)

Refer to Chicken with Bean Sauce and Nuts for details on stir-frying in advance and doubling the recipe.

SUBSTITUTIONS : For the pork you can substitute the following cuts: veal shoulder or leg (scallops); beef flank, skirt, sirloin, shell, filet mignon, club, or rib; lamb leg, or shoulder.

For the green pepper you can substitute snow peas, zucchini, or asparagus, slant-cut.

For the red pepper you can substitute slant-cut carrots, which require blanching.

Instead of the yellow onion, you can substitute 1 full cup shredded leeks (white part only); ½ cup slant-cut scallions (white and green parts); or 14 shallots, peeled and left whole.

TIPS : Use curry paste and not curry powder. Madras Genuine Sun Brand Curry Paste is the best brand. It should be stored in the refrigerator and will keep for over a year.

The marinade (water chestnut powder, sherry, and egg white) affects the texture and not the taste of the pork. It acts as a tenderizing agent and gives the meat a velvety texture. Be sure to measure the water chestnut powder carefully, leveling off the tablespoon with a chopstick.

It is important to let the oil heat in the wok for 20 to 30 seconds before you add the pork, in order to avoid excessive sticking.

## BRAISED GINGERED SPARERIBS
YIELD: 3 TO 4 SERVINGS IF SERVED ALONE; 6 TO 8 SERVINGS IF SERVED WITH 3 OTHER DISHES

2 pounds spareribs (1-inch pieces)

**Marinade**
1 clove garlic, minced
2 teaspoons light soy sauce
1 teaspoon sugar

⅓ cup dry sherry

¾ cup chicken stock
2½ tablespoons Japanese bean paste (dark)
2 to 3 scallions (white and green parts)
2 slices ginger root
2 tablespoons peanut oil

### PREPARATION
Have butcher chop spareribs into 1-inch pieces.

Trim ribs of excess fat.

Mince garlic.

Marinate spareribs in garlic, soy sauce, and sugar for at least 30 minutes, longer if possible (up to 12 hours).

Mix sherry, stock, and bean paste in a bowl.

Slant-cut scallions.

Slice ginger.

### COOKING PROCEDURE
Place wok over high flame for 30 seconds.

Add 2 tablespoons oil, and heat for 20 seconds or until oil is very hot but not smoking.

Restir spareribs in marinade with chopsticks.

Add 1 pound spareribs, letting them brown and tossing them with two wooden spoons or chopsticks for 2 to 3 minutes.

Remove spareribs from wok.

Add scallions and ginger and let sizzle for a few seconds.

Add remaining 1 pound of spareribs; repeat the browning procedure.

Return the first pound of spareribs to the wok, and add the stock, sherry, and bean paste.

Bring to a boil; then cover and cook at a fast simmer over a medium-low flame for 45 minutes, checking every 15 minutes.

Tilt wok or saucepan to remove fat or refrigerate until the fat has solidified to facilitate removal.

Empty contents of wok into serving dish and serve.

TIMING: This dish can be prepared a day or two in advance. If refrigerated or completely cooked, rewarm in a loosely covered casserole, in a preheated oven at 350° for 10 or 15 minutes. If you want to keep it warm right after cooking, put it in the oven at 225° for no more than 10 minutes.

Leftover spareribs can be rewarmed by placing them on a rack resting on a cookie sheet and broiled for 5 to 7 minutes. That will make them crisp.

SUBSTITUTIONS: For the pork spareribs you can substitute the following cuts: beef short ribs, brisket, or chuck; veal breast or shoulder; pork loin or Boston butt.

The timing will vary a few minutes, depending on the cut of meat and on whether it has bones. When the meat is tender, it is done; to test it, pierce the meat with a poultry skewer, which should go through easily.

For the scallions, you can substitute 6 whole shallots; 1 cup leeks, white part only, cut in 1-inch pieces; or ½ cup yellow onion, sliced.

TIPS : If all the liquid evaporates and the spareribs are done, remove the spareribs from the wok and put them in a serving dish. Pour about ½ cup chicken stock in the wok and turn the flame to high. Let the liquid boil down while you stir with a wooden spoon, scraping up all the brown bits.

When the liquid forms a syrupy glaze, pour it over the spareribs and serve, or refrigerate if you are preparing the spareribs ahead of time. If the pan drippings have burned, this technique cannot be used.

Japanese bean paste is made from soy beans, rice, and salt. It is not an authentic Chinese seasoning sauce, but it adds an excellent flavor to this dish, and it aids in the glazing. There are at least two types available, the dark and the light. It is preferable to use the dark in this recipe, but if you can only get the light, add 1 tablespoon of dark soy sauce to it. If you cannot find either, you can substitute 2 tablespoons (Chinese) bean sauce, or 3 tablespoons dark soy sauce.

Since this dish can be prepared a day in advance, it is wise to include it when you are preparing a multicourse Chinese dinner.

It is important to brown no more than 1 pound spareribs at a time in order for them to brown properly.

To double the recipe, brown 1 pound spareribs in a 12-inch wok, heavy skillet, or dutch oven. Remove spareribs to a wok large enough to hold 4 pounds of spareribs. Repeat with the second, third, and fourth pound of spareribs, adding more oil to the wok if needed. Add scallions and ginger before browning the last pound of spareribs. After the 4 pounds of spareribs have been browned and added to the larger wok, add 1 cup chicken stock, 5 tablespoons bean paste, and ⅔ cup sherry to the wok in which the spareribs have been browned. Let the liquid boil down while you circulate the spatula around the sides of the wok to gently scrape up the brown bits. Pour the liquid over the spareribs and bring to a boil.

Let simmer 45 minutes or until tender. They can be prepared and served in an enamel or copper casserole.

Each time the spareribs are reheated, more fat will be rendered. Be sure to remove it by blotting with paper towels.

The finished dish should have enough liquid barely to glaze the spareribs. If the liquid is too plentiful after the 45-minute cooking period, drain the liquid into a separate container. Remove fat, then pour the liquid back into the wok with the spareribs. Turn the flame high and boil down the liquid, shaking the wok every 5 seconds (to avoid spareribs burning or sticking) until the liquid becomes a syrupy glaze.

## PEKING SPARERIBS

YIELD: 3 TO 4 SERVINGS IF SERVED ALONE; 6 TO 8
SERVINGS IF SERVED WITH 3 OTHER DISHES

*This dish has converted many students who thought they disliked the anise flavor. Although the sauce is reminiscent of sweet and sour, it has its own unique taste that makes this an unusual dish. It differs from sweet and sour in that the sauce is not overly sweet and not plentiful.*

1¼ pounds spareribs

**Marinade**
1 *tablespoon sherry*
2 *tablespoons light soy sauce*

4 tablespoons brown sugar
3 tablespoons Chinese red vinegar
½ teaspoon five-spice powder
1 whole star anise (8 pods)
3 tablespoons chicken stock

2 scallions (white and green parts)

**Binder**
1 *teaspoon sesame-seed oil*
1 *teaspoon water chestnut powder*
1 *teaspoon chicken stock*

½ cup water chestnut powder (for dredging)
2 cups peanut oil

## PREPARATION

Have butcher cut spareribs into 1-inch pieces. Remove excess fat.

Marinate them in 1 tablespoon sherry and 2 tablespoons light soy sauce for at least 30 minutes (up to 12 hours).

In a small saucepan put sugar, vinegar, five-spice powder, star anise, and chicken stock. Bring to a boil, then turn off flame and let sauce steep for 1 hour. Remove star anise.

Shred scallions.

Make binder: mix 1 teaspoon sesame-seed oil, 1 teaspoon water chestnut powder, and 1 teaspoon stock to a fine paste.

Drain spareribs, reserving marinade to add to sauce steeping in pan.

Coat spareribs with water chestnut powder.

## COOKING PROCEDURE

Heat 2 cups of oil to 325°.

Add spareribs and fry for 5 minutes over a medium-high flame. Oil should maintain a temperature of 300°.

Stir spareribs gently with chopsticks once in a while while they are frying.

Remove spareribs from oil with wire strainer and drain on several layers of paper towels. Strain the oil and then return it to the wok.

When spareribs are cool (after about 30 minutes), heat oil to 375° and fry them a second time for 1 or 2 minutes, until they are brown and crisp.

Drain spareribs again on fresh paper towels.

Remove oil from wok, leaving 1 tablespoon. Do *not* wash wok.

In the same wok, heat remaining oil over high flame and add shredded scallions.

Stir-fry for 30 seconds, then add sauce to the wok.

Bring the sauce to a boil. Restir binder and add to sauce with one hand while mixing with the other until the sauce thickens.

Again add spareribs and mix well for 1 minute.

Empty contents of wok into a heated serving dish, and serve immediately.

TIMING: The spareribs can be cut the day ahead, and marinated up to 12 hours ahead.

The first frying of the spareribs can be done up to 4 hours ahead. Drain on paper towels and allow to cool in a single layer. When cool, cover with wax paper but do not refrigerate.

The sauce—which includes sugar, vinegar, five-spice powder, star anise, and chicken stock—can be brought to a boil, allowed to steep for 1 hour, and have the star anise removed, early in the day.

Remember to add leftover marinade from spareribs to the sauce.

You can shred the scallions and mix the binder early in the day.

The second frying of the spareribs should be done in thirds, making sure the oil temperature remains at 375°. That means you have to heat the oil for about 30 seconds after you remove the first ⅓ of the total quantity of spareribs before you add the second ⅓, and so on. It is important that the oil temperature be maintained. The purpose of the first frying is to cook the ribs; the purpose of the second frying is to make them crisp.

Once the dish is completed it must be served immediately. Do not keep it warm.

After the oil has reached 375°, the remaining part of the recipe requires about 3 or 4 minutes.

TIPS: The last part of this recipe requires an adept stir-fryer. There is a small amount of sauce; it is actually a coating for the spareribs. When the spareribs are again added to the wok (after the second frying), they must be tossed quickly and efficiently in order for them to be evenly coated with the small amount of sauce.

When doubling this recipe, double the amount of all the ingredients except the oil and follow the recipe as indicated.

Leftovers are best eaten cold.

## TWICE-FRIED SWEET AND SOUR PORK

YIELD: 3 TO 4 SERVINGS IF SERVED ALONE; 6 TO 8
SERVINGS IF SERVED WITH 3 OTHER DISHES

1 pound boneless pork (lean part of Boston butt or loin)

**Marinade**
1½ tablespoons light soy sauce
1 tablespoon sherry

**Vegetables**
¼ pound snow peas
1 medium-size sweet red pepper
2 scallions (white and green parts)
½ cup water chestnuts (fresh if possible)
¼ cup bamboo shoots
½ cup fresh mango or pineapple

**Sweet and Sour Sauce**
¾ cup chicken stock

3 tablespoons honey
3 tablespoons wine vinegar
1 tablespoon Chinese red vinegar
1 tablespoon Chenkong vinegar
1 tablespoon dark soy sauce
1 tablespoon chili sauce (Heinz or Del Monte)
1 clove garlic, minced

**Binder**
¼ cup pineapple juice
1½ tablespoons water chestnut powder

¼ cup nuts (pine, almonds, or cashews)
¾ cup water chestnut powder for dredging
3 to 4 cups peanut oil for deep-frying

## PREPARATION

Cut pork into ¾-inch cubes.

Place pork in a bowl and marinate in sherry and light soy sauce.

Mix with chopsticks and let marinate at least 1 hour, up to 12 hours.

String snow peas and slant-cut each snow pea in 2 or 3 pieces depending on size.

Seed and triangle-cut red pepper.

Slant-cut scallions in 1-inch pieces.

Peel and slice water chestnuts.

Roll-oblique-cut bamboo shoots.

Peel, then roll-oblique-cut mango, or cut pineapple in chunks.

Mix ingredients for sweet and sour sauce in a bowl: chicken stock, honey, vinegars, soy sauce, chili sauce, and garlic.

Mix binder.

Roast nuts (refer to Ingredients, page 65).

Spread ¾-cup water chestnut powder over a cookie sheet and dredge the pork cubes, one at a time. Massage gently with fingers to coat well.

## COOKING PROCEDURE

Heat oil in wok to 325°.

Lower pork pieces into the oil, ½ pound at a time with a wire strainer, turning them with chopsticks for 5 minutes.

Pork should fry at 300°.

Lift pork pieces out of oil with wire strainer and drain well over several layers of paper towels. Let cool in a single layer at least 20 minutes. If desired, this step can be done 4 to 5 hours ahead. Do not refrigerate pork.

When oil has cooled, strain through a sieve lined with cheesecloth.

Heat oil to 375°.

While oil is heating, bring the sweet and sour sauce to a boil in a saucepan over a high flame.

Restir binder.

Add binder and stir vigorously with a wire whisk until the sauce thickens.

Set aside.

Refry pork pieces in ¼-pound quantities, making sure to bring the oil temperature back to 375° before adding additional pieces.

Drain pork pieces on several layers of paper towels.

While pork is draining, bring sweet and sour sauce back to a boil.

Add bamboo shoots, red pepper, scallions, and mango. Continue to cook sauce, stirring with a wooden spoon or chopsticks for ½ minute.

Add snow peas and water chestnuts.

Allow sauce to return to a boil.

Pour sauce and vegetables into a serving dish and sprinkle with nuts.

Put the pork cubes on top. If you combine the pork and the sauce, the crisp pork pieces will become soggy.

# BEEF

---

## BEEF WITH BLACK BEAN SAUCE
YIELD: 3 TO 4 SERVINGS IF SERVED ALONE; 6 TO 8
SERVINGS IF SERVED WITH 3 OTHER DISHES

1 pound boneless beef (flank or skirt)

*Marinade*
*1 tablespoon sherry*
*2 teaspoons light soy sauce*
*1 teaspoon sugar*
*1 teaspoon water chestnut powder*
*1 egg white, beaten slightly*

2 tablespoons fermented black beans
2 cloves garlic

2 teaspoons ginger root, minced
¾ cup yellow onions, sliced
2 scallions (white and green parts)
1 cup very ripe tomatoes, diced

*Binder*
*1 tablespoon dark soy sauce*
*2 tablespoons sherry*
*1 teaspoon water chestnut powder*

3 tablespoons peanut oil

## PREPARATION

If using flank steak, trim the fat, cut in thirds with the grain, then cut each piece in half crosswise against the grain. Freeze the 6 pieces in a single layer (do not pile on top of each other) in 1-pound quantities. Cut whatever pieces are needed into ¼-inch-thick slices, against the grain.

If using skirt steak, trim fat, cut in half crosswise, and freeze in the same way. When meat is partially frozen (1½ to 3 hours, depending on the temperature of your freezer), remove from freezer and cut into ¼-inch-thick slices, with the grain.

Marinate beef in 1 tablespoon sherry, 2 teaspoons light soy sauce, 1 teaspoon sugar, 1 teaspoon water chestnut powder, and egg white.

Refrigerate at least ½ hour, up to 12 hours.

Mince black beans, garlic, and ginger. Mix together in a bowl.

Slice onions.

Shred scallions.

Dice tomatoes.

Mix binder in a small cup.

## COOKING PROCEDURE

Place wok over high flame for 30 seconds.

Add 1 tablespoon oil and heat 20 seconds, or until oil is hot but not smoking.

Restir beef in marinade with chopsticks.

Add half of beef and stir-fry until both sides of beef are well browned, about 2 minutes. Empty contents of wok into a heated serving dish.

Do not wash wok.

Heat 1 tablespoon oil in wok over high heat and add black beans, garlic, and ginger. Stir-fry a few seconds.

Add remaining half of beef and stir-fry until beef is well browned.

Empty contents of wok into the same serving dish.

Deglaze, wash, and dry wok. Pour deglazing liquid over beef. The entire dish can be prepared ahead up to this point.

If you are browning the meat more than 2 hours ahead of time, it should be refrigerated. Allow it to cool 30 minutes before refrigerating.

Stir-fry onions and scallions in 1 tablespoon oil over medium-high flame for 2 minutes.

Add tomatoes and stir-fry another minute.

Remix binder, then add with one hand while mixing with the other for 30 seconds.

Add browned beef mixture and stir-fry over high flame for about 1 minute or until mixture is hot.

Empty contents of wok into heated serving dish.

Serve immediately.

TIMING : This dish can be kept warm for 5 to 8 minutes, uncovered, in a preheated 225° oven.

The beef can be marinated up to 12 hours in advance.

The vegetables can all be prepared early in the day or the day before if wrapped well and refrigerated.

The garlic should not be minced more than 1 hour before stir-frying.

The beef can be fried (and the wok deglazed and washed) up to 4 hours in advance. Remove beef to a serving dish, pour deglazing liquid over beef, allow to cool, then cover with wax paper. Refrigerate beef if you are browning it more than 2 hours in advance.

The remaining part of this recipe, which consists of stir-frying the onions and tomatoes and combining them with the beef and binder, requires only a few minutes.

S U B S T I T U T I O N S : For the flank or skirt steak you can substitute the following cuts: pork loin or Boston butt; veal shoulder, sliced thin against the grain, or scallops from the leg, cut in large dice.

You could also use more tender cuts of beef, such as filet mignon, sirloin, shell, club, rib, and so on. With these cuts, slice the beef in ½-inch-thick pieces. Eliminate the water chestnut powder and egg white from the marinade, since they act as tenderizing agents. Do *not* brown the beef any longer than 2 minutes, because a tender cut of meat should be served medium rare.

For the onion and scallions, you can substitute 1 cup leeks, shredded (white part only), or Chinese chives, cut in 2½-inch lengths.

For the tomatoes, you can substitute shredded green or red pepper.

It is important to choose a bright-colored vegetable to contrast with the dark brown meat.

T I P S : To deglaze, add 3 tablespoons liquid (sherry or chicken stock) to the wok immediately after removing the beef. Let the liquid boil down while stirring with the spatula until the liquid reduces to a thick syrupy glaze. Pour over the beef.

Wash and dry wok. If you are doubling the recipe, you will have to deglaze the wok twice, remembering to wash and dry out the wok well after deglazing.

You can stir-fry twice the quantity of vegetables at one time.

If thinning occurs, drain sauce from beef and vegetables, and boil down. Thicken again with an emergency binder (refer to Cooking Techniques), then pour thickened sauce over beef-and-vegetable mixture, and serve. There should be no more than ¼ cup sauce.

Skirt steak (also called diaphragm) is a little-known cut of beef. It is available and frequently on sale in many supermarkets. To my taste, it has more flavor and is more tender than flank steak. It can also be marinated in one piece, then broiled and sliced as London broil.

## SZECHUAN SHREDDED BEEF
### YIELD: 2 TO 3 SERVINGS IF SERVED ALONE; 4 TO 6 SERVINGS IF SERVED WITH 3 OTHER DISHES

¾ pound boneless beef
  (flank or skirt)

**Marinade**
2 teaspoons light soy sauce
1 tablespoon water chestnut
  powder
1 tablespoon sherry
½ egg white, beaten slightly

½ cup carrots, shredded
1 cup broccoli (middle part
  of stem), shredded
½ cup sweet red pepper,
  shredded
1 fresh hot pepper, shredded
4 scallions (white part only),
  shredded

1 clove garlic, minced
2 teaspoons ginger root,
  minced

**Seasoning Sauce**
1 tablespoon hoisin sauce
1 tablespoon bean sauce
2 teaspoons plum sauce
1 tablespoon sherry
1 tablespoon Chinese red
  vinegar
1 or 2 teaspoons hot sauce
1 tablespoon dark soy sauce
1 teaspoon water chestnut
  powder

3 tablespoons peanut oil

## PREPARATION

Slightly freeze beef, then shred it. (Refer to page 23.)

Marinate beef in light soy sauce, water chestnut powder, sherry, and the slightly beaten egg white.

Refrigerate for at least ½ hour or up to 12 hours.

Peel, then shred, carrots and broccoli, and place them in a bowl.

Seed, then shred, sweet and hot peppers, and place them in a bowl.

Shred scallions and place them in the same bowl with the peppers.

Mince garlic and ginger, and place in a small cup.

Mix together in a bowl ingredients for the seasoning sauce: hoisin sauce, bean sauce, plum sauce, sherry, vinegar, hot sauce, soy sauce, and water chestnut powder.

## COOKING PROCEDURE

Place wok over medium flame for 30 seconds.

Add 1 tablespoon of oil, and heat for 20 seconds or until oil is hot but not smoking.

Add garlic and ginger and stir-fry for 15 seconds.

Add broccoli and carrots and stir-fry one minute. Turn flame to high.

Add peppers and scallions and stir-fry one minute.

Empty contents of wok into a heated serving dish.

Do *not* wash wok.

Stir marinated beef with chopsticks.

Heat remaining 2 tablespoons of oil in the same wok.

Add beef and stir-fry about 2 minutes or until the beef loses its redness. Remove beef from the wok.

Restir seasoning sauce and add along with vegetables and stir-fry one more minute or until thoroughly mixed and hot.

Empty contents of wok into a heated serving dish. Serve immediately.

TIMING: The beef can be trimmed and frozen several months ahead or as little as several hours ahead. The purpose of slightly freezing the beef is to facilitate the slicing and shredding. It can be marinated up to 12 hours ahead.

The seasoning sauce and the vegetables can be prepared early in the morning or the day before. Cover and refrigerate.

If desired, the beef can be stir-fried up to 4 hours ahead of time, emptied into a serving dish, allowed to cool, then covered and refrigerated. In this case, follow procedure for doubling recipe listed under tips. Remove from the refrigerator 15 minutes before stir-frying the vegetables. Cooking the beef is a great help if you are preparing a multicourse meal, or if you are doubling the recipe and must stir-fry ¾ pound of beef at a time, which requires you to deglaze the wok after stir-frying the first ¾ pound of beef. The deglazing liquid is then poured over the beef (refer to Cooking Techniques, page 31).

Do not mince the garlic more than 1 hour before cooking, since its flavor weakens when peeled and exposed to air.

This dish is best served immediately, but if necessary it can be kept warm in a preheated oven at 200° for 3 to 5 minutes, uncovered. If you are planning to keep it warm, slightly undercook the vegetables.

SUBSTITUTIONS: Instead of flank or skirt steak, you can substitute more tender cuts of beef, such as sirloin, shell, rib, and filet. Thicker shreds are preferable in these cases because they are more tender. Other substitutes include the following cuts: veal shoulder or leg; pork boneless loin or Boston butt.

You can also substitute poultry, using boned chicken breasts or dark meat, boned duck or turkey. Poultry must be raw.

TIPS: If you would like to make the dish spicier, increase the amount of minced ginger to 1 tablespoon, and the hot sauce from 2½ to 3 teaspoons, depending on the type of hot sauce you are using—each brand varies in strength.

If the vegetables are scorching, turn down the flame under the wok, or turn off completely for ½ minute.

To double the recipe, follow this procedure: stir-fry ¾ pound beef; empty beef into a heated serving dish. Deglaze wok and pour deglazing liquid over beef. Wash and dry wok. Stir-fry double the amount of vegetables in 2 tablespoons of oil; empty vegetables into the same serving dish; do not wash wok. Stir-fry another ¾ pound of beef in the wok; again add first ¾ pound of beef, along with vegetables and seasoning sauce and stir-fry until hot, 1 or 2 minutes.

Unless the flame on your stove is extremely high, do not attempt to triple this recipe. Even though you brown the beef ¾ pound at a time, the meat and vegetables will create too much steam and the final dish will not be as successful. If you want to double the recipe and brown all the beef ahead of time, you will have to deglaze twice. When ready to serve, start with the stir-frying of the vegetables, then add the browned beef along with seasoning sauce and cook until hot.

## BEEF WITH TEA SAUCE

1 pound boneless beef
(flank or skirt steak)

*Marinade*
*½ egg white*
*1 tablespoon sherry*
*1 tablespoon water chestnut
  powder*

2 bunches watercress
4 scallions (white part only)
2 teaspoons ginger root,
  minced
2 cloves garlic

*Seasoning Sauce*
*1 to 2 teaspoons hot sauce*
*1 tablespoon Satay paste*
*2 teaspoons dark soy sauce*
*1 tablespoon sherry*
*1 tablespoon brewed tea*
*1 tablespoon bean sauce*
*1 teaspoon water chestnut
  powder*
*1 teaspoon sesame-seed oil*
*1 teaspoon fish sauce*

*3½ tablespoons peanut oil*

## PREPARATION

Partially freeze beef.

Slice beef ⅜ inch thick. Flank steak is first cut with the grain and then against the grain; skirt steak is cut with the grain (see instructions for Beef with Black Bean Sauce).

Marinate beef in egg white, 1 tablespoon sherry, and 1 tablespoon water chestnut powder. Refrigerate for ½ hour or up to 12 hours.

Cut 1½ inches off the stems of the watercress.

Wash and drain the watercress well, leaving whole.

Shred scallions.

Mince ginger and garlic.

Place scallions, ginger, and garlic in a small bowl.

Mix together in a bowl the ingredients for the seasoning sauce: hot sauce, Satay paste, soy sauce, sherry, tea, bean sauce, water chestnut powder, sesame-seed oil, and fish sauce.

## COOKING PROCEDURE

Place wok over high flame for 30 seconds.

Add 1 tablespoon oil, and heat for 20 seconds or until oil is very hot but not smoking.

Add watercress and stir-fry for 1 minute.

Empty contents of wok into a heated serving dish.

Spread watercress around the edges of the serving dish.

Wash and dry wok.

Heat wok over high flame and add ½ tablespoon oil.

When oil is hot but not smoking, add garlic, scallions, and ginger, and stir-fry for 1 minute.

Empty contents of wok into the small bowl.

Do not wash wok.

Heat remaining 2 tablespoons oil over high flame until very hot but not smoking.

Restir marinated beef with chopsticks and add to wok.

Stir-fry beef for 2 to 3 minutes.

Restir seasoning sauce, add to wok, and mix briefly.

Again add garlic, scallions, and ginger, and stir-fry 1 more minute or until it is thoroughly mixed and very hot.

Place beef over watercress, leaving some watercress around the side to form a border.

Serve immediately.

**TIMING**: This recipe must be served immediately.

All preparations can be made early in the day, with the exception of mincing the garlic.

If desired, you can stir-fry the beef up to 4 hours ahead, in which case the wok must then be deglazed, washed, and dried. The deglazing liquid is poured back over the beef (refer to Cooking Techniques, page 31 for deglazing instructions). Allow the beef to cool for 30 minutes, then cover it to avoid it drying out. Refrigerate the cooked beef if you have stir-fried it more than 2 hours ahead.

**SUBSTITUTIONS**: For the flank or skirt steak you can substitute the following cuts: beef sirloin, shell, rib, or filet mignon; veal shoulder, scallops, loin, or rib; pork loin or Boston butt; poultry—white and/or dark meat.

**TIPS**: If you want to make this dish spicier, increase the amount of hot sauce to 1 tablespoon and the ginger root to 1 tablespoon.

If Satay paste is not available, increase bean sauce to 2 tablespoons.

If fish sauce is not available, it can be omitted.

When doubling this recipe, refer to notes on Szechuan Shredded Beef.

Satay paste is available at Chinese grocery stores, such as the Chinese American Trading Company, 91 Mulberry Street, New York, New York 10013, and United Market, 84 Mulberry Street, New York, New York 10013. It is sold in a jar and may be stored for 6 months in the refrigerator. It contains soy sauce, meat extract, chili, and other spices.

Fish sauce is also available in Oriental grocery stores. It is a concentrated, strong-smelling sauce from fish essences, and should be used sparingly. It is sold in a jar and can be stored for 6 months in the refrigerator.

## BARBECUED SHORT RIBS OF BEEF

YIELD: 6 SERVINGS IF SERVED ALONE AS APPETIZER;
8 SERVINGS IF SERVED WITH OTHER APPETIZERS;
3 TO 4 SERVINGS IF SERVED ALONE AS ENTRÉE

2 pounds short ribs
  (flanken), lean and meaty

*Marinade*
*2 tablespoons brown sugar*
*3 tablespoons light soy sauce*
*1 tablespoons sherry*
*1 tablespoon sesame-seed oil*

*2 cloves garlic, minced*
*1 teaspoon ginger root, minced*
*2 scallions, chopped (white and green parts)*
*¼ teaspoon freshly ground pepper*
*2 tablespoons sesame seeds*

### PREPARATION

Have butcher cut short ribs in small, 1½- × 2-inch pieces.

Trim fat from ribs.

Score each rib on all sides, every ½ inch.

Mix ingredients for marinade in a bowl.

Place ribs in a shallow rectangular pan and pour marinade over ribs.

Turn the ribs over in the marinade, making sure that the marinade touches all surfaces and cuts.

Marinate for 6 to 8 hours, turning the ribs every 2 hours.

### COOKING PROCEDURE

Preheat oven to broil for 15 minutes.

Remove ribs from marinade and place on a rack set over a shallow roasting pan.

Broil ribs 4 inches from the broiler flame for 8 to 10 minutes on each side.

Serve hot or cold.

TIMING : Short ribs of beef can be served as an appetizer or as part of dinner, either hot or cold.

If desired, they can be cooked early in the day or the day before, allowed to cool on a rack and then rewarmed in a preheated oven at 425° for 5 to 7 minutes. If you plan to rewarm, only cook them for 6 minutes on each side.

SUBSTITUTIONS : This is an excellent marinade which can be used on many different types of meat. For the ribs you can substitute pork—spareribs, country-style spareribs cut in 1½-inch pieces, or loin chops, cut 1 inch thick (these cuts do not need scoring).

To substitute beef, use skirt steak, flank, shell, sirloin, filet mignon, club or rib. After marinating any of the above, broil as you would an American steak to desired done-ness.

If you prefer veal, buy loin, rib, or shoulder chops, cut 1 to 1½ inches thick. Broil 8 to 10 minutes on each side.

To use lamb, select loin or shoulder chops, cut 1½ inches thick. Broil 5 to 8 minutes on each side. You can also use chunks of lamb cut from the leg, as for shish kebab: make 1½-inch cubes, and broil 4 minutes on each side. For lamb add 1 tablespoon freshly squeezed lemon juice to the marinade.

TIPS : Any of these meats can be grilled on an outdoor barbecue, which will greatly enhance the flavor.

If a natural sauce is desired after you remove the meat from the rack, add ½ cup liquid (sherry, white wine, vermouth, chicken, veal, pork, or beef stock) to the roasting pan, and boil down until the liquid in the pan reduces to half, stirring constantly with a wooden spoon. Pour the liquid into a Pyrex measuring cup and remove the fat (refer to Cooking Techniques, page 51). Serve the ribs with the natural sauce on the side to be used on the white rice. Or reserve the sauce and use in stir-fried vegetable dishes.

When turning over the ribs after the first 8 to 10 minutes of broiling, pour a little water in the bottom of the roasting pan to prevent the pan juices from burning.

## FIVE-SPICE BRAISED BEEF
YIELD: 4 TO 6 SERVINGS IF SERVED WITH RICE AND VEGETABLE;
8 TO 12 SERVINGS IF SERVED WITH 3 OTHER DISHES

*The Chinese are not as well known to Americans for their casserole or braised dishes as for their stir-fried dishes, but this type of dish is frequently enjoyed. In China it may be served with a vegetable such as duck apples.*

1 brisket of beef (5 pounds)          ¼ cup dark soy sauce
2 cloves garlic                       1 teaspoon five-spice powder
4 slices ginger root                  1 cup sherry
2 cups leeks (white and green         1 cup stock
   parts)                             4 tablespoons peanut oil
2 tablespoons bean sauce

### PREPARATION
Crush garlic.

Slice ginger.

Cut off root end of leeks and wash well to remove sand.

Cut leeks in 1-inch pieces.

Mix together the bean sauce, soy sauce, five-spice powder, sherry, and stock.

### COOKING PROCEDURE
In a large dutch oven or wok, heat the 4 tablespoons oil until very hot but not smoking.

Add brisket and brown well on all sides. That should take about 5 minutes.

Remove brisket and place on a plate.

Pour off oil, leaving one tablespoon.

Turn flame to medium-low.

In the remaining oil, stir-fry garlic, ginger, and leeks for 1 minute.

Place the brisket on top of the garlic, ginger, and leeks.

Pour the combined bean sauce, soy sauce, five-spice powder, sherry, and stock over the brisket, and bring to a boil.

Cover and turn the flame to low.

Simmer the brisket for about 3 hours or until tender.

While the brisket is simmering, set the timer every 30 minutes—to baste, to check that there is enough liquid, and to make sure that the brisket is not sticking to the bottom of the pot.

When brisket is tender, remove liquid and defat.

Pour liquid back into the cooking vessel and boil down the juices over a medium-high flame until it forms a thick syrupy glaze.

Remove the brisket from the pot and place on a serving platter.

Pour the thickened juices over the meat and serve.

TIMING: This recipe can be made a day or 2 in advance and then rewarmed in a preheated 250° oven for 15 to 20 minutes when ready to serve. Any leftover portion of the beef can be rewarmed in the same manner.

SUBSTITUTIONS: For the brisket you can substitute the following cuts: beef chuck or shin, rump roast, bottom round, short ribs, or flanken; veal shoulder; or pork loin, Boston butt, or fresh (not smoked) shoulder (also called picnic shoulder or cali).

TIPS: For the five-spice powder, you can substitute 1 whole star anise (8 pods).

For the leeks, you can substitute 1 cup scallions (white and green parts), slant-cut in 1-inch pieces, or 1 cup sliced onions.

When the Chinese serve a whole piece of braised meat, they actually overcook it by about 30 to 45 minutes, so that when it is brought to the table it is so tender it can be broken apart with chopsticks. If you wish to serve it in this manner, place a rack in the bottom of the cooking vessel after the leeks, garlic, and ginger have cooked for a minute. Then place the brisket on the rack. When it is finished, lift the rack out of the pot with the brisket on top of it. Slide the meat off the rack and onto the serving platter, then pour the juices over the meat. Put a pair of chopsticks in the middle of the brisket and move them in a circular motion. The meat should fall apart.

If you prefer, slice the meat as you would an American or French braised cut of meat. For this purpose, the meat is tender when it is pierced easily with a poultry skewer. When browning the meat, use two wooden spoons or spatulas to turn it over. A metal fork would pierce the meat, causing it to lose some of its natural juices and flavor.

Duck apples are a seasonal starchy vegetable eaten in China. They can be purchased in Oriental markets in the United States. They are also referred to as arrowheads. They are shaped like water chestnuts, though slightly pointed at one end, and are prepared in the following manner: peel and rinse under cold running water, leave whole, and add in the last ½ hour of cooking.

# VEAL WITH SHALLOTS

YIELD: 2 TO 3 SERVINGS IF SERVED ALONE; 4 TO 6
SERVINGS IF SERVED WITH 3 OTHER DISHES

1 pound veal scallops (from leg)

*Marinade*
*½ egg white*
*1 tablespoon sherry*
*2 teaspoons water chestnut powder*

14 to 16 shallots, depending on size
1 tablespoon ginger root, minced
1 clove garlic

1½ tablespoons fermented black beans
2 tablespoons sherry
¾ tablespoon light soy sauce
¾ tablespoon dark soy sauce
½ teaspoon sugar

*Binder*
*1 tablespoon sherry*
*1 teaspoon water chestnut powder*

3 tablespoons peanut oil

## PREPARATION

Have butcher pound the veal scallops to tenderize them.

Dice veal large (1 inch × 1 inch).

Marinate veal in egg white, 1 tablespoon sherry, and 2 teaspoons water chestnut powder. Refrigerate at least ½ hour, up to 12 hours.

Peel shallots and leave whole.

Mince ginger and garlic.

Chop black beans coarsely and then soak them in 2 tablespoons sherry.

Place shallots, ginger, and garlic in small bowl.

Place the light and dark soy sauces and the sugar in a small cup.

Mix binder.

## COOKING PROCEDURE

Place wok over high flame for 30 seconds.

Add 2 tablespoons oil and heat for another 30 seconds. Oil should be hot but not smoking.

Restir veal in marinade with chopsticks, add to wok, and stir-fry for about 3 minutes or until veal is thoroughly cooked.

Empty contents of wok into a heated serving dish.

Deglaze wok with ¼ cup sherry (refer to Cooking Techniques, page 31).

Pour deglazing liquid over veal.

Wash and dry wok.

The entire dish can be prepared ahead up to this point.

Heat 1 tablespoon oil over medium flame for 30 seconds.

Add shallots, ginger, and garlic, and stir-fry for 2 minutes.

Move the shallots, ginger, and garlic to the side of the wok and add the black beans and sherry, mashing them with the back of the spatula for 30 seconds.

Add the light and dark soy sauces and sugar and mix for 5 seconds.

Again add the veal, and mix for ½ minute.

Restir binder, then add with 1 hand while mixing with the other for 1 more minute, or until the mixture is hot.

Empty contents of wok into a heated serving dish and serve immediately.

TIMING: The veal can be marinated up to 12 hours ahead.
The remaining preparations can be done early in the day, except mincing the garlic, which should not be done more than 1 hour before stir-frying.

The veal can be cooked up to 4 hours ahead. If you are stir-frying the veal more than 2 hours ahead of time, it should be covered and refrigerated.

Allow to cool for 30 minutes before refrigeration.

This recipe is best served immediately, but if necessary can be kept warm *uncovered* for 3 to 5 minutes in a preheated oven at 225°.

SUBSTITUTIONS: For the veal scallops you can substitute veal: boneless loin, rib, or shoulder. (The shoulder must be partially frozen and sliced ⅜ inch thick, against the grain, in order for it to be tender.)

Another choice is pork: Boston butt or boneless loin. (The loin should be cut the same way as shoulder of veal.)

You can substitute chicken: white or dark meat, diced as for Chicken with Bean Sauce and Nuts (2 chicken breasts, weighing between 14 and 16 ounces each, or one 3- to 3½-pound chicken, yield about 1 pound of boneless chicken meat).

With lamb, use the leg, cut like the shoulder of veal.

TIPS: If possible, buy plume de veau (white veal) from a good French or Italian butcher. Cut into a piece of veal before removing it all from the wok after 3 minutes to make sure it is cooked all the way through. Veal requires less intense heat than pork, beef, or lamb, which makes it possible to stir-fry 1 pound at a time. When substituting other meat for this recipe, stir-fry ½ pound at a time.

When doubling recipe, stir-fry 1 pound of veal at a time. Deglaze wok, wash and dry, then repeat.

## SZECHUAN TWICE-COOKED VEAL

YIELD: 3 TO 4 SERVINGS IF SERVED ALONE; 6 TO 8
SERVINGS IF SERVED WITH 3 OTHER DISHES

1 pound boneless veal (filet or shoulder)

½ cup sherry

Scant ½ cup veal juices (from sherry in which the veal was cooking)

2 slices ginger root

6 scallions, slant-cut in 1-inch pieces (white and green parts)

¾ cup red pepper, triangle-cut

¾ cup snow peas

1 clove garlic, minced

1½ tablespoons bean sauce

1 teaspoon dark soy sauce

¾ teaspoon horse beans with chili

*Binder*

*1 teaspoon water chestnut powder*

*2 teaspoons sherry*

2 to 3 tablespoons peanut oil

### PREPARATION

Cut veal in slices, 3 inches × 5 inches × 1 inch.

Pour sherry into a heavy sauté pan and bring to a boil.

Add veal slices, ginger, and 2 of the slant-cut scallions.

Cover, turn flame to low and simmer 30 minutes or slightly longer.

When veal is very tender, remove from wok and let cool.

Boil down liquid in wok, if necessary, to a scant ½ cup.

Strain liquid into a cup and reserve.

While the veal is simmering, cut the remaining vegetables. Slant-cut the 4 scallions. Triangle-cut the red pepper. Mince the garlic.

Mix together the bean sauce, soy sauce, and horse beans with chili.

When veal is cool, slice it against the grain into pieces ⅜ inch thick and 1½ inches long.

Mix binder.

## COOKING PROCEDURE

Place wok over high flame for 30 seconds.

Add 1 tablespoon oil and heat for 20 seconds or until oil is very hot but not smoking.

Add red peppers and scallions and stir-fry 1 minute. Add snow peas and stir-fry one minute. Turn off flame.

Empty contents of wok into a heated serving dish. Do not wash wok.

Add 1 tablespoon oil to the wok over high flame, add veal slices, and stir-fry for 1 minute. Empty veal slices into the same serving dish. Turn off flame.

Do not wash wok.

Add 1 more tablespoon oil to the wok if the veal has absorbed it all. (If about 1 tablespoon of oil remains in the wok, you can eliminate this last tablespoon.) Turn flame to high and add garlic. Let sizzle a few seconds.

Add mixture of bean sauce, soy sauce, and horse beans, and let sizzle for 30 seconds, stirring slowly.

Add peppers, scallions, and veal again, and stir-fry another 30 seconds. Add reserved veal liquid and binder, mix another minute, and serve immediately.

TIMING: All preparations can be made early in the day or the day before, including the simmering and slicing of the veal.

The garlic should not be minced more than 1 hour before cooking.

This dish can be kept warm, uncovered, in a preheated 200° oven for 3 to 5 minutes or on a hot tray (low setting) for 3 to 4 minutes. If you plan to keep it warm, undercook the vegetables slightly.

SUBSTITUTIONS: For the veal you can substitute pork—Boston butt or loin—or lamb—leg, shoulder, or loin.

For the snow peas, you can substitute ¾ cup green pepper, triangle-cut; ¾ cup asparagus or zucchini, slant-cut; or ¾ cup broccoli, slant-cut and blanched. When making vegetable substitutions in this recipe, bear in mind the contrasting colors of red and green.

TIPS: If you want to make this dish spicier, increase the horse beans with chili from ¾ teaspoon to 1½ teaspoons, according to taste.

This recipe can have a more interesting flavor if the liquid in which the veal is simmered is allowed to evaporate completely after the veal is tender. Proceed as follows. Pierce the veal with a poultry skewer to see if it is tender. Remove cover and boil down any remaining liquid over a medium-high flame until all the liquid evaporates. When the pan drippings start to turn brown, remove the veal pieces and pour in a full ½ cup unsalted, home-made chicken or veal stock. With a wooden spoon or spatula, continue to boil liquid until it reduces to a scant ½ cup. Remove liquid from the sauté pan and reserve to add with binder when recipe indicates. It is the brown juices that give the recipe a richer flavor. In order to avoid burning the pan drippings, watch the pan closely while you are boiling them down. This procedure will take 3 to 5 minutes.

Horse beans with chili is a prepared sauce that comes in a jar. It is available at the Chinese American Trading Company, 91 Mulberry Street, New York, New York 10013. Once opened, it will last in the refrigerator for a year. Horse beans are a legume native to China. They are also sold dried and salted to be eaten as snacks. Substitute 1 to 2 teaspoons of hot sauce if horse beans with chili is not available.

## LAMB WITH HOT PEPPERS AND SCALLIONS

YIELD: 3 TO 4 SERVINGS IF SERVED ALONE; 6 TO 8
SERVINGS IF SERVED WITH 3 OTHER DISHES

1 pound boneless lamb (from the butt end of the leg)

**Marinade**

1 egg white, beaten slightly
1 tablespoon water chestnut powder
1 tablespoon sherry

2 teaspoons ginger root, minced
3 to 4 fresh hot peppers or 10 dried hot peppers
6 to 7 scallions (white part only)

**Seasoning Sauce**

2 tablespoons dark soy sauce
2 teaspoons Chinese red vinegar
3 tablespoons sherry
1 clove garlic, minced
¼ teaspoon black pepper, ground fresh

**Binder**

2 teaspoons water chestnut powder mixed with 1 tablespoon sherry

3 to 4 cups peanut oil for frying (in 14-inch wok)
1 teaspoon sesame-seed oil

### PREPARATION

Cut lamb with the grain in strips about 1½ inches wide. Partially freeze, then cut against the grain into ¼-inch-thick slices.

Blend the slightly beaten egg white with 1 tablespoon water chestnut powder and 1 tablespoon sherry.

Mix with the lamb and marinate in the refrigerator for at least ½ hour, or up to 12 hours.

Mince ginger.

Seed fresh hot peppers, then shred along with scallions. Place scallions and peppers in the same bowl as the ginger. If using dried peppers, cut off the stem end and shake out seeds. Leave whole, but remove before serving.

Measure out all ingredients for the seasoning sauce and place in a bowl: soy sauce, vinegar, sherry, garlic, pepper, and binder.

## COOKING PROCEDURE

Heat oil in wok to 300°, over a medium flame.

Stir the lamb slices in the marinade and then add them to the oil, stirring constantly with chopsticks for about 1 minute.

Remove lamb with a wire strainer and place in another wire strainer or sieve which has been placed over a bowl to catch the drippings.

Empty the oil from the wok into another bowl, leaving 1 tablespoon in the wok. Do not wash wok.

Using the same wok that the lamb was fried in, stir-fry the peppers, scallions, and ginger over a high flame for 1 minute.

Return the drained lamb to the wok and mix briefly.

Stir the seasoning sauce and add it to the lamb in the wok.

Stir-fry for another minute or until the sauce has thickened and everything is heated through.

Add the sesame-seed oil and mix again for 5 seconds.

Empty contents of wok into a heated serving dish and serve immediately.

TIMING: The lamb can be trimmed and frozen several months ahead or as little as several hours ahead. The lamb will become partially frozen in 1 to 4 hours, depending on the temperature of your freezer. It can be marinated up to 12 hours ahead. The seasoning sauce and the vegetables can be prepared early in the morning or the day before. Cover and refrigerate the vegetables. The lamb can be fried up to 4 hours ahead. If that is done, refrigerate the drippings and remove fat. Add the defatted lamb drippings to seasoning sauce. After the lamb pieces have cooled thoroughly, cover them well to avoid drying out.

Do not mince the garlic more than 1 hour before stir-frying.

This dish is best served immediately, but if necessary it can be kept warm in a preheated oven at 200° for 5 minutes, *uncovered*.

If you are planning to keep it warm, slightly undercook the vegetables.

SUBSTITUTIONS : For the lamb you can substitute beef flank, skirt (diaphragm), sirloin, rib, shell, club, or filet mignon (skirt is cut with the grain; all others cuts are cut against the grain).

Or try veal—shoulder, rib, loin, or leg (scallops), or pork—Boston butt or loin.

Wine vinegar can be substituted for the Chinese red vinegar.

TIPS : If a spicier dish is desired, increase the number of fresh hot peppers to 5 or the number of dried hot peppers to 12.

This technique of frying lamb differs from deep-frying. It is called *passing through*. It serves two purposes. First, it cooks the lamb about 80 percent and seals in all the juices. The lamb can then be left without refrigeration for several hours, which is a prime consideration in China. Second, it prevents the lamb from sticking when it is returned to the wok later to be stir-fried with the vegetables.

If the oil temperature is too hot, the pieces of lamb will stick together. If that happens, turn off the flame immediately. If the oil is too cool, the lamb will sink to the bottom of the wok and absorb too much oil. Working with a Taylor deep-fat-frying thermometer is recommended.

It is important to remove all the lamb from the oil within 30 seconds, by using a wire strainer. If it is not possible to accomplish this in such a short amount of time, take the wok by its handles and pour the meat and the oil into a strainer set over a bowl. That is how they handle such a dish in a restaurant, but take extreme caution, since the oil is very hot. A good way to practice removing meat from oil is to place cereal in a bowl of water and remove it with a wire strainer as quickly as possible. The Mongolians include lamb regularly in their diet; it is rarely, if ever, a part of the Chinese diet.

When doubling this recipe, never fry more than 1 pound of lamb at a time because the oil temperature will cool down too rapidly. Fry lamb in oil heated to 300°. Remove lamb from oil with a wire strainer and place in another wire strainer or sieve set over a bowl. Heat oil back to 300° and fry the second pound of lamb in oil. Remove lamb from oil and put in the same strainer or sieve in which the first batch is draining. Empty oil into another bowl or pot, leaving 2 tablespoons of oil in the wok. Do not wash wok. In the same wok, stir-fry vegetables according to the recipe. Add seasoning sauce and the drained lamb, and stir-fry until hot.

Unless the flame on your stove is extremely high, do not attempt to triple this recipe. Even if you fry the lamb 1 pound at a time, the lamb and vegetables will create too much steam and the final dish will not be as successful.

# VEGETABLES

Few Americans realize how exciting vegetables can be. The Chinese are masters at cutting and cooking every vegetable that grows. Any and all vegetables can be stir-fried (some have to be blanched first if they are very hard) and served as an accompaniment to a meal, be it American, French, Italian, Greek, or whatever. When I cater nine-course banquets, frequently the most popular dish is the vegetable combination I always include. Americans do not expect anything from vegetables except vitamins, but ironically they almost always overcook them, thus destroying all the nutritive value. They do not realize the endless possibilities of contrasting color, crunch, and texture.

Try as many different vegetables as there are in season. Taste them in the raw. Many are great in salads, such as minced broccoli or shredded kohlrabi. Sometimes a touch of shredded pork or minced ham can add an unusual flavor to an otherwise common vegetable dish. I hope the recipes I have included will inspire you to concoct your own favorite combination, which will be based on what is freshest.

## STIR-FRIED SNOW PEAS AND CARROTS

YIELD: 4 SERVINGS

*This is an example of the basic stir-fried vegetable dish, one which does not call for the addition of a prepared seasoning sauce such as oyster, soy, or hoisin. It allows the natural taste of the included vegetables to come out, retaining their color, crunch, and vitamins.*

¾ pound snow peas
½ pound carrots
½ cup scallions, chopped
  (white and green parts)
2 slices ginger root
1 clove garlic

*Binder*
*1 teaspoon water chestnut*
  *powder*
*1 tablespoon sherry*

1½ tablespoons peanut oil or
  chicken fat
1 teaspoon salt
½ teaspoon sugar

### PREPARATION

String and slant-cut snow peas in 2 or 3 pieces.

Peel and slant-cut carrots.

Bring 1 quart of water to a boil and blanch carrots for one minute. (Start timing the minute after the water has come to a boil.)

Remove carrots from the water with a wire strainer and plunge them into a bowl of ice water. Drain them in a colander.

Place carrots on a paper towel to dry.

Chop scallions.

Slice ginger; crush garlic, but leave whole.

Mix binder.

## COOKING PROCEDURE

Place wok over medium-high flame for 30 seconds.

Add 1½ tablespoons oil and heat for 20 seconds or until oil is very hot but not smoking.

Add scallions, ginger, and garlic and let sizzle for 15 seconds.

Add carrots and stir-fry 2 minutes.

Add snow peas and stir-fry 1 minute.

Add salt and sugar.

Mix well.

Restir binder and add with one hand while you stir-fry with the other for 1 minute.

Remove ginger and garlic.

Empty contents of wok into a heated serving dish and serve immediately.

TIMING: This, like all vegetable dishes, should be served immediately or emptied into a heated serving dish for not more than 3 or 4 minutes before serving. Do *not* keep warm on a hot tray or in the oven; if you do, you will lose the vital qualities of color, crunch, and freshness.

SUBSTITUTIONS: For the snow peas you can substitute any of the following vegetables: slant-cut young zucchini (not more than 1 inch in diameter); roll-oblique-cut carrots and zucchini; American peas; slant-cut or roll-oblique-cut asparagus (add 1 more minute to the stir-frying time for asparagus); broccoli; or string beans. For the last 2, slant-cut in 1¼-inch pieces, then blanch for 1 minute after the water has returned to a boil.

You can add 2 tablespoons of oyster sauce, bean sauce or hoisin sauce.

TIPS: A teaspoon of hot sauce can always be added to the binder if spicy vegetables are preferred.

Chinese vegetables are interesting not only for their taste and texture but also for their esthetic qualities. This dish, which is nutritional, and easy to prepare, also serves as an illustration of visual excitement due to the contrasting colors (bright orange and green) of the two vegetables. Try to choose bright colors whenever possible.

Pick out young snow peas.

Always save the water in which any vegetable was blanched to add to stock or to cook rice, because it contains water-soluble vitamins.

# STIR-FRIED SHANTUNG CABBAGE
# WITH MINCED HAM

YIELD: 4 SERVINGS

1½ pounds Shantung
  cabbage
2 ounces ham
2 scallions (white and green
  parts)

**Binder**
1 *teaspoon water chestnut
  powder*

1 *tablespoon sherry*

1½ tablespoons peanut oil
  or chicken fat
1 teaspoon salt
½ teaspoon sugar
¼ teaspoon freshly ground
  pepper

## PREPARATION

Wash, drain, and dry cabbage.

Cut cabbage into 1-inch pieces, separating the stems from the leafy parts.

Mince ham.

Chop scallions.

Mix binder.

## COOKING PROCEDURE

Place wok over medium-high flame for 30 seconds.

Add 1½ tablespoons oil and heat for 20 seconds or until oil is hot but not smoking.

Add scallions and let sizzle a few seconds.

Add cabbage stems and stir-fry for about 2 minutes.

Add leafy part of cabbage and stir-fry another minute.

Add salt, sugar, and pepper.

Mix again.

Add ham and mix well.

Turn flame to high, restir binder and add with one hand as you stir-fry with the other.

Cook until any remaining liquid in the wok has thickened.

Empty contents of wok into a heated serving dish and serve immediately.

TIMING : If you still have 1 more dish to stir-fry, this dish can be kept warm in a preheated serving dish for 3 to 5 minutes. Do *not* keep the vegetables warm in the oven or on a hot tray. Do *not* cover, as the steam will cause the cabbage to become soggy.

SUBSTITUTIONS : Instead of Shantung cabbage, you can use any of the vegetables in the choy family: bok choy, Shanghai bok choy, or hung choy.

American-Chinese celery cabbage is another possibility that is widely available.

You can also substitute fresh spinach, which requires 1 or 2 minutes less cooking. To prepare spinach, cut off 1 inch from the bottom part of the stems, keeping the leaves whole.

To wash spinach or any of the choy vegetables, proceed as follows: wash out sink and fill with cold water. Add ¼ cup white vinegar. Place spinach in sink and soak for several minutes. With your hands, lift spinach out of the water and let drain in a colander set over a bowl. Let water and sand drain out of sink. Repeat until there is no trace of sand.

TIPS : Make sure the cabbage is drained and dried well before stir-frying. That will minimize 2 undesired effects: spattering, and the accumulation of liquid in the bottom of the wok. The finished dish should not have more than a few tablespoons of liquid. If there is too much liquid in the wok and the cabbage is done, remove the cabbage with a wire strainer and boil down the liquid until it reduces to 2 to 3 tablespoons. Pour liquid over cabbage.

# STIR-FRIED ZUCCHINI WITH YELLOW SUMMER SQUASH

YIELD: 4 SERVINGS

4 cups zucchini
4 cups yellow squash
4 scallions (white and green parts)
2 tablespoons fresh dill, minced

**Binder**
1 *teaspoon water chestnut powder*

1 *tablespoon sherry*
1 *tablespoon dark soy sauce*

1½ tablespoons peanut oil or chicken fat
1 teaspoon salt
½ teaspoon sugar

## PREPARATION

Slant-cut zucchini and yellow squash.

Chop scallions.

Mince dill.

Mix binder.

## COOKING PROCEDURE

Place wok over high flame for 30 seconds.

Add 1½ tablespoons oil and heat for 20 seconds or until oil is hot but not smoking.

Add scallions and let sizzle for 15 seconds.

Add zucchini and squash and stir-fry 2 minutes.

Add salt and sugar and mix well.

Add dill and stir-fry 1 minute.

Restir binder and add with one hand while stir-frying with the other for another minute.

Empty contents of wok into a heated serving dish and serve immediately.

TIMING: This, like all vegetable dishes, must be served immediately since the vegetables become soggy when kept warm or reheated. If the vegetables are emptied into a heated serving dish they will stay warm for 3 to 5 minutes.

TIPS: Pick young zucchini and squash, no more than 1 inch diameter, if possible, for looks as well as for taste.

Roll-oblique-cut the squash for esthetic appeal, and stir-fry another minute or two. The heat will take a little longer to penetrate the vegetables if you use this cut.

Alternate seasonings for the soy sauce include 2 tablespoons of master sauce, bean sauce, spicy bean sauce, hoisin sauce, or oyster sauce. If any of these are used, omit the chopped fresh dill. The dill is a western seasoning, and its addition to a stir-fried vegetable dish would make it go very well with any Occidental meal.

## STIR FRIED CHINESE BROCCOLI WITH OYSTER SAUCE

YIELD: 4 SERVINGS

1½ pounds broccoli
1 clove garlic
1 teaspoon ginger root, minced
1½ tablespoons oyster sauce
1 tablespoon dark soy sauce

*Binder*
1 tablespoon sherry
1 teaspoon water chestnut powder

2 tablespoons peanut oil or chicken fat

## PREPARATION

Wash and drain broccoli, discarding any brown or yellow leaves.

Peel about 1½ inches of tough outer layer off bottom of broccoli stem.

Slant-cut in 2-inch lengths, placing leafy part and stems in two different bowls.

Mince garlic and ginger.

Measure the oyster and soy sauce in a small cup.

Mix binder.

## COOKING PROCEDURE

Bring 2 quarts of water to a boil and blanch the broccoli stems for 1 minute.

Add the leafy parts and continue to cook for another minute.

Lift the broccoli out of the boiling water with a wire strainer and plunge in a bowl of ice water for one minute; drain in colander and then on paper towels to dry thoroughly.

Place wok over high flame for 30 seconds.

Add 2 tablespoons oil and heat for 20 minutes or until oil is hot but not smoking.

Add garlic and ginger; let sizzle a few seconds.

Add broccoli and stir-fry for 2 minutes.

Add sugar, oyster sauce, and soy sauce; mix well.

Add binder and cook for another minute. Serve immediately.

TIMING : The broccoli can be blanched early in the day or a day ahead. All other preparations can be done early in the day, except for the mincing of the garlic, which should not be done more than 1 hour before stir-frying.

Like all stir-fried vegetables, this dish cannot be kept warm in the oven or on a hot tray, but can be emptied into a preheated serving dish, covered loosely, and allowed to stand for 3 to 5 minutes.

SUBSTITUTIONS : American broccoli can be used instead of Chinese. In that case, separate the florets from the stems and add the florets when the recipe calls for the addition of the leafy part.

The purpose of blanching the Chinese broccoli is to soften it and to remove some of its characteristic bitter flavor. American broccoli does not have that bitterness and can therefore be stir-fried without blanching. If the blanching is omitted, increase the stir-frying time and add stock as follows:

Heat oil in wok over medium flame and stir-fry stems for 2 minutes.

Add garlic and ginger and stir-fry a few seconds.

Add florets and stir-fry 1 more minute.

Add ¼ cup chicken stock and stir-fry another 2 minutes.

Add sugar, oyster sauce, and soy sauce; mix well.

Add binder and cook for another minute.

Other substitutions for the Chinese broccoli are: American string beans or Chinese long beans. Cut the string beans in 2-inch pieces and follow the same recipe. When preparing the string beans, be sure to remove the fat end that is attached to the plant, not the thin one, since the thin end contains many vitamins.

Other possible substitutions are slant-cut asparagus, snow peas, or American peas. Blanching is not necessary for any of these vegetables.

TIPS: Chopped scallions (white and green parts), leeks (white part), or minced shallots can be added along with the garlic and ginger.

Bean sauce or hoisin can be substituted for the oyster sauce.

Broccoli should always have a deep, rich green color with no trace of yellow.

Ideally, Chinese broccoli stalks should be no larger in diameter than medium-size asparagus. That will vary according to season. Always look at the end of the broccoli in order to judge its freshness: if it looks dried, brown, or moldy, don't buy it.

## STIR-FRIED SING QUA WITH SHALLOTS
## AND MASTER SAUCE

YIELD: 3 SERVINGS IF SERVED WITH 1 MEAT ENTRÉE;
6 SERVINGS IF SERVED WITH 3 OTHER DISHES

6 cups sing qua
¼ cup shallots, minced

**Binder**
1 teaspoon water chestnut
  powder

1 tablespoon sherry

1½ tablespoons peanut oil or
  chicken fat
¼ cup master sauce

## PREPARATION

Peel and roll-oblique-cut sing qua.

Mince shallots.

Mix binder.

## COOKING PROCEDURE

Place wok over medium flame for 30 seconds.

Add 1½ tablespoons oil and heat for about 20 seconds, until oil is hot but not smoking.

Add shallots and stir-fry 2 minutes.

Turn flame to high.

Add sing qua and stir-fry for 2 to 3 minutes.

Add master sauce and stir-fry 1 minute.

Restir binder and add with one hand while stir-frying with the other for ½ minute.

Empty contents of wok into a heated serving dish and serve immediately.

TIMING: If the empty serving dish is warmed first in a preheated oven, when the sing qua is put in it warm, uncovered, it will stay for 3 to 5 minutes. This gives you time to stir-fry one more dish.

Do not place the vegetables in the oven or on a hot tray.

SUBSTITUTIONS: For the sing qua you can substitute hairy melon, which must also be peeled; zucchini; or summer yellow squash. If thin, young squash or zucchini are available, peeling is *not* necessary.

TIPS: Alternatives to the master sauce include 2 tablespoons dark soy sauce, 2 tablespoons bean sauce, or 2 tablespoons oyster sauce. Master sauce is described on page 148.

Remove the tough green skin of the sing qua with a vegetable peeler.

## SEASONAL STIR-FRIED VEGETABLES

YIELD: 6 SERVINGS IF SERVED WITH 1 MEAT ENTRÉE;
10 TO 12 SERVINGS IF SERVED WITH 3 OTHER DISHES

4 carrots
4 cups asparagus
1 can baby corn, drained
1 medium-size sweet red
　pepper
8 to 10 fresh water chestnuts
16 gingko nuts
1 cup leeks, in 1-inch pieces
　(white part only)
1 can straw mushrooms,
　drained
⅓ cup chicken stock

3 tablespoons miso
1 tablespoon dark soy sauce

*Binder*
*1½ teaspoons water chestnut*
　*powder*
*1 tablespoon sherry*

2½ tablespoons peanut oil or
　chicken fat
1 teaspoon salt
¼ teaspoon black pepper
½ teaspoon sugar

### PREPARATION

Slant-cut carrots, asparagus, and baby corn (leave corn whole if small).

Triangle-cut red pepper.

Slice each fresh water chestnut in two or three parts.

Shell gingko nuts by cracking them, and pouring boiling water over them. Let stand 10 minutes, remove brown peel, and drain. If you are not using gingko nuts, use roast peanuts, cashews, or almonds.

Cut leeks in 1-inch pieces.

Mix mushroom stock with bean sauce and soy sauce.

Mix binder.

## COOKING PROCEDURE

Place wok over high flame for 30 seconds.

Add 2½ tablespoons oil and heat for 20 seconds or until oil is very hot but not smoking.

Add carrots, leeks, and gingko nuts, and stir-fry for 2 minutes.

Add salt, ground black pepper, and sugar.

Add asparagus and cook another 2 minutes.

Add stock and bean sauce mixture, and bring to a boil.

Continue cooking over a high flame for another 2 minutes.

*Do not cover.*

Add straw mushrooms, baby corn, red pepper, and fresh water chestnuts.

Cook over high flame until all vegetables are thoroughly heated, and barely tender, about 2 minutes.

Restir binder and add with one hand while stir-frying with the other for another minute.

Empty contents of wok into a heated serving dish. Serve immediately.

TIMING : Considering that the beauty of stir-fried vegetables lies in the preservation of their color, crunch, and freshness, it is never a good policy to keep them warm. They will soon overcook, become soggy, and begin to lose vitamins. At the most, you can keep vegetables warm for 3 to 4 minutes if you preheat the serving dish. Those few minutes will give you enough time to finish, for example, a stir-fried beef and vegetable dish. Never cover the vegetables, since the steam will continue to cook them.

SUBSTITUTIONS : When making vegetable substitutions, always use fresh vegetables, not frozen.

When asparagus is not in season, you may use another fresh green vegetable, such as snow peas or American peas, zucchini, Chinese or American broccoli, or string beans. Broccoli and string beans require blanching (refer to Vegetables). Snow peas, American peas, and zucchini require about 1 minute less stir-frying time than the asparagus and do not require blanching.

If roasted nuts are preferred to gingko nuts, sprinkle on top as a garnish after the vegetables have been emptied into the serving dish.

If fresh water chestnuts are not available, increase the green vegetable to 5 cups and use 1½ red peppers.

If too many of these vegetables are out of season, try another vegetable recipe in this book.

For the leeks you can substitute ½ cup scallions, slant-cut, or ⅓ cup shallots, left whole.

Straw mushrooms and baby corn are available in cans and should be part of your Chinese staples. The shelf life of all canned ingredients is 6 months. They are included in this recipe for esthetic reasons. All other vegetables should be fresh.

Alternative seasonings for the bean sauce are spicy bean sauce, hoisin sauce, oyster sauce, or dark soy sauce.

TIPS : If the sauce is not thickening properly, lift out vegetables with a wire strainer and boil down remaining liquid. Then pour liquid over vegetables. That precaution is wise in the case of any stir-fried vegetable or meat dish, to prevent the sauce from becoming either too thin or too plentiful. The technique helps retain the color, crunch, texture, and nutritional value of the fresh vegetables.

If the vegetables are scorching, turn off the flame for a few seconds, then turn it on again at a lower setting.

Take care to cut all vegetables with precision, in size as well as shape.

This dish is colorful, esthetically pleasing, and delicious.

After you have added the stock-bean sauce mixture, the vegetables may *not* require a full 2 minutes' cooking. It depends on how intense your flame is, how thin you have slant-cut the carrots, and whether you are using asparagus, snow peas, or broccoli. If you can't judge accurately by looking, then taste a piece of asparagus or carrot. It should be slightly undercooked before you add the straw mushrooms, baby corn, and red pepper.

When doubling this recipe, increase the stock to ½ cup and double the amount of all other ingredients. The reason for this is that more stock will take longer to evaporate, and the finished dish should have very little sauce.

Vegetables stir-fried in chicken fat are very flavorful, but much higher in cholesterol.

Save the drippings from any roasted meat or poultry to use when a recipe calls for stock to add to stir-fried vegetables. To make this stock, use the following deglazing method: after removing roast from the pan, pour off fat and add about ½ cup stock or white wine to the roasting pan. Then boil down the liquid, scraping up all the brown bits, until it is reduced by half. Freeze this stock until you are ready to use it (up to 6 months). This same procedure can be followed after roasting meat or poultry.

Mastering the art of stir-frying vegetables is probably the most difficult of all Chinese cooking techniques. A vegetable recipe such as this can only guide you; you will have to discover through trial and error how to judge the exact timing of the dish. Eventually you will trust your senses, and will be able to tell just by looking when the vegetables are done. A lapse of 30 seconds can mean the difference between crisp and soggy asparagus. Confidence comes with familiarity and experience.

## SPICY SEASONAL STIR-FRIED VEGETABLES

YIELD: 3 SERVINGS IF SERVED WITH 1 MEAT DISH;
5 TO 6 SERVINGS IF SERVED WITH 3 OTHER DISHES

¼ cup dried straw mush-
  rooms
¼ cup Smithfield ham, sliced
½ cup winter bamboo shoots
2½ cups sing qua (¾ pound)
8 to 10 fresh water chestnuts
1 medium-size sweet red
  pepper
1 or 2 fresh hot peppers
8 to 10 shallots

*Binder*
1 *tablespoon water chestnut*
  *powder*

1 *tablespoon sherry*
½ cup stock (liquid in which
  dried mushrooms were
  soaked)
1½ tablespoons oyster sauce
2 teaspoons dark soy sauce
2 tablespoons chicken fat or
  peanut oil
½ teaspoon salt
½ teaspoon sugar
¼ teaspoon black pepper

## PREPARATION

Rinse mushrooms, cover with warm water, and soak for 30 to 60 minutes or until soft.

Remove tough outer layer of mushroom and leave whole. (See illustration, page 64.)

Slice Smithfield ham in 1-inch × 1-inch pieces.

Roll-oblique-cut bamboo shoots.

Peel, then roll-oblique-cut, sing qua.

Peel, then slice, fresh water chestnuts.

Seed, then triangle-cut sweet and hot peppers.

Peel shallots and leave whole.

Mix binder.

Mix together stock, oyster sauce, and soy sauce.

## COOKING PROCEDURE

Place wok over medium flame for 30 seconds.

Add 2 tablespoons oil and heat for 20 seconds or until oil is hot but not smoking.

Add shallots and stir-fry ½ minute.

Add sing qua and stir-fry 1 minute.

Add bamboo shoots and peppers, and stir-fry 1 minute.

Add mushrooms and Smithfield ham, and stir-fry 1 minute.

Add salt, sugar, and pepper.

Add water chestnuts, and mix.

Add mixture of stock, soy sauce, and oyster sauce, and bring to a boil.

Restir binder, then add with one hand while stir-frying with the other, until sauce thickens.

Empty contents of wok into a heated serving dish. Serve immediately.

TIMING: Vegetables can never be kept warm without running the risk of becoming soggy. If the serving dish is preheated in the oven, the vegetables will remain hot in it for about 3 to 4 minutes. Never cover the vegetables after they have been emptied into the serving dish because the steam will continue to cook them.

SUBSTITUTIONS: When making vegetable substitutions, always use fresh vegetables, not frozen. Fresh American mushrooms (¼ pound) can be used instead of the dried Chinese straw mushrooms, in which case you would use chicken stock or any leftover stock saved from drippings (refer to Seasonal Stir-Fried Vegetables), instead of the stock from the soaked dried mushrooms.

Instead of the sing qua, you can use zucchini, summer yellow squash, hairy melon, or a combination of any two.

Instead of the shallots, you can use ½ cup scallions, slant-cut, or 1 cup leeks (white part only), cut in ½-inch pieces.

Prosciutto or Westphalian ham can be used instead of Smithfield ham.

TIPS : Hoisin or bean sauce can be used instead of the oyster sauce.

Refer to Tips on Seasonal Stir-Fried Vegetables for additional information.

## AMERICAN SEASONAL STIR-FRIED VEGETABLES

YIELD: 6 SERVINGS IF SERVED WITH 1 MEAT ENTRÉE

12 SERVINGS IF SERVED WITH 3 OTHER DISHES

2 carrots
2 cups leeks (white part only)
4 cups American broccoli
2 cups cauliflower
1 sweet red pepper
¼ pound fresh mushrooms
⅓ cup stock
1 tablespoon bean sauce
1 tablespoon hoisin sauce

*Binder*
*1½ teaspoons water chestnut*
   *powder*
*1 tablespoon sherry*
¼ cup peanuts

2 tablespoons peanut oil or
   chicken fat
1 teaspoon salt
½ teaspoon sugar
¼ teaspoon white pepper,
   ground fresh

## PREPARATION

Peel and slant-cut carrots.

Wash leeks to remove all sand. Cut the white part only into 1-inch pieces.

Cut 3 inches off the stems of the broccoli. Slant-cut the broccoli until you reach the flower portion. Break the florets apart.

Separate the stems from the florets.

Break off and cut cauliflower into the same size pieces as the broccoli.

Triangle-cut red pepper.

Slice mushrooms.

Mix ⅓ cup stock with 1 tablespoon bean sauce and 1 tablespoon hoisin sauce.

Mix binder.

Roast nuts and cool (refer to Ingredients, page 65).

## COOKING PROCEDURE

Place wok over medium-high flame for 30 seconds.

Add 2 tablespoons of oil and heat until oil is hot but not smoking.

Add carrots and leeks and stir-fry for 1 minute.

Add salt, sugar, and pepper.

Add broccoli and cauliflower, and stir-fry for 2 to 3 minutes.

Add mushrooms and red pepper, and stir-fry 1 minute.

Turn flame high.

Add mixture of stock, bean sauce, and hoisin sauce. Bring to a boil.

Stir binder, then add it with one hand while you stir-fry with the other until the sauce thickens.

Empty contents of wok into a heated serving dish.

Sprinkle with roasted peanuts and serve immediately.

# DRY SAUTÉED STRING BEANS, SZECHUAN STYLE
YIELD: 3 TO 4 SERVINGS IF SERVED WITH 1 MEAT ENTRÉE;
6 TO 8 SERVINGS IF SERVED WITH 3 OTHER DISHES

1 teaspoon dried shrimp
1 pound string beans

**Seasoning Sauce Mixture**
*1 tablespoon dark soy sauce*
*1 teaspoon honey*
*1 tablespoon sherry (that in which shrimp was soaking)*
*1 teaspoon sesame-seed oil (plain or with chili)*

1 tablespoon Szechuan preserved vegetable, minced
1 scallion (white and green parts)
2 cups peanut oil
6 ounces (¾ cup) ground pork

## PREPARATION
Rinse shrimp in water, then soak in 1 tablespoon sherry for 1 hour.

Cut off ends of string beans, then cut into 2-inch lengths.

Mix seasoning sauce ingredients in a bowl and set aside (soy sauce, honey, sherry, and sesame-seed oil).

Rinse Szechuan preserved vegetable with water, then mince.

Mince shrimp, reserving the sherry in which they were soaking to add to the seasoning sauce mixture.

Chop scallion.

## COOKING PROCEDURE
Heat 2 cups of oil in wok to 375°.

Add string beans and deep-fry until they wrinkle (about 3 minutes).

Remove string beans from the oil with a wire strainer and drain on several layers of paper towels.

Empty all but 1 tablespoon oil into a bowl. Do not wash wok.

In the 1 tablespoon oil that remains, stir-fry the ground pork for 3 to 4 minutes, or until it turns white.

Add the dried shrimp and preserved vegetable; cook for 1 more minute.

Add the cooked string beans, scallion, and seasoning sauce mixture to the wok.

Stir continuously until the liquid has evaporated and the sauce coats the ingredients.

Empty contents of wok into a heated serving dish.

Serve immediately, or keep warm in preheated 200° oven.

TIMING : This recipe can be kept warm in a preheated 200° oven, or uncovered on the low setting of a hot tray for 3 minutes.

The string beans can be fried 1 hour in advance.

All the other preparations can be done early in the day or the day ahead.

SUBSTITUTIONS : Use either Chinese long beans or American string beans.

For pork, you can substitute shoulder or breast of veal.

TIPS : There should be almost no liquid left in the bottom of the wok when the recipe is completed.

This is an economical as well as delicious way of preparing string beans. For low-calorie but less authentic version, proceed as follows:

Steam the string beans instead of frying them. The string beans will steam in 5 to 7 minutes. Plunge them into ice water after steaming, then drain and dry well. That will stop the cooking and hold the color.

When choosing string beans, always snap one before buying them. If it is fresh, beads of moisture will appear at the place it has been broken.

Chinese long beans are almost always too dry, which is why I prefer the American variety.

# EGGPLANT IN GARLIC SAUCE

YIELD: 3 TO 4 SERVINGS IF SERVED WITH 1 MEAT DISH;
6 TO 8 SERVINGS IF SERVED WITH 3 OTHER DISHES

1 teaspoon dried shrimp
2 tablespoons sherry
6 small Chinese mushrooms
2 fresh green hot peppers
1 green bell pepper or sweet
   red pepper
2 cloves garlic

### Seasoning Sauce
1 to 2 teaspoons hot sauce
½ tablespoon dark soy sauce
½ tablespoon light soy sauce
1 tablespoon red wine vinegar
1 teaspoon sugar

1 tablespoon tomato sauce
1 tablespoon tomato paste
2 tablespoons sherry (in
   which the dried shrimp
   was soaking)

1 medium eggplant (1 to 1¼
   pounds)
2 teaspoons salt
3 tablespoons oil or chicken
   fat
½ cup stock (combine
   chicken and mushroom)

## PREPARATION

Rinse the dried shrimp. Soak for 1 hour in 2 tablespoons sherry.

Rinse mushrooms, cover with warm water, and soak for 30 to 60 minutes or until soft. Cut off stems and leave whole. Save stock.

Triangle-cut peppers.

Mince garlic.

Prepare seasoning sauce: blend together the hot sauce, soy sauces, vinegar, sugar, 1 tablespoon tomato sauce, 1 tablespoon tomato paste, and the 2 tablespoons sherry in which dried shrimp was soaked.

Trim off ends of eggplant and discard. Cut the eggplant into eighths lengthwise. Cut the slices into 1½- to 2-inch cubes. Sprinkle with 2 teaspoons salt and place on cookie sheet, with paper towels and chopping block on top. Let stand for 30 minutes.

Rinse, drain, and dry eggplant slices well.

Mince dried shrimp.

## COOKING PROCEDURE

Place wok over high flame for 30 seconds.

Add 3 tablespoons of oil, and heat for 20 seconds or until oil is very hot but not smoking.

Add eggplant cubes; stir and press lightly to aid browning.

Cook over a medium flame until lightly browned, about 5 minutes.

Add drained and minced shrimp and continue to stir-fry for 30 seconds.

Add garlic.

Add mushrooms and peppers. Stir-fry until tender, about 1 to 2 minutes.

Add ½ cup stock. Cook, stirring about 5 seconds.

Add seasoning sauce.

Cook over medium flame, stir-frying about 3 to 5 minutes, or until juices have thickened.

Empty contents of wok into a serving dish.

Serve hot, warm, or cold.

TIMING: This recipe can be kept warm if necessary, uncovered, in a preheated 225° oven for 5 to 7 minutes. Eggplant in Garlic Sauce makes an excellent appetizer served cold or hot. It will keep, if refrigerated, for 5 days.

SUBSTITUTIONS: If dried shrimp is not available, omit and follow recipe as indicated. For the eggplant you can substitute zucchini. Roll-oblique-cut zucchini and cook for only 1 minute instead of 5 in the first step.

TIPS : During the last minute of cooking, add ¾ cup cooked and cooled white rice to the mixture. The bland rice absorbs some of the spicy sauce, which results in quite a pleasing combination. To make the recipe spicier or less spicy, increase or decrease the hot sauce or the hot peppers accordingly.

The purpose of salting the eggplant (or the zucchini) is to remove any bitter taste and to draw out excess moisture; the weighing down further aids the dehydration and minimizes the amount of oil that is needed in the sautéing process.

When doubling this recipe, use a high flame throughout the entire cooking process. Increase fat to 5 tablespoons and stock to ¾ cup. This recipe goes very well with various roasted or barbecued cuts of meat, such as roast leg of lamb.

## BEAN SPROUT SALAD

YIELD: 4 SERVINGS

¼ cup pine nuts
1 cup carrots, shredded
½ cup sweet red pepper, shredded
2 scallions, shredded (white and green parts)
2 cups mung bean sprouts

**Dressing**
2 tablespoons wine vinegar
1 tablespoon Chenkong vinegar

1 tablespoon rice vinegar
1 tablespoon Chinese red vinegar
2 tablespoons light soy sauce
½ tablespoon sesame-seed oil
3 tablespoons peanut oil
¼ teaspoon pepper, ground fresh

## PREPARATION

Roast nuts and cool (refer to Ingredients, page 65).

Shred all vegetables, with the exception of the mung bean sprouts.

Refrigerate until ready to use.

Mix salad dressing in a bowl.

Just before serving salad, toss dressing and vegetables together until well mixed. Serve immediately.

TIPS : If a spicy dressing is desired, use sesame-seed oil with chili in place of regular sesame-seed oil.

Other raw vegetable possibilities include snow peas, green pepper, broccoli, and kohlrabi. The last two require peeling.

Other roasted nut possibilities include cashews, almonds, or 1 tablespoon sesame seeds. Refer to Ingredients, page 65, for roasting of nuts.

## SZECHUAN BEAN CURD
### YIELD: 4 TO 6 SERVINGS IF SERVED WITH 3 OTHER DISHES

*This recipe is economical, nutritious, and tasty. It is an excellent illustration of how far the Chinese can stretch ¼ pound meat.*

¼ pound lean fresh pork, ground (½ cup)
1 tablespoon dark soy sauce
1 tablespoon sherry
½ teaspoon sugar
1 teaspoon ginger root, minced
1 clove garlic
½ cup scallion, chopped (white and green parts)
4 pieces fresh Chinese bean curd

½ teaspoon Szechuan peppercorns
⅓ cup chicken stock
1 to 2 teaspoons hot sauce
1½ tablespoons bean sauce

*Binder*
*1 tablespoon sherry*
*2 teaspoons water chestnut powder*

1 teaspoon sesame-seed oil
1½ tablespoons peanut oil

## PREPARATION
Combine pork, soy sauce, sherry, and sugar.

Mince ginger and garlic.

Chop scallion.

Cut bean curd into ½-inch pieces.

Set a wok or 10-inch skillet over high flame, without using any oil, and drop in the Szechuan peppercorns.

Turn flame to medium and cook, stirring constantly for about 5 minutes, or until they are browned.

Crush the peppercorns to a fine powder with a rolling pin.

Shake through a fine stainer into a small bowl and set aside.

Mix together stock, hot sauce, and bean sauce.

Mix binder: water chestnut powder dissolved in 1 tablespoon sherry.

## COOKING PROCEDURE

Place wok over high flame for 30 seconds.

Add the 1½ tablespoon oil, and heat for 20 seconds or until oil is very hot but not smoking.

Add garlic, scallions and ginger.

Add pork mixture and stir-fry for 2 to 3 minutes, breaking it into small pieces.

Add bean sauce, hot sauce, and chicken stock, and mix well.

Drain bean curd and add to mixture of sauce and stock.

Return to a boil, then cook over moderate heat for 2 minutes.

Remix binder and add with one hand while stirring with the other until sauce thickens.

Turn flame off and add sesame-seed oil. Mix well.

Empty contents of wok onto a heated serving dish.

Sprinkle with Szechuan Peppercorn Powder and serve immediately.

TIMING : This dish can be kept warm in a preheated 225°
oven for 5 to 10 minutes.

SUBSTITUTIONS : For the ground pork you can substitute veal—breast or shoulder—or pork—shoulder or loin.

TIPS : Have the butcher grind the pork only once, or mince
it yourself by partially freezing, then shredding and mincing it
(refer to Cutting Techniques).

In China the pork is never ground by a machine, but is
minced by hand with a cleaver, resulting in a coarse texture. If it
were ground twice by machine, it would be too fine and lack
sufficient texture.

When doubling this recipe, change oil from 1½ to 2 tablespoons; change stock from ⅓ cup to ½ cup; and keep flame on
high throughout entire cooking procedure.

# RICE AND NOODLES

---

## BOILED WHITE RICE

YIELD: 4 SERVINGS

1 cup raw rice                    1¼ cups water

### COOKING PROCEDURE

Place the water and the rice in a heavy 1½- to 2-quart saucepan.

Bring to a boil over high flame and stir with chopsticks in a figure-eight motion.

Cover, and turn flame very low.

Simmer rice for 15 minutes.

Turn off flame and let rice remain in covered pot for 20 minutes. This is called letting the rice relax. Do not remove saucepan from burner.

Remove cover and stir with chopsticks.

**TIMING**: Boiled white rice will stay warm up to 30 minutes after the relaxing period if you leave it on the burner. Rice can be made early in the day or rewarmed even if several days old.

Here are two methods of warming precooked rice. One way is to sprinkle 2 or 3 tablespoons of water, or mushroom or chicken stock, over rice. Cover saucepan and place in a preheated 225° oven for 15 minutes. Another method is to place the covered saucepan in a frying pan with 2 inches of water in it (to create your own double boiler). Turn flame high. When water boils, turn flame to medium-low and simmer for 15 minutes or until rice is hot.

**TIPS**: Leftover rice will keep up to 5 days in the refrigerator; it will keep in the freezer for 1 month. It can then be used for fried rice.

Other uses for leftover rice include soup, stuffing, and rice pudding.

If you are using an electric stove, preheat 2 different burners to high and low. Change burners as recipe indicates.

If you prefer a softer rice, use more water—up to 1¾ cups— and simmer the rice longer—up to 20 minutes.

Carolina rice has whiter grains than Uncle Ben's; in Uncle Ben's the grains are more separate and therefore more difficult to eat with chopsticks.

## PEKING DOILIES

YIELD: 10 DOILIES

1½ cups flour                    Sesame-seed oil
⅔ cup (scant) boiling water

### PREPARATION

Measure 1½ cups flour in a mixing bowl. Do not sift.

Gradually add boiling water until flour is well mixed and batter is slightly sticky.

Cover with a damp paper towel or dishcloth and let stand 10 minutes.

Knead dough 5 minutes.

Cover again and let stand 15 minutes.

Roll out dough ⅛ inch thick.

Cut circles, using a round cookie-cutter 4 inches in diameter, or the top of a jar.

Brush lightly with sesame-seed oil and put 2 circles on top of each other with the oil sides facing each other.

Roll out 4 to 6 inches in diameter. Continue until all circles are cut and rolled.

## COOKING PROCEDURE

In an ungreased heavy flat pan or wok, over a low flame, dry-cook each circle until it bubbles slightly. Turn over and dry-cook the other side.

Remove from the pan and pull the 2 pieces apart.

Wrap in a damp dishtowel and steam before serving (about 5 minutes).

N O T E : Peking Doilies are used for Peking Duck and Mo Sho Ro. These can be frozen for several months after they have been pulled apart. Refer to instructions for Shanghai Spring Roll.

# SHRIMP FRIED RICE

YIELD: 5 TO 6 SERVINGS

1¼ cups raw rice (or 3 cups cooked rice)

⅓ pound raw shrimp (in shell)

*Marinade*
*1 teaspoon sherry*
*½ teaspoon salt*
*¼ egg white*
*1 teaspoon water chestnut powder*

¼ cup scallions (white and green parts)

1 cup diced vegetables (fresh)

¾ cup mung bean sprouts

1½ tablespoons dark soy sauce

2 teaspoons oyster sauce

½ teaspoon sugar

3 eggs, beaten slightly

4½ tablespoons peanut oil

¼ teaspoon salt

## PREPARATION

Place rice and 1½ cups cold water in a heavy 2-quart saucepan.

Bring to a rapid boil. Stir with chopsticks, cover, and turn flame down as low as possible. Cook for 15 minutes.

Turn flame off. Leave rice on burner and allow to relax for 20 minutes.

Remove cover and stir well with chopsticks.

Refrigerate until rice is cold.

While rice is cooling, prepare the shrimp.

Shell, devein, wash, drain, dry, and dice shrimp.

Marinate shrimp in the sherry, salt, egg white, and water chestnut powder.

Refrigerate shrimp for at least ½ hour, up to 12 hours.

Chop scallions.

Dice vegetables.

Measure soy sauce, oyster sauce, and sugar in a small cup.

Scramble eggs in 1 tablespoon oil. Remove from wok and place in a bowl.

Stir-fry 1 cup diced vegetables in ½ tablespoon oil for 1 minute.

Add ¼ teaspoon salt and mix well.

Empty contents of wok into a dish. Do not wash wok.

Stir-fry shrimp in 1 tablespoon oil for about 1 minute or until pink. Remove from wok. If nothing has stuck to the wok, do not wash it.

## COOKING PROCEDURE

Place wok over high flame for 30 seconds.

Add 2½ tablespoons oil, and heat for 20 seconds or until oil is hot but not smoking.

Add cold rice and stir-fry for 2 minutes.

Add soy sauce, oyster sauce, and sugar; mix 1 minute.

Add eggs, breaking into little bits with the spatula.

Add scallions, shrimp, diced vegetables, and bean sprouts.

Stir-fry 1 more minute.

Empty contents of wok into a heated serving dish.

Fried rice can be kept warm in a preheated 200° oven for 15 minutes.

*Do not cover.*

TIMING : The rice should be made in advance so it can cool thoroughly. Fried rice can be made with any leftover rice you might have. Cooked rice will keep in the refrigerator up to 7 days. It will keep in the freezer for one month. Fried Rice can be kept warm in a preheated 200° oven for 15 minutes. *Do not cover,* or else the rice will steam, the vegetables will become soggy, and the scallions and eggs will soften. While the rice is being kept warm, you will have time to stir-fry 2 dishes.

SUBSTITUTIONS : The vegetable possibilities are really limitless. Some suggestions are red pepper, snow peas, zucchini, yellow squash, bok choy, Shantung cabbage, string beans, and broccoli. The last two should be diced very small and stir-fried for an extra minute, because they are much harder vegetables.

Leftover scrambled eggs from a Sunday brunch can be used.

For the shrimp, you can substitute leftover meat, fish, or poultry. Since these have been cooked, they do not have to be marinated and should be added in the last minute of stir-frying, along with the vegetables.

Ham, roast pork, or bacon (rendered until crisp and broken into little pieces) work well. Also, try a combination of 2 or more of the above suggestions.

## ROAST PORK LO MEIN

*In China, noodles are traditionally served on birthdays. The long noodles are never cut, since they symbolize longevity.*

*The authentic Chinese lo mein recipe calls for a very high proportion of noodles to vegetables and meat; I have adapted this recipe to American taste and increased the proportion of vegetables and meat.*

YIELD: 3 TO 4 SERVINGS IF SERVED ALONE; 6 TO 8
SERVINGS IF SERVED WITH 3 OTHER DISHES

4 or 5 Chinese mushrooms
1 full cup roast pork, shredded
2½ cups vegetables, such as:
  1 cup bok choy
  ½ cup zucchini or hairy
    melon

½ cup snow peas
½ cup bean sprouts
1 clove garlic
2 slices ginger root
2 scallions (white and green
    parts)

1 tablespoon oyster sauce

2 tablespoons dark soy sauce
   (or ¼ cup master sauce)

½ cup plus 2 tablespoons
   stock

**Binder**

1 *tablespoon water chestnut
   powder*

1 *tablespoon sherry*

⅓ pound fresh egg noodles
   (lo mein)

3 tablespoons peanut oil

1 teaspoon salt

½ teaspoon sugar

## PREPARATION

Rinse mushrooms, cover with warm water, and soak for 30 to 60 minutes or until soft.

Shred the mushrooms.

Shred pork, bok choy, zucchini or hairy melon, and snow peas. Leave bean sprouts whole.

Mince garlic and ginger.

Shred scallions.

Separate green and white parts of bok choy.

In a saucepan, combine oyster sauce, soy sauce, or master sauce, and stock.

Mix binder.

## COOKING PROCEDURE

Boil at least 2 quarts water in a saucepan and add noodles.

Bring to boil again and boil 3 to 4 minutes, stirring with chopsticks occasionally.

Drain noodles and rinse in cold water.

Toss noodles in bowl with ½ tablespoon oil.

Cut noodles in 4- to 6-inch pieces.

Place wok over high flame for 30 seconds.

Add 1½ tablespoons oil and heat for 20 seconds or until oil is hot but not smoking.

Stir-fry noodles, adding 1 teaspoon salt, and cook 3 to 4 minutes or until very hot.

Empty contents of wok into serving platter and keep warm, un-covered, in preheated 250° oven.

Bring mixture of stock and sauce to a boil in a saucepan; at the same time start stir-frying the mushroom shreds in 1 tablespoon oil for 1 minute.

Add scallions, garlic, and ginger.

Add white part of bok choy, zucchini or hairy melon, and snow peas.

Stir-fry 1 minute.

Add ½ teaspoon sugar and mix well.

Add boiling stock-sauce mixture and let it come to a boil again.

Restir binder and add to vegetable mixture along with bean sprouts, green part of boy choy, and roast pork. Mix well.

Put vegetable-pork mixture over noodles and toss at table and serve immediately.

TIMING: Lo mein falls under the category of last-minute dishes. You are working with shredded vegetables which cook in a few seconds. The difference of ½ minute could determine the suc-cess or failure of the recipe. Many of my students ask how they can tell when the vegetables are done. That comes with practice. In the beginning, I recommend tasting; eventually you will be able to de-tect a slight change in color and transparency which signifies the degree of done-ness.

The noodles can be boiled, drained, rinsed, tossed with ½ tablespoon oil, and then cut in 4- to 6-inch pieces early in the day, or the day before. They can be stir-fried and kept warm, uncovered, in a preheated 250° oven for up to 30 minutes. It is better to stir-fry ½ the amount of noodles at a time because that way they will brown slightly, which is desirable.

The roast pork can be made (or purchased) in advance and frozen (refer to Roast Pork).

The vegetables can be prepared early in the day, or the day before, if wrapped well and refrigerated.

The garlic should not be minced more than 1 hour before stir-frying.

SUBSTITUTIONS: Substitutions for roast pork are endless. You could use 1 cup of any meat, fish, or fowl, as long as it has been thoroughly cooked. It is a great way to use up leftover roast beef, turkey, chicken, veal, and so on. If you are not using leftover meat, fish or fowl, here are some ideas.

Partially freeze ½ pound beef, pork, or veal; shred it; then marinate in 1 teaspoon water chestnut powder, ½ tablespoon sherry, and 1 tablespoon light soy sauce. Stir-fry in 1 tablespoon oil for 2 to 3 minutes. Remove meat from wok and deglaze (reserve deglazing liquid to add at the end with stock). The meat can be cooked hours ahead or even the day ahead.

Another possibility is ½ pound shrimp or scallops. Use the marinade for the meat given above, substituting ¾ teaspoon salt for the light soy sauce.

There are as many substitutions for vegetables as there are vegetables in season. Go to the best source you have for *fresh* vegetables, be it Chinatown, your own garden, or the specialty shop down the block. Always bear in mind color, crunch, and freshness. If Oriental vegetables are not available, try red pepper, zucchini, yellow squash, carrots, broccoli, or kohlrabi. (If using broccoli, use just the stems, not the florets.) Scallions are just one possible representative of the onion family. Shredded leeks (¾ cup, white part only), or ¼ cup minced shallots, also work very well.

You can substitute dried Chinese or Japanese noodles for the fresh. After tossing the noodles with 1 tablespoon oil, remove about 1 cup of noodles, which will increase the proportion of vegetables and meat to noodles.

Leftover noodles (plain) can be stir-fried days later with a few tablespoons of master sauce and any member of the onion family.

TIPS: Choose an oven-proof platter such as an enamel or copper paella dish. The lo mein can then be served in the same platter which was used to keep the noodles warm in the oven.

If the sauce is not thickening fast enough after you have added the binder, remove the vegetable-meat mixture from the wok with a wire strainer and let the sauce drain into the wok. Place the vegetable-meat mixture over the noodles while the sauce boils down and thickens. Take this precaution to prevent the vegetables from becoming soggy.

Use stock made from the roast pork or roast duck drippings (refer to notes on Roast Pork).

To cut the noodles, after they have been cooked, drained, and rinsed in cold water, cut through them in 2 or 3 places with a cleaver.


## BANQUET LO MEIN
YIELD: 3 TO 4 SERVINGS IF SERVED ALONE; 6 TO 8
SERVINGS IF SERVED WITH 3 OTHER DISHES

2¼ cups shredded meat, such as:
  1 to 1¼ pound fresh lobster (¾ cup lobster meat)
  ¾ cup roast duck (½ duck)
  ¾ cup roast pork

¼ cup Chinese mushrooms
1 cup kohlrabi, peeled and shredded
1 carrot, peeled
1 cup leeks (white part only)
1 cup snow peas, strung
1 cup Chinese broccoli, peeled and shredded

1 cup hairy melon, peeled
½ cup fresh water chestnuts
1 cup mung bean sprouts
2 teaspoons ginger root, minced
2 cloves garlic
1 cup stock (chicken, duck, lobster, or a combination of all three)
3 tablespoons dark soy sauce, or 6 tablespoons master sauce

1½ tablespoons oyster sauce

**Binder**
*1½ tablespoons water chestnut powder*
*2 tablespoons sherry*

5 tablespoons peanut oil
¾ pound fresh Chinese egg noodles
2 teaspoons salt
1 teaspoon sugar

## PREPARATION

To prepare lobster:
Bring 1 cup water to a boil in a pot large enough to hold the lobster.

When water boils, add the lobster and cook over high flame 5 minutes or until the lobster turns red.

Remove lobster from pot and let cool 15 minutes.

Boil down stock (water in which lobster was cooked) to a scant ½ cup.

Remove all lobster meat; shred and place in a bowl.

To prepare duck:
Either buy Chinese roast duck or roast one yourself (refer to Barbecued Roast Duck).

Split duck in half, and remove wing and leg. Remove skin and meat from duck carcass.

Shred duck meat and place in bowl.

Place duck skin on a rack and roast in a shallow roasting pan for

10 to 15 minutes in a preheated 375° oven. Skin should be very crisp. Remove from oven and let cool 5 minutes. Shred skin, and place in a small bowl.

Shred roast pork, and place in same bowl as lobster and duck meat.

Rinse mushrooms, cover with warm water and soak for 30 to 60 minutes or until soft; then shred.

Boil down mushroom stock (water in which dried mushrooms were soaking) to ¼ cup and add to lobster stock.

Shred kohlrabi, mushrooms, carrot, leeks, snow peas, broccoli, and hairy melon.

Slice water chestnuts.

Measure bean sprouts and place in bowl with water chestnuts.

Mince ginger and garlic, and place in a small cup.

Place kohlrabi, carrot, and broccoli in a bowl.

Place mushrooms and leeks in a bowl.

Place hairy melon and snow peas in a bowl.

Mix 1 cup stock with soy sauce (or master sauce) and oyster sauce.

Mix binder.

To prepare noodles:
Bring to a boil 4 quarts water and ½ tablespoon oil.

Add noodles and boil for 3 to 5 minutes, depending on the size of the noodle and the intensity of the flame. Stir noodles occasionally with chopsticks to prevent sticking together.

Pour noodles into a colander and rinse with cold water.

Mix noodles with ½ tablespoon oil.

Cut noodles with a cleaver into 6-inch lengths.

## COOKING PROCEDURE

Place wok over high flame for 30 seconds.

Add 2 tablespoons oil, and heat for 20 seconds or until oil is hot but not smoking.

Add noodles and stir-fry for 2 minutes.

Add 1 teaspoon salt and continue to fry until noodles are very hot (2 to 3 minutes more). Empty noodles onto a flat, heated serving dish, and place *uncovered* in a preheated 250° oven for up to 30 minutes.

In the same wok, heat 2 tablespoons oil over high heat, and add garlic and ginger. Stir-fry a few seconds.

Add kohlrabi, broccoli, and carrot. Stir-fry 3 minutes.

Add mushrooms and leeks, and stir-fry another minute.

Add the hairy melon and snow peas and stir-fry 1 more minute.

Add 1 teaspoon each of salt and sugar.

Add boiling stock-sauce mixture.

Remix binder and add with one hand, while continuing to stir-fry with the other.

Add bean sprouts, fresh water chestnuts, lobster, duck, and roast pork. Mix well.

The mixture should be sizzling hot, and the sauce should be thick.

Place vegetable-meat mixture over noodles and garnish with roast duck skin.

Mix well *after* serving at the table, as you would a salad.

TIMING : Refer to Roast Pork Lo Mein.

SUBSTITUTIONS : Refer to Roast Pork Lo Mein.

TIPS : Choose an oven-proof platter such as an enamel paella pan, or a copper or porcelain flat serving dish.

The roast duck and the lobster can be prepared a day in advance. The vegetables can be prepared early in the day or the day before if wrapped well and refrigerated.

When doubling recipe, use the 2 wings and 2 legs from the roast duck as a garnish.

An ideal combination of stock would be equal parts of mushrooms, lobster, duck, and roast pork juices.

Roast pork and roast duck can be made (pages 208 and 157), or purchased in Chinatown.

For cutting noodles, refer to Roast Pork Lo Mein.

## SPICY COLD NOODLES WITH SESAME-SEED PASTE

YIELD: 4 SERVINGS

1 tablespoon peanut oil
½ pound fresh egg noodles
1 tablespoon sesame-seed oil
1 cup mung bean sprouts

**Sauce**
2 tablespoons sesame-seed paste
2 tablespoons dark soy sauce
1 tablespoon brewed tea

½ tablespoon Chinese red vinegar
½ tablespoon chili oil
½ tablespoon sesame-seed oil
½ teaspoon sugar
1 teaspoon ginger root, minced
1 clove garlic
2 scallions (white and green parts)

### PREPARATION

In a 6-quart saucepan, bring 4 quarts of water to a rapid boil.

Add 1 tablespoon peanut oil.

Boil noodles for 3 to 5 minutes, stirring occasionally with chopsticks.

Drain noodles in a colander and rinse with cold water.

Cut noodles in 6-inch pieces.

Mix the noodles with 1 tablespoon sesame-seed oil and set aside.

Rinse the bean sprouts, then drain and dry well.

In a bowl, mix the sesame-seed paste, soy sauce, and tea until well blended.

Add the red vinegar, chili oil, sesame-seed oil, and sugar.

Mince the ginger and garlic.

Chop scallions.

Add ginger, garlic, and scallions to previously mixed sauce ingredients; combine well.

When ready to serve, mix the bean sprouts and the noodles with 2 wooden spoons.

Stir the sauce again and pour it over the noodles, tossing until the noodles and bean sprouts are well coated.

Serve immediately.

TIMING : All the preparations can be made early in the day or the day before.

Do *not* mix the noodles, bean sprouts, and sauce until immediately before serving.

SUBSTITUTIONS : For the sesame-seed paste you can substitute peanut butter, which is also flavorful.

For the fresh egg noodles you can substitute dried egg noodles or any type of fresh pasta.

TIPS : If you do not want the spiciness, omit the ½ tablespoon chili oil and increase the sesame-seed oil in the sauce to 1 tablespoon.

One cup of leftover (cooked) shredded meat can be added along with the bean sprouts, such as chicken, duck, or pork.

Chili oil is available at all Chinese grocery stores. It is a clear red oil (red from the chili peppers, which are removed), and will keep in the refrigerator for one year.

Sesame-seed paste is also available in Chinese grocery stores. It is made from roasted sesame seeds and sesame-seed oil. It will keep in the refrigerator for one year.

The easiest way to cut noodles is to place them on a flat surface, after you have cooked, drained, and rinsed them, and cut through them in 2 or 3 places with a cleaver.

# DESSERTS

The American taste for sweets of all kinds, at any time of day or night and particularly after a meal, is not shared by the Chinese. That is partially due to the lack of dairy products in China, because of the expense of feeding cattle. The Chinese do make cookies and certain types of pastry, but they use lard instead of butter, and the results are heavier and harder to digest, hardly an appropriate end to a multicourse meal. Such cakes are eaten as between-meal snacks, with tea.

The most commonly served sweet is a soup which is drunk at the end of a meal and between the courses of a meal. When served between courses, it functions as does the French "sorbet," to clear and refresh the palate. It can be made from fruits, such as oranges or pineapple; it can also be made from nuts, such as almonds, walnuts, peanuts, or lotus seeds.

The other authentic end to a meal is any type of fruit: fresh, canned, or preserved. Some of the more popular fruits are fresh lichee, pineapple, kumquats, loquats, plums, mangoes, starfruit, and peaches. I like to combine elements of both East and West, serving a fresh fruit that has been lightly sprinkled with a liqueur such as Grand Marnier or Amaretto. Another possibility, which is popular in Chinese-American restaurants, is to section fresh fruit, dip the sections in batter, and then deep-fry them. They are then immersed in a thick syrup and finally plunged into ice water, which crystallizes them.

There are a few elaborate desserts, such as the classic Almond Float (which has a gelatin base) or the Eight-Precious Rice Pudding (so-called because of the 8 different fruits and nuts used to decorate the glutinous rice-based pudding). These are esthetically stunning, since they contain a great variety of colors and shapes, but are not that interesting to the American palate because the taste and texture is bland.

A good Chinese meal, such as any one listed on the dinner plans in this book, is well-balanced and includes a variety of tastes, including the sweet, so a heavy dessert would be inappropriate. That is why I recommend a light, refreshing dessert such as a fresh fruit sherbet. I include a recipe for mango sherbet, which is a classic recipe and can serve as the basis for any other type of fruit sherbet, fresh or canned.

## ALMOND CREAM

YIELD: 6 SERVINGS

4 cups milk
1 cup raw blanched almonds, pulverized in a blender
¾ cup sugar
¼ cup rice flour

½ teaspoon almond extract
Fresh berries as garnish, such as strawberries, raspberries, or blueberries

## PREPARATION

Put 1 cup blanched almonds in a blender and mix at medium speed until finely ground.

## COOKING PROCEDURE

In a 2- to 3-quart saucepan, combine 3½ cups of the milk with the almonds and sugar.

Bring to a boil over a medium-low flame, stirring occasionally.

Remove the pan from the heat, cover, and let the almonds steep for 45 minutes.

Strain the mixture through a sieve set over a bowl, pressing down hard on the almonds with the back of a wooden spoon to extract their moisture before discarding them.

Return the almond-flavored liquid to the saucepan.

Dissolve the rice flour in the remaining ½ cup of milk, stir it into the liquid, and set the pan over low heat.

Stirring frequently, simmer for about 15 minutes, or until the custard thickens enough to coat the spoon.

Add almond extract and stir to blend.

Strain through a sieve and spoon the custard into 6 individual dessert bowls, or 1 glass serving bowl. Cover and chill in the refrigerator for at least 2 hours.

Before serving, garnish with berries.

TIMING : This can be prepared a day in advance.

TIPS : Straining the custard through a sieve allows some of the crushed almonds to pass through, which gives the custard a more interesting texture.

You can use the almond cream as you would a crème anglaise. In that case, give each person a bowl of fresh berries, letting the individual spoon the cream over the fruit.

Instead of almond extract, you can substitute 2 to 3 tablespoons almond liqueur, such as Amaretto. If you do, decrease the quantity of sugar to ½ cup.

Rice flour is also labelled rice powder.

To avoid a skin forming, cover the custard with plastic wrap touching the surface.

## MANGO SHERBET

YIELD: 6 SERVINGS

2 medium-size mangoes, or 2 cups purée

2 egg whites, at room temperature

½ cup sugar

2 tablespoons lemon juice

## PREPARATION

Peel and dice mangoes.

Put the diced mangoes through the blade of a food mill or purée them in a blender.

Measure out two cups mango purée.

Beat egg whites until soft peaks form, and reserve.

Beat the sugar and lemon juice into the mango purée until the sugar dissolves (about 3 to 4 minutes).

Add the reserved beaten egg whites and continue to beat for another 2 minutes.

Place the sherbet and the bowl in the freezer covered with aluminum foil.

Freeze for 2 to 3 hours, or until the sherbet has begun to set. The time will depend on the temperature of your freezer, which should ideally be at o° or below.

When partially set, beat again for 2 or 3 minutes. If sherbet has become too solid, let soften at room temperature. Cover and freeze sherbet for another hour, beat it again, then turn it into a bowl, individual dishes, or a mold lightly greased with sesame-seed oil. Let the sherbet soften for about ½ hour in the refrigerator before you serve it.

SUBSTITUTIONS: For the mango, you can substitute 1 quart hulled strawberries or raspberries, put through a food mill. That procedure retains some of the natural berry texture. (If you put them in a blender, the berries will be mashed into too fine a texture.)

You can also substitute loquats. Use a 14-ounce can of loquats.

Drain the fruit, reserving the liquid.

Put the loquats through a food mill.

Measure the puréed fruit and add enough of the juice from the can to make 2 cups. Follow the above recipe.

TIPS: If you are using a mold, first grease it lightly with sesame-seed oil. When ready to serve, hold the mold in a large bowl of cool water for 5 seconds. Then place a serving dish over the mold and turn the mold upside down. Shake it vigorously, until the sherbet slides out.

If it is not to be served immediately, cover with an inverted bowl and return to freezer.

If a richer dessert is preferred, fold 1 cup freshly beaten heavy cream into sherbet after the first freezing. Then place in a large mold or in individual dishes, and freeze until firm. A second beating is not necessary.

## ALMOND COOKIES

YIELD: 40 COOKIES

40 whole almonds
2½ cups flour, sifted
1 teaspoon double-acting
  baking powder
¼ teaspoon salt
1¼ cups sugar
2 cups blanched almonds,
  ground fine

¾ cup butter
1 tablespoon sesame-seed oil,
  plus a little extra for glazing
2 eggs, beaten
1 teaspoon almond extract

## PREPARATION

Roast 40 almonds in a preheated 325° oven for 12 to 15 minutes. Do not coat with oil or sprinkle with salt.

Sift the flour, baking powder, salt, and sugar into a bowl.

Mix in the ground, blanched almonds, then work in the butter and sesame-seed oil with the hands or a pastry blender.

Add the beaten egg and almond extract and stir a minute.

Break off tablespoon-size pieces of dough and shape into balls.

Arrange on a greased cookie sheet, leaving at least 1 inch between each cookie. Brush each cookie lightly with sesame-seed oil. Place one almond in the center of each cookie, pressing down lightly.

## COOKING PROCEDURE

Bake cookies for 5 minutes at 375°, then reduce oven temperature to 325° and continue to bake for another 8 to 12 minutes.

Remove cookies from the oven with a spatula and cool on a rack.

N O T E : If you don't have racks on which to cool cookies, turn them upside down.

# DINNER PARTY PLANS

Planning and executing parties has always caused great anxiety among hosts and hostesses. That is especially true of Chinese dinner parties because of all the last-minute cooking. Questions run through your mind, such as: Will the food be good? Will the guests like the chosen menu? How much time is needed for the preparation? How much time must be spent in the kitchen after the guests arrive? How much food is needed? What kind of table arrangements should be made? What beverage goes well? Is it worth all the trouble?

Preparing Chinese dinner parties can be a highly gratifying experience. I have been catering them for the past 7 years and have calmed, surprised, and delighted many a host, hostess, and guest. People are impressed by an Occidental who can prepare an authentic as well as delicious Oriental meal. They tend to take good Continental or American cooking for granted but are awed by the preparation and presentation of a home-made Oriental dinner. The result of the evening is that your guests will notice the meal more, comment upon it, and compliment it.

Your guests can share the preparation of the meal as well as the eating. Instead of one person spending many hours in the kitchen preparing food for the family or company, a few or several people can make a joint effort. Since there is so much preparation and very little cooking involved in Chinese cooking, it lends itself to group participation. You only have to invest in a few extra chopping blocks and cleavers for guests or family members. As a cook, you will never feel alienated again.

In my cooking classes everyone chops, everyone cooks, everyone eats! We compare our shredded meat and vegetables, understand and appreciate every step involved in the preparation, and consequently enjoy the food to a far greater extent. It becomes more than oral gratification. The idea of group preparation can be applied to almost any situation, whether you are planning a romantic dinner for two, your usual family meal, or a festive dinner party. I have planned communal banquets to which every person brings all the prepared components of a dish and stir-fries it on the spot. These occasions engender a feeling of warmth between everyone involved and a real sense of contribution.

Whether you are cooking communally or by yourself, the key to a successful dinner is *organization*. The first step is to make a detailed plan of the menu, from a shopping list with all necessary ingredients, to an outline of the chronological sequence of steps. You can follow one of mine until you have the confidence to create your own. Since no main course is served at Chinese dinners, planning a menu can be great fun. Choose one or two appetizers; a soup; one poultry course; one fish course; one beef, veal, or pork course; a vegetable course; rice or noodles; dessert; a white wine or beer with the meal; and tea with the dessert.

Try not to repeat the same ingredient in two different dishes if it plays a major role. If you choose beef with black bean sauce, do not also serve a steamed bass with fermented black beans. You can omit the black beans from the fish recipe and add a little more hoisin, oyster, or bean sauce. A dish of Roast Pork and another of Chicken with Bean Sauce and Nuts would not go well together either, since the hoisin sauce is the predominating ingredient in both recipes. A shredded beef dish and a lo mein dish would look too much alike. A whole duck should not be served with a whole fish. Select some light and some heavy dishes. Plan variety in all areas: various colors of vegetables; various textures, achieved by different methods of cooking (stir-frying, deep-frying, steaming, or braising); and various tastes, by selecting dishes that are rich, light, spicy, bland, sweet, and sour. That variety makes it easier to plan a multicourse dinner in which all the dishes come out at the same time.

Do not plan on doing more than 2 last-minute stir-fried dishes if you are the only cook.

The dinner plans which are presented here are just a small sample of the infinite variety possible when you are coordinating a dinner. At times I have departed slightly from the basic recipes given in Part II, and I call for a variation. All variations and substitutions appear in the Substitutions section that follows most recipes. These form a crucial part of my teaching and of this book, for they offer suggestions for a wide range of experimentation and improvisation. When I include a recipe in a dinner plan that differs from the original, however, I note the title of the original directly below.

I usually ask my guests before I complete my plans for the menu if they have any strong likes or dislikes. Don't wait until they arrive at your home to find someone is allergic to shrimp and someone else doesn't eat pork. Since you will be dealing with several courses, calculating the amount of food required is quite different from planning a European or American dinner. I have devised the following system.

Select one or two appetizers and one soup. The soup recipes in this book will serve four to six people. The appetizer recipes indicate how many pieces they will yield. For example, the recipe for Shanghai Spring Rolls yields 9 to 10 pieces, and you should allow 1 to 1½ per person; for Shrimp Toast, 24 pieces, allow 3 per person. The following chart will help you determine how much food is required for your entrées. I always allow at least ½ pound meat per person for company meals, less for family meals. After you know how many people are coming, decide how many dishes to prepare. Then multiply the number of people times ½ pound of meat, fish, or fowl, and divide by the number of dishes. An example of a menu for twelve people would be:

Shrimp with Wine Rice: double recipe
Lamb with Hot Peppers and Scallions: double recipe
Cantonese Fried Chicken: use a 5-pound chicken

The most time-consuming part of the dinner is the preparation of ingredients, for which you should allow about 1 hour per dish. Some dishes require much less time (Steamed Fish with Hoisin Sauce) and some a much longer time (Boneless Stuffed Duck, Canton Style). I like to overestimate the time needed in case of complications. If you want to enjoy the preparation of your Chinese dinner, do all the shopping and house-cleaning the day before. Start your preparation early in the morning. Set up one tray for each dish. Cut all the vegetables and put the necessary ingredients on each tray, according to the order in which they will be used. Follow each recipe up to the point indicated for advance preparation. Then take a break. Run a few miles, or read a book, but avoid working up to the last minute. The evening will be much more enjoyable.

You are now ready to follow your plan. Having a plan will help quell most of those panicky feelings we all have just before the guests arrive. Efficient organization decreases the possibility of failure. I make a plan for every dinner I am responsible for, whether it is a professional assignment or a gathering of friends. Read it over several times, trying to get a visual picture of how it will work. Place 2 woks or 1 wok and a steamer on your stove to see if they fit. Try them diagonally, and if that doesn't work, use other pans. Make sure all the cooking utensils, serving spoons, and platters you are going to use are out, and go over all ingredients on the trays. In most cases, each dish will have its own tray. If you

The numbers in the chart represent the quantity of pounds of meat, fish, or fowl collectively.

Formula: Number of People × ½ pound per Person ÷ number of dishes.

Example: Number of People: 12  Pounds of meat, fish, or fowl: 6  Number of Dishes: 3  Pounds per dish: 2

| Total Pounds Meat, Fish, Fowl | People | 2 | 3 | 4 | 5 | 6 | 7 |
|---|---|---|---|---|---|---|---|
| | | Pounds per Dish | | | | | |
| 2 | 4 | 1 | — | — | — | — | — |
| 3 | 6 | 1½ | 1 | — | — | — | — |
| 4 | 8 | 2 | 1½ | 1 | — | — | — |
| 5 | 10 | 2½ | 2 | 1½ | 1 | — | — |
| 6 | 12 | 3 | 2 | 1½ | 1½ | 1 | — |
| 7 | 14 | 3½ | 2½ | 2 | 1½ | 1½ | 1 |
| 10 | 20 | 5 | 3½ | 2½ | 2 | 2 | 1½ |
| 12 | 24 | 6 | 4 | 3 | 2½ | 2 | 2 |
| 15 | 30 | 8½ | 5 | 4 | 3 | 2½ | 2½ |
| 18 | 36 | 9 | 6 | 4½ | 4 | 3 | 2½ |
| 20 | 40 | 10 | 7 | 5 | 4 | 3½ | 3 |

work during the day, do all the cutting and marinating the night before. When you return home the following evening, you only have to do the cooking. That makes a Chinese dinner party an ideal way of entertaining for anyone who enjoys cooking.

Your favorite white wine is the perfect accompaniment to any Chinese meal. You may prefer beer or tea. I allow ⅓ to ½ bottle of wine per person. In China they drink soup as their beverage, and tea at the end of the meal or throughout the day as we drink coffee. The Chinese do not have a taste for alcoholic beverages or sweets. Fresh fruit is served at the end of the meal. As a dessert, I can think of nothing more satisfying than a fresh Hawaiian pineapple sprinkled with a touch of Grand Marnier, or fresh lichee fruit (they are in season only during the month of June or July). I love pastries, but not immediately after a big meal, and especially not after a Chinese meal. Fresh pineapple, mango, loquat, or raspberry sherbet would also be appropriate.

Even though I encourage my students to experiment on guests, unless you have some experience in preparing Chinese dinners, I would not advise trying more than one experiment at a time. It is best to cook each dish once before you coordinate it into one of the following dinner plans.

I can not overemphasize the importance of the trays. As you are making the preparations for any one recipe, place all the ingredients on a tray. You should have the same number of trays as you have dishes. Before you are ready to cook, read over all the ingredients in the recipe to double-check you have not forgotten anything.

I have tried to estimate the approximate time it will take you to prepare a dinner, based on the speed of my beginning students. Every time you prepare a dish and become more familiar with the techniques, it will take you less time. My time estimates do not allow for the shopping and washing of vegetables since, as previously mentioned, this should be done the day before the dinner.

Although most of these dinners are suggested for eight to

twelve people, by following the chart you will be able to scale up or down the quantity of food according to your specific needs. In general, one dish is enough for two to three people depending on the size of the individual's appetite. A small dinner party for four people could include an appetizer or a soup and two entrées.

When you are making your own dinner plan, ask yourself two main questions: What to do first? What is the order of subsequent preparations? The answer to the first question is often: *marinate*. Then read over each recipe and see what the preparations are and how far in advance they can be done. Some dishes, or a significant part of them, can be prepared and cooked a day in advance, such as Braised Gingered Spareribs, Roast Pork, or the Shrimp Dumplings for the Fresh Spinach Soup.

Other questions you should ask yourself are: What dish can be cooked first and kept warm without deteriorating? Is there a dish that is already cooked and needs only to be rewarmed? Is there a dish that can be served cold or at room temperature? If there is a steamed entrée involved, coordinate it so the last 10 or 15 minutes of your cooking (perhaps 2 stir-fried dishes) will be finished at the same time as the steamed entrée. And finally, determine which is the most fragile dish—usually the fish recipe, which must be served immediately. Save it for last. Never plan more than 2 stir-fried dishes in one dinner plan unless you have 2 cooks in the kitchen.

Tack up your dinner plan on a wall or cabinet in the kitchen where you can easily refer to it while you are cooking. Unless you have someone to read to you, it also helps to post your recipes where you can read them.

There are two ways to eat a Chinese meal: banquet style, in which each course is served separately; or family style, in which all the food is served simultaneously. If you are at a restaurant or having a sit-down dinner catered by Karen Lee, it is much more enjoyable to savor one dish at a time. Family style, however, enables the cook to join his or her guests at the table, which most people prefer. The effort to coordinate cooking and dining served as the impulse for this chapter and the book as a whole. If you understand how to plan and organize, you will soon find your own answers to the most crucial question of all: how to get it together.

# THE TWELVE
# DINNER PARTY
# PLANS

BEGINNER'S DINNER FOR EIGHT
*Hot and Sour Soup*
*Roast Pork Lo Mein*
*Soy Sauce Whole Chicken*
*Steamed Bass with Hoisin Sauce*
*Mango Sherbet*

ECONOMICAL DINNER FOR SIX
*Cantonese Stuffed Bean Curd*
*Home-Style Egg Drop Soup*
*Shredded Szechuan Beef*
*Dry Sautéed String Beans, Szechuan Style*
*Sea Trout with Bean Sauce*
*White Rice*
*Seasonal Fresh Fruit*

ECONOMICAL DINNER FOR EIGHT
Pan-Fried Stuffed Peppers
Lemon Chicken
Braised Gingered Spareribs
Szechuan Spicy Bean Curd
Stir-Fried Spinach with Minced Ham
White Rice
Fresh Mango Slices

FIVE-COURSE DINNER FOR EIGHT
Spring Rolls
Pork Curry
Stir-Fried Shrimp with Asparagus
Crisp Fried Squab
White Rice
Almond Cream and Raspberries

SIX-COURSE DINNER FOR EIGHT TO TWELVE
Barbecued Short Ribs of Beef
Shrimp with Wine Rice
Szechuan Diced Chicken
Roast Pork Fried Rice
Stir-Fried Snow Peas and Carrots
Strawberry Sherbet

SEVEN-COURSE DINNER FOR EIGHT TO TWELVE
Deep-Fried Wontons
7-Ingredient Winter Melon Soup
Barbecued Roast Duck
Lamb with Hot Peppers and Scallions
Steamed Cantonese Shrimp
Spicy Seasonal Stir-Fried Vegetables
White Rice
Loquat Sherbet with Almond Cookies

## LOW-CHOLESTEROL DINNER FOR EIGHT
*Pearl Balls (Made with veal)*
*Hot and Sour Soup (Made with veal and egg white)*
*Lemon Sole with Lobster Sauce*
*Chicken with Bean Sauce and Nuts*
*Eggplant with Garlic Sauce*
*White Rice*
*Fresh Pineapple and Strawberries*

## LOW-CHOLESTEROL DINNER FOR TWELVE
*Flounder Toast*
*Vegetable Wonton Soup*
*Steamed Red Snapper with Bean Sauce*
*Veal with Hot Peppers and Scallions*
*American Seasonal Stir-Fried Vegetables*
*White Rice*
*Fresh Lichees*

## LOW-CHOLESTEROL DINNER FOR TWENTY
*Grilled Lamb*
*Fresh Spinach Soup*
*Szechuan Peppercorn Chicken*
*Sweet and Sour Flounder Balls*
*Szechuan Twice-Cooked Veal*
*White Rice*
*Strawberry Sherbet or Seasonal Fresh Fruit*

## SPECIAL OCCASION: DINNER FOR EIGHT
*Minced Squab in Lettuce Leaves*
*7-Ingredient Winter Melon Soup*
*Veal with Shallots*
*Boneless Stuffed Duck, Canton Style*
*Spiced Filet of Sea Bass with Broccoli*
*Fresh Papaya Slices*

BANQUET DINNER FOR TWELVE

*Fresh Spinach Soup with Ham and Shrimp Dumplings*
*Banquet Lo Mein*
*Sizzling Shrimp on Rice Patties*
*Seasonal Stir-Fried Vegetables*
*Peking Spareribs*
*Szechuan Twice-Cooked Veal*
*Peking Duck*
*Mango Sherbet and Almond Cookies*

COCKTAIL PARTY FOR FORTY

*Cantonese Fried Chicken*
*Pearl Balls*
*Deep-Fried Wontons*
*Barbecued Spareribs*

## Beginner's Dinner for Eight

| | |
|---|---|
| *Soup* | Hot and Sour Soup (2 times recipe) |
| *Entrées* | Roast Pork Lo Mein (2 times recipe) |
| | Soy Sauce Whole Chicken (4- to 5-pound chicken) |
| | Steamed Bass with Hoisin Sauce (Variation on Steamed Fish with Hoisin Sauce) (2½- to 3-pound fish, weighed before cleaning) |
| *Dessert* | Mango Sherbet (1½ times recipe) |
| | Tea |

### 1 DAY BEFORE

1. Go over all recipes and make a detailed shopping list. Make separate categories: butcher, fruit and vegetable market, fish market, and supermarket.
2. Wash all vegetables, drain, and refrigerate.
3. Make Mango Sherbet, and freeze.

Approximate preparation time: 2 hours.

### MORNING PREPARATIONS — DAY OF THE DINNER

1. Soak mushrooms, tree ears, and lily buds.
2. Cut all vegetables and place in separate bowls, then cover and refrigerate.
3. Prepare Soy Sauce Whole Chicken up to the "cooling" step.
4. Prepare soup up to the step before adding bean curd.
5. Complete remaining preparations for all dishes. Place all ingredients for each recipe (unless requiring refrigeration), in the order they will be used, on a corresponding tray. For this plan you only need to set up 2 trays: 1 for the soup and 1 for the Roast Pork Lo Mein.
6. Boil egg noodles, drain, rinse with cold water, and toss with oil.
7. Set up necessary cooking equipment: one 14-inch wok; a steamer with a rack; 1 pot for soup.
8. Select serving pieces and platters and set the table.

9. Refrigerate wine.
10. Measure 8 teaspoons tea leaves in tea pot.
11. Reread all recipes to make sure that you haven't omitted any ingredients or steps.

Approximate preparation time: 2½ to 3 hours.

### 2 HOURS BEFORE SERVING DINNER

Set up steamer with rack and water. Place bass on a dish appropriate for both steaming and serving, and pour seasoning sauce over fish. Garnish with scallions, ginger, and black beans. Cover with plastic wrap and place dish in refrigerator.

### 1 HOUR BEFORE SERVING DINNER

Cut up Soy Sauce Whole Chicken (which has been cooling at room temperature for 3 hours), and place on Chinese or American parsley. Cover with plastic wrap. Do not refrigerate.

### 25 MINUTES BEFORE SERVING DINNER

1. Preheat oven to 250°.
2. Boil water in steamer.
3. Take fish out of refrigerator and baste a few times with sauce.
4. Fry noodles, put in serving dish, and keep warm in oven, *uncovered*.
5. Finish preparation of soup.
6. Put fish in steamer.
7. Open the wine.
8. Serve the soup. The fish takes 15 minutes to cook, which means you can join your guests for soup for 10 minutes. Set the timer.
9. When the timer goes off, return to the kitchen and reset it for 5 minutes.
10. Heat stock for lo mein in a saucepan while stir-frying vegetable-pork mixture for Roast Pork Lo Mein. Take noodles out of the oven. If the timer goes off for the fish, simply turn off

the flame, but do *not* remove cover. Place vegetable-pork mixture over noodles in a serving dish.

11. Serve the Soy Sauce Whole Chicken, Steamed Bass, and Roast Pork Lo Mein together.

**30 MINUTES BEFORE SERVING DESSERT**
Take sherbet out of the freezer and put in the refrigerator.

**10 MINUTES BEFORE SERVING DESSERT**
1. Boil water for tea, pour over tea leaves, and let steep for 5 minutes.
2. Unmold the Mango Sherbet and serve with tea.

## ECONOMICAL DINNER FOR SIX

| | |
|---|---|
| *Appetizer* | Cantonese Stuffed Bean Curd |
| *Soup* | Home-Style Egg Drop Soup |
| *Entrées* | Szechuan Shredded Beef (use flank or skirt steak) |
| | Dry Sautéed String Beans, Szechuan Style |
| | Sea Trout with Bean Sauce (variation of Steamed Fish with Hoisin Sauce) |
| | White Rice (1½ cups raw) |
| *Dessert* | Seasonal Fresh Fruit |
| | Tea |

**1 DAY BEFORE**
1. Go over all recipes and make a detailed shopping list. Make separate categories: butcher, vegetable and fruit market, fish market, and supermarket.
2. Wash all vegetables, drain, and refrigerate.

Approximate preparation time: 1 hour.

MORNING PREPARATIONS — DAY OF THE DINNER

1. Trim beef of fat; freeze, slice, marinate, then refrigerate.
2. Marinate sea trout and refrigerate.
3. Soak dried shrimp and mushrooms.
4. Weigh down bean curd.
5. Cut all vegetables and place in separate bowls, then cover and refrigerate.
6. Mix all seasoning sauces and binders.
7. Make stuffing for the bean curd.
8. Stuff bean curd and refrigerate.
9. Place ingredients for each recipe (unless requiring refrigeration) in the order they will be used on a corresponding tray; for this plan you should set up a total of 4 trays (the trout does not require a separate tray).
10. Set up necessary cooking equipment: two 12- or 14-inch woks; 1 pot for the soup; 1 pot for the rice; and a steamer (make sure the platter on which you will be serving the fish fits into the steaming arrangement).
11. Select serving pieces and platters and set the table.
12. Pour soup stock in soup pot.
13. Refrigerate the wine or beer.
14. Measure 6 teaspoons of tea leaves in tea pot.

Approximate preparation time: 3 hours.

3 HOURS BEFORE SERVING DINNER

1. Rinse sea trout, place on a dish appropriate for both steaming and serving, and pour seasoning sauce over fish; garnish and refrigerate.
2. Put 2 inches water in steamer.
3. Stir-fry the marinated beef shreds, deglaze wok and pour deglazing liquid over beef. Wash and dry wok. Let beef cool for 30 minutes, then cover and refrigerate.
4. Prepare Seasonal Fruit; put in serving dish and refrigerate.
5. Reread all recipes to make sure that you haven't omitted any ingredients or steps.

1 HOUR BEFORE SERVING DINNER

1. Remove all prepared ingredients from the refrigerator (except the sea trout) and set them up on each corresponding tray.
2. Heat 2 cups oil in wok to 375°, and fry string beans. Remove them with a wire strainer and drain well on paper towels. Remove oil from wok. Do not wash wok; you will use the same wok to stir-fry the string beans when ready to serve.
3. Make White Rice.

20 MINUTES BEFORE SERVING APPETIZER

1. Preheat oven to 250°.
2. Fry Cantonese Stuffed Bean Curd and serve.
3. Turn oven temperature to 225°.

30 MINUTES BEFORE SERVING DINNER

1. Remove sea trout from the refrigerator.
2. Open wine.
3. Prepare soup and serve.
4. Turn flame to high under the steamer.
5. Place rice and 2 serving dishes in oven to warm.
6. Join your guests for the soup course (about 5 minutes).
7. Return to the kitchen and start steaming fish.
   Set the timer for 15 minutes.
8. Join your guests for the soup course (another 5 minutes).
9. Return to the kitchen and stir-fry the string beans. Empty into a heated serving dish and return to the oven, *uncovered*. Turn off oven.
10. Finish the beef dish, stir-frying the vegetables and then adding the already cooked beef and the seasoning sauce.
11. When the timer for the fish goes off, remove the fish from the steamer. If the timer goes off too early, turn the flame off but leave the cover on. The fish will keep for 5 minutes.
12. Serve the Sea Trout with Bean Sauce; Dry Sautéed String Beans, Szechuan Style; Szechuan Shredded Beef; and White Rice together.

10 MINUTES BEFORE SERVING DESSERT

1. Boil water for tea, pour over tea leaves, and let steep for 5 minutes.
2. Serve tea and Seasonal Fresh Fruit together.

## ECONOMICAL DINNER FOR EIGHT

*Appetizer*   Pan-Fried Stuffed Peppers
*Entrées*   Lemon Chicken
         Braised Gingered Spareribs
         Szechuan Bean Curd
         Stir-Fried Spinach with Minced Ham (variation on
            Stir-Fried Shantung Cabbage with Minced Ham)
         White Rice (2 cups raw)
*Dessert*   Fresh Mango Slices in Grand Marnier
         Tea

1 DAY BEFORE

1. Go over all recipes and make a detailed shopping list. Make separate categories: butcher, fruit and vegetable store, fish market, and supermarket.
2. Wash all vegetables, drain, and refrigerate.
3. Make stuffing for peppers and refrigerate.
4. Seed peppers.
5. Prepare and cook spareribs; then refrigerate the finished dish.

Approximate preparation time: 2½ hours.

MORNING PREPARATION—DAY OF THE DINNER

1. Bone, marinate, and refrigerate chicken breasts.
2. Cut all vegetables and place in separate bowls, then cover and refrigerate.
3. Make lemon sauce for the chicken.
4. Make sauce for the peppers. Mix all binders.

5. Complete remaining preparations for all dishes. Place all ingredients for each recipe (unless requiring refrigeration) in the order they will be used on a corresponding tray; for this plan you should set up a total of 5 trays.

6. Set up necessary cooking equipment: two 12- or 14-inch woks, a heavy dutch oven for the spareribs, a pot for the rice, and a small saucepan for the Lemon Chicken sauce.

7. Select serving pieces and platters; set the table.

8. Refrigerate the wine.

9. Heat 2 to 3 cups oil to 325° in wok and fry the chicken for the first time. Remove breasts from the oil and let drain well on several layers of paper towels. Do not refrigerate. When oil is cool, strain into another wok. (You can fry the chicken up to 4 hours before dinner.) Wash wok in which the chicken was fried.

10. Stuff peppers and refrigerate.

11. Measure 8 teaspoons of tea leaves in tea pot.

12. Remove fat from spareribs and place spareribs in a heat-proof uncovered serving dish.

13. Reread all recipes to make sure that you haven't omitted any ingredients or steps.

Approximate preparation time: 2½ to 3 hours.


1 HOUR BEFORE SERVING DINNER

1. Remove all prepared ingredients from the refrigerator, and set them up on each corresponding tray.

2. Make White Rice.

3. Slice 4 medium mangoes and marinate in 8 teaspoons Grand Marnier.

4. Shred cabbage (garnish) and place on Lemon Chicken platter.


30 MINUTES BEFORE SERVING APPETIZER

1. Put a low flame under the pot containing the spareribs.

2. Fry the peppers and serve.

3. Preheat oven to 225° and put in the rice to warm.
4. Join your guests for the appetizer.
5. Return to the kitchen.

15 MINUTES BEFORE SERVING DINNER
1. Turn oven up to 250° and put in spareribs.
2. Place 2 serving dishes in the oven to warm.
3. Stir-fry bean curd and place in the oven uncovered.
4. Turn on a medium flame under the wok containing 2 to 3 cups of oil for the second frying of the chicken. Put a low flame under the saucepan containing the lemon sauce.
5. Stir-fry the spinach and empty it into a heated serving dish.
6. Thicken the lemon sauce, but do not add vegetables. Turn flame off under sauce.
7. Refry the chicken and make 6 or 7 cuts crosswise. Place on platter over the shredded cabbage.
8. Add vegetables to the lemon sauce and pour over chicken.
9. Serve the Lemon Chicken, Braised Gingered Spareribs, Szechuan Bean Curd, Stir-Fried Spinach with Minced Ham, and White Rice together.
10. Open wine.

30 MINUTES BEFORE SERVING DESSERT
1. Boil water for tea, pour over tea leaves, and let steep for 5 minutes.
2. Serve the fresh Mango Slices in Grand Marnier with the tea.

## FIVE–COURSE DINNER FOR EIGHT

| | |
|---|---|
| *Appetizer* | Shanghai Spring Rolls with Plum Sauce Dip and Mustard Sauce |
| *Entrées* | Pork Curry |
| | Stir-Fried Shrimp with Asparagus |

Crisp Fried Squab with Szechuan Peppercorn Powder
(variation on Cantonese Fried Chicken)
White Rice (2 cups raw)

*Dessert*      Almond Cream and Raspberries
Tea

For eight people, use 1½ times recipe, except for the Crisp Fried Squab, which requires 2 squabs.

### SEVERAL MONTHS TO 1 DAY BEFORE
1. Make Plum Sauce Dip and Mustard Sauce, and refrigerate.
2. Make Szechuan Peppercorn Powder.

### 1 DAY BEFORE
1. Go over all recipes and make a detailed shopping list. Make separate categories: butcher, fruit and vegetable store, fish market, and supermarket.
2. Wash all vegetables, drain, and refrigerate.

Approximate preparation time: 1 hour.

### MORNING PREPARATION — DAY OF THE DINNER
1. Freeze pork (to be used in both Pork Curry and Spring Roll filling).
2. Slice and marinate pork for curry, then refrigerate.
3. Devein, butterfly, and marinate the shrimp, then refrigerate.
4. Soak mushrooms.
5. Make Spring Roll filling, and allow to cool.
6. Cut up and marinate squabs for no more than 4 hours in the refrigerator.
7. Set up necessary cooking equipment: two 12- or 14-inch woks, and 1 pot for the rice.
8. Select serving pieces and platters, and set the table.
9. Refrigerate wine.

10. Place Plum Sauce Dip and Mustard Sauce in separate bowls for serving.
11. Make Almond Cream and refrigerate. Rinse raspberries, dry, and refrigerate.
12. Cut all vegetables and place in separate bowls, then cover and refrigerate.
13. Place ingredients for each recipe (unless requiring refrigeration) in the order they will be used on a corresponding tray; for this plan you should set up only 2 trays: 1 for the pork and 1 for the shrimp.
14. Mix binders and seasoning sauces for Pork Curry and Stir-Fried Shrimp with Asparagus.
15. Remove Spring Roll wrappers from refrigerator.
16. Heat 2 to 3 cups oil to 325° in a wok and fry the squab for the first time. Drain on paper towels. Do not refrigerate. Strain oil into another wok. It will be used to fry Spring Rolls and then again to fry the squab a second time.
17. Roll the Spring Rolls. Place them on a cookie sheet, cover with a damp towel, and refrigerate (up to 3 hours ahead).
18. Measure 8 teaspoons of tea leaves in tea pot.
19. Reread all recipes to make sure that you have not omitted any ingredients or steps.

Approximate preparation time: 5 hours (if you cut vegetables and stir-fry Spring Roll filling ahead).


1 HOUR BEFORE SERVING DINNER
1. Remove all prepared ingredients from the refrigerator and set them up on each corresponding tray.
2. Make White Rice.


15 MINUTES BEFORE SERVING APPETIZER
Heat oil in wok to 325°, and fry Spring Rolls. Drain well on paper towels, cut, and serve with Plum Sauce Dip and Mustard Sauce.

30 MINUTES BEFORE SERVING DINNER
(15 MINUTES BEFORE SOUP)

1. Preheat oven to 225°.
2. Heat 2 to 3 cups oil to 375° in wok.
3. Start heating chicken stock.
4. Refry squab for the second time. Drain on paper towels.
5. Place rice and serving dishes in the oven to warm.
6. Open wine.
7. Return to the kitchen and stir-fry the Pork Curry. Place in a heated serving dish and return to the oven, uncovered. Turn off the oven.
8. Stir-fry the shrimp with asparagus.
9. Serve at the same time: Crisp Fried Squab, Pork Curry, Stir-Fried Shrimp with Asparagus, and White Rice.

10 MINUTES BEFORE SERVING DESSERT

1. Boil water for tea, pour over tea leaves, and let steep for 5 minutes.
2. Serve the Almond Cream, raspberries, and tea.

## Six–Course Dinner for Eight to Twelve

| | |
|---|---|
| *Appetizer* | Barbecued Short Ribs of Beef |
| *Entrées* | Shrimp with Wine Rice |
| | Szechuan Diced Chicken |
| | Roast Pork Fried Rice (variation on Shrimp-Fried Rice) |
| | Stir-Fried Snow Peas and Carrots |
| *Dessert* | Strawberry Sherbet (variation on Mango Sherbet) |
| | Tea |

For eight people, use 1½ times recipe; for twelve people, use 2 times recipe, except for the chicken, which should be 3 times the recipe.

**1 WEEK BEFORE**
1. Buy or make Roast Pork, and freeze.
2. Make Wine Rice.

**1 DAY BEFORE**
1. Go over all recipes and make a detailed shopping list. Make separate categories: butcher, fruit and vegetable store, fish market, and supermarket.
2. Wash all vegetables, drain, and refrigerate.
3. Make Strawberry Sherbet, and freeze.
4. Make White Rice (for fried rice), let cool, and refrigerate.
5. Make marinade for Barbecued Short Ribs of Beef.
6. Mix sauce for shrimp.

Approximate preparation time: 2 hours.

**MORNING PREPARATIONS—DAY OF THE DINNER**
1. Bone, dice, marinate, then refrigerate chicken.
2. Shell, devein, split, wash, drain, dry, marinate, then refrigerate shrimp.
3. Marinate short ribs 6 hours before dinner.
4. Cut all vegetables and place in separate bowls, then cover and refrigerate.
5. Mix seasoning sauce for chicken. Mix all binders.
6. Complete remaining preparations for all dishes. Place all ingredients for each recipe (unless requiring refrigeration) in the order they will be used on a corresponding tray; for this plan you should set up a total of 5 trays.
7. Set up necessary cooking equipment: three 12- or 14-inch woks, a roasting pan with a rack, and a pot for the rice.
8. Select serving pieces and platters, and set the table.
9. Refrigerate wine.
10. Broil short ribs, and let cool on a rack. Do not refrigerate.
11. Measure 8 to 12 teaspoons of tea leaves in tea pot.

12. Reread all recipes to make sure that you have not omitted any ingredients or steps.

Approximate preparation time: 3½ hours.

## 2 HOURS BEFORE SERVING DINNER

1. Heat 2 to 3 cups of oil in wok to 325°. Fry marinated, diced chicken pieces. Remove from oil with a wire strainer and let drain. Spread chicken pieces apart to avoid steaming. Let chicken cool. Do not refrigerate. Strain oil into a container and refrigerate for another use. Do not wash wok. The same wok will be used to stir-fry chicken when ready to serve.
2. Set up short ribs on a rack placed in a roasting pan to rewarm when ready to serve.
3. In the second wok, stir-fry marinated shrimp until not quite done. (The shrimp should be slightly pink, but still translucent.) Empty shrimp onto a plate. Do not wash wok. The same wok will be used to finish stir-frying the shrimp when ready to serve.

## 1 HOUR BEFORE SERVING DINNER

Remove all prepared ingredients from the refrigerator, and set them up on each corresponding tray.

## 20 MINUTES BEFORE SERVING APPETIZER

1. Preheat oven to 450° for 10 minutes.
2. Place short ribs in oven to re-warm for 5 minutes. Serve with Plum Sauce Dip and Mustard Sauce.
3. Open wine.
4. Turn oven temperature down to 225°.

## 20 MINUTES BEFORE SERVING DINNER

1. Place 3 serving dishes in the oven to warm.
2. In a third wok, stir-fry rice; when done, place in the oven un-covered (still at 225°).
3. Stir-fry snow peas and carrots. Empty them into a heated serv-

ing dish and cover loosely, but do *not* keep warm in the oven lest the snow peas become soggy.

4. Finish stir-frying the chicken, empty into a heated serving dish, and return to the oven uncovered to keep warm. Turn off the oven.

5. Finish the shrimp dish and empty into a heated serving dish. Serve the Shrimp with Wine Rice, Szechuan Diced Chicken, Roast Pork Fried Rice, and Stir-Fried Snow Peas and Carrots together.

### 30 MINUTES BEFORE SERVING DESSERT

Take the Strawberry Sherbet out of the freezer and put in the refrigerator.

### 10 MINUTES BEFORE SERVING DESSERT

1. Boil water for tea, pour over tea leaves, and let steep for 5 minutes.

2. Unmold the Strawberry Sherbet and serve with tea.

## SEVEN–COURSE DINNER FOR EIGHT TO TWELVE

| | |
|---|---|
| *Appetizer* | Deep-Fried Wontons with Plum Sauce Dip and Mustard Sauce |
| *Soup* | Seven-Ingredient Winter Melon Soup |
| *Entrées* | Barbecued Roast Duck |
| | Lamb with Hot Peppers and Scallions |
| | Steamed Cantonese Shrimp |
| | Spicy Seasonal Stir-Fried Vegetables |
| | White Rice (2 to 3 cups raw) |
| *Dessert* | Loquat Sherbet (variation on Mango Sherbet) |
| | Almond Cookies |
| | Tea |

For eight people, follow proportions indicated in each recipe; for twelve people, use 1½ times recipe.

### 1 MONTH TO 1 DAY BEFORE
1. Make Plum Sauce Dip and Mustard Sauce.
2. Make Wontons and freeze, using crab meat or lobster instead of shrimp as part of the filling if desired.

### 1 DAY BEFORE
1. Go over all recipes and make a detailed shopping list. Make separate categories: butcher, fruit and vegetable store, fish market, and supermarket.
2. Wash all vegetables, drain, and refrigerate.
3. Defrost duck by putting it in the refrigerator.
4. Make Loquat Sherbet.
5. Make Almond Cookies.

Approximate preparation time: 3 hours.

### MORNING PREPARATIONS—DAY OF THE DINNER
1. Hang duck from 8:00 A.M. to 3:00 P.M.
2. Freeze lamb; cut, marinate, and refrigerate.
3. Set up necessary cooking equipment: two 12- or 14-inch woks, a pot for the soup, another for the rice, a steamer, and a roasting pan with a rack.
4. Select serving pieces and platters, and set the table.
5. Soak the mushrooms.
6. Marinate shrimp.
7. Complete remaining preparations for all dishes. Place ingredients for each recipe (unless requiring refrigeration) in the order they will be used on a corresponding tray; for this plan you need 3 trays.
8. Pour chicken stock into soup pot.
9. Place pork mixture in rectangular dish for steaming, cover, and refrigerate.

10. Marinate duck at 3:00 P.M. and refrigerate.
11. Remove Wontons from the freezer if you have made them ahead. Place them on a cookie sheet lined with paper towels while they are defrosting.
12. When they have defrosted, fry them for the first time and let drain on paper towels. Allow to cool. Do *not* cover or refrigerate.
13. Refrigerate the wine.
14. Measure 8 to 12 teaspoons tea leaves in tea pot.
15. Reread all recipes to make sure that you have not omitted any ingredients or steps.

Approximate preparation time: 4½ hours.


3 HOURS BEFORE SERVING DINNER
Preheat oven to 325°.


2½ HOURS BEFORE SERVING DINNER
Place duck in oven and set timer, being sure to note position of bird and temperature changes in the recipe.


2 HOURS BEFORE SERVING DINNER
1. Remove all ingredients from the refrigerator and set them up on corresponding trays.
2. Fry lamb, remove from oil with a wire strainer, and let drain. Do not wash wok. You will be using the same wok to complete the lamb dish when ready to serve.
3. Make White Rice.
4. Place Plum Sauce Dip and Mustard Sauce in bowls.


15 MINUTES BEFORE SERVING APPETIZER
1. Heat oil in wok to 375°.
2. Fry Wontons, drain, and serve with Plum Sauce Dip and Mustard Sauce.

30 MINUTES BEFORE SERVING DINNER
( 10 MINUTES BEFORE SOUP )

1. Remove dish with pork mixture from the refrigerator.
2. Check duck and see if there is enough water in the bottom of the roasting pan.
3. Place dish containing pork mixture in steamer. Turn flame to high and set timer for 25 minutes (which allows 5 minutes for the water to come to a boil).
4. Make soup and serve.
5. If you have a second oven, put in rice at 225° for 10 minutes; if you have to put it in the oven with the duck, put the rice in a double boiler, but do not leave it in for more than 15 minutes.
6. Join your guests or family for 5 minutes. Then return to kitchen.
7. Check the duck. If it is done, remove it from the oven and place it on a rack over a serving platter while you cook the remaining 3 dishes.
8. When the timer for the steamer goes off, remove pork mixture from the steamer and arrange the shrimp around the edges.
9. Open wine.
10. Complete the stir-frying of the lamb. Place on a hot tray if you do not have a second oven, while you stir-fry the vegetable dish. Lamb will keep warm for 5 minutes.
11. Return dish containing shrimp and pork to steamer. Set the timer for 3 minutes.
12. Stir-fry vegetable dish. If the timer for the shrimp goes off before you have finished stir-frying the vegetable dish, remove the steamer cover and turn off the flame. The shrimp dish will stay warm for 5 minutes.
13. Serve the Steamed Cantonese Shrimp, Barbecued Roast Duck, Lamb with Hot Peppers and Scallions, Spicy Seasonal Stir-Fried Vegetables, and White Rice at the same time. There are two ways of serving the duck after you have presented it for everyone to see: first, while they are helping themselves to the 3 other dishes, return to the kitchen to cut up the duck

with a heavy cleaver and mallet; second, cut it up with poultry shears at the table.

½ HOUR BEFORE SERVING DESSERT
Remove Loquat Sherbet from the freezer and place it in the refrigerator.

10 MINUTES BEFORE SERVING DESSERT
1. Boil water for tea, pour over tea leaves, and let steep for 5 minutes.
2. Serve tea, Loquat Sherbet, and Almond Cookies.

### LOW–CHOLESTEROL DINNER FOR EIGHT

| | |
|---|---|
| *Appetizer* | Pearl Balls (using Ground Shoulder of Veal) with Soy Sauce–Vinegar Dip |
| *Soup* | Hot and Sour Soup (using Veal and Egg White) |
| *Entrées* | Lemon Sole with Lobster Sauce (variation on Shrimp with Lobster Sauce) |
| | Chicken with Bean Sauce and Nuts |
| | Eggplant in Garlic Sauce |
| | White Rice (2 cups raw) |
| *Dessert* | Fresh Pineapple and Strawberries |
| | Tea |

For eight people, use 1½ times recipe, except for the Pearl Balls, which require 1¼ times recipe, and the Hot and Sour Soup, which should be doubled.

1 DAY BEFORE
1. Go over all recipes and make a detailed shopping list. Make separate categories: butcher, fruit and vegetable store, fish market, and supermarket.
2. Wash all vegetables, drain, and refrigerate.

3. Prepare Pearl Balls and steam for 20 minutes. Place them on a cookie sheet, cool for 30 minutes, cover, and refrigerate.
4. Make Soy Sauce–Vinegar Dip.

Approximate preparation time: 2 hours.

MORNING PREPARATIONS — DAY OF THE DINNER
1. Freeze shoulder of veal for soup. When partially frozen, shred it as you would the pork.
2. Cut sole and marinate.
3. Bone and skin chicken breasts and marinate.
4. Soak mushrooms, tree ears, lily buds, and dried shrimp.
5. Cut all vegetables and place in separate bowls, then cover and refrigerate.
6. Mix all seasoning sauces and binders.
7. Complete remaining preparations for all dishes. Place all ingredients for each recipe (those not requiring refrigeration) in the order they will be used on corresponding tray; set up a total of 4 trays.
8. Set up necessary cooking equipment: two 14-inch woks, a steamer, a pot for the soup, and a pot for the rice.
9. Select the serving pieces and platters, and set the table.
10. Refrigerate the wine.
11. Pour chicken stock in soup pot.
12. Rinse strawberries, drain, dry, and hull, leaving them whole.
13. Measure 8 teaspoons tea leaves into tea pot.
14. Prepare soup up to the step before adding bean curd.
15. Reread all recipes to make sure that you have not omitted any ingredients or steps.

Approximate preparation time: 3½ hours (if Pearl Balls are done ahead).

1½ HOURS BEFORE SERVING DINNER
1. Remove all prepared ingredients from the refrigerator, and set them up on each corresponding tray.

2. Make White Rice.
3. Stir-fry ½ the amount of chicken breasts in wok. Empty contents of wok onto a plate. Deglaze wok. Repeat with remaining ½ of chicken, making sure to spread out the chicken pieces to avoid steaming.
4. Heat 2 to 3 cups oil in another wok and fry ½ the amount of sole pieces. Remove from wok and let drain on paper towels for 15 minutes. Place fish pieces in a single layer on a plate, in order to avoid steam.
5. Set up Pearl Balls in steamer.
6. Pour oil in which you have fried the fish into a sieve set over a pot. Do not wash wok in which the fish was fried. You will complete the stir-frying of the Lemon Sole with Lobster Sauce in the same wok.

### 20 MINUTES BEFORE SERVING APPETIZER

1. Turn flame to high and steam Pearl Balls for 20 minutes. That allows 5 minutes for the water to come to a boil.
2. Remove Pearl Balls from the steamer with a spatula, and place on a flat, heated serving dish with the Soy Sauce–Vinegar Dip in a bowl in the center of the dish.

### 25 MINUTES BEFORE SERVING DINNER

1. Preheat oven to 225° for 5 minutes.
2. Place rice in oven to rewarm.
3. Put a low flame under the chicken stock.
4. Make eggplant and keep warm, uncovered, in the oven.
5. Place 2 serving dishes in the oven to warm: one for the flounder and one for the chicken.
6. Open the wine.
7. Finish making the soup and serve. That will take about 5 minutes. Join your guests at the dining table for about 5 minutes of the soup course. Then return to the kitchen to prepare the remaining two dishes.
8. Follow the recipe for Chicken with Bean Sauce and Nuts,

starting with the stir-frying of the vegetables. Since the chicken has already been stir-fried, the remaining part of the recipe will take about 3 minutes.

9. Keep the chicken warm on a heated serving platter while you finish the Lemon Sole with Lobster Sauce. It should be cooked in the same wok used to fry the sole pieces. It is necessary to have 2 woks for this dinner.

10. Serve the Lemon Sole with Lobster Sauce, Chicken with Bean Sauce and Nuts, Eggplant in Garlic Sauce, and White Rice at the same time.

### 10 MINUTES BEFORE SERVING DESSERT

1. Boil water for tea, pour over tea leaves, and let steep for 5 minutes.

2. Cut off the top of the pineapple and set in the center of a round serving platter. Cut the remaining body of the pineapple into 6 sections, lengthwise. On each of the sections, remove the hard inner core. Make a single horizontal cut, separating the fruit from the rind; then make about 6 vertical cuts. Arrange the 6 sections around the center, radiating outward to resemble the spokes of a wheel. Scatter the strawberries around the spokes.

### LOW–CHOLESTEROL DINNER FOR TWELVE

*Appetizer*    Flounder Toast with Soy Sauce–Vinegar Dip (2½ times recipe for Shrimp Toast)

*Soup*    Vegetable Wonton Soup (1½ times recipe) (made with ground shoulder of veal)

*Entrées*    Steamed Red Snapper with Bean Sauce (two-pound fish) (variation on Steamed Fish with Hoisin Sauce)

Veal with Hot Peppers and Scallions (2 times recipe) (variation of Lamb with Hot Peppers and Scallions)

American Seasonal Stir-Fried Vegetables (2 times recipe)

White Rice (3 cups raw rice)

*Dessert*    Fresh Lichees (in season in June or July; substitute other fresh fruit if unavailable)
            Tea

### 1 MONTH TO 1 DAY BEFORE

1. Make Wontons and freeze.
2. Make Soy Sauce–Vinegar Dip.

### 1 DAY BEFORE

1. Go over all recipes and make a detailed shopping list. Make separate categories: butcher, fruit and vegetable store, fish market, and supermarket. Choose fresh vegetables in season for the stir-fried vegetable dish.
2. Wash all vegetables, drain, and refrigerate.

Approximate preparation time: 1 hour.

### MORNING PREPARATIONS — DAY OF THE DINNER

1. Slice veal (use scallops from the leg), marinate, refrigerate.
2. Make mixture for Flounder Toast and refrigerate.
3. Cut stale bread into triangles and cover.
4. Soak mushrooms.
5. Make sauce for fish, substituting bean sauce for hoisin sauce.
6. Cut all vegetables and place in separate bowls, then cover and refrigerate.
7. Mix all seasoning sauces and binders.
8. Complete remaining preparations for all dishes. Place all ingredients for each recipe (unless requiring refrigeration) in the order they will be used, on a corresponding tray; for this plan you should set up a total of 4 trays (a tray for the fish is not necessary).
9. Set up necessary cooking equipment: cookie sheets for Wontons and Flounder Toast; a steamer for the fish; two 14-inch woks; a pot for the soup and another for the rice.
10. Select serving pieces and platters, and set the table.

11. Refrigerate wine.
12. Pour chicken stock in soup pot.
13. Measure 12 teaspoons tea leaves in tea pot.
14. Rinse lichees. Place in glass serving bowl and refrigerate.
15. Reread all recipes to make sure that you have not omitted any ingredients or steps.

Approximate preparation time: 3½ hours (if Wontons have been made ahead)


2 HOURS BEFORE SERVING DINNER

1. Set up steamer with rack and water. Place the 2 red snappers in the dish in which they will be served, and pour sauce over them; garnish with scallions, ginger, and black beans. Place dish as is in refrigerator.
2. Boil Wontons as recipe indicates. (If made ahead and frozen, do *not* defrost before boiling.) Drain well and place them in a single layer on a greased cookie sheet. Cover with plastic wrap. Refrigeration is not necessary.
3. Spread flounder mixture on bread. Place triangles in a single layer on a cookie sheet. Cover with wax paper and refrigerate.
4. Heat 2 to 3 cups of safflower oil in a wok to 300° and fry ½ the total quantity of marinated veal (1 pound). Remove veal from oil with a wire strainer; let drain in another strainer set over a bowl. Repeat another time for the second pound.
5. Make White Rice.
6. Pour oil in which you have fried the veal into a sieve and let it drain into the second wok. This wok will be used to fry the flounder toast. Do not wash the wok in which you have fried the veal. You will complete the stir-frying of the Veal with Hot Peppers and Scallions just before serving dinner.


1 HOUR BEFORE SERVING DINNER

Remove all prepared ingredients from the refrigerator and set them up on each corresponding tray.

10 MINUTES BEFORE SERVING APPETIZER

Heat oil in wok (strained safflower oil) to 375° and fry the Flounder Toast. Drain well on paper towels. Serve with Soy Sauce–Vinegar Dip.

30 MINUTES BEFORE SERVING DINNER

1. Preheat oven to 225°. Place 2 serving dishes in the oven to
   warm.
2. Pour oil out of wok into a container and let cool. Wash and
   dry wok. This wok will be used later to stir-fry the vegetable
   dish.
3. Bring water in steamer to a boil, then turn flame to low.
4. Take fish out of refrigerator and baste a few times with the
   sauce.
5. Bring chicken stock to a boil. Add cooked Wontons. When
   soup returns to a boil, let Wontons simmer for ½ minute. Remove Wontons with a wire strainer and place in a soup tureen.
6. Place rice in oven to rewarm.
7. Blanch soup vegetables in boiling chicken stock and remove.
   Pour chicken stock over Wontons and garnish with vegetables.
8. Serve soup.
9. Open wine.
10. Put the 2 fish in the steamer. They take 18 minutes to cook.
11. Join your guests for 8 minutes for the soup course.
12. Return to the kitchen and stir-fry the vegetables. Place them
    in a heated serving dish.
13. If the timer goes off for the fish before you have finished stir-
    frying the Veal with Hot Peppers and Scallions, turn off the
    flame and keep the fish covered (up to 5 minutes).
14. Complete stir-frying the veal dish.
    The remaining part of the recipe takes about 3 minutes.
15. Serve the Steamed Red Snapper, Veal with Hot Peppers and
    Scallions, American Seasonal Stir-Fried Vegetables, and White
    Rice together.

10 MINUTES BEFORE SERVING DESSERT

1. Boil water for tea, pour over tea leaves, and let steep for 5 minutes.
2. Serve tea and Fresh Lichees.


## Low–Cholesterol Dinner for Twenty

| | |
|---|---|
| *Appetizer* | Grilled Lamb (2½ pounds) (variation on Roast Pork) |
| *Soup* | Fresh Spinach Soup (without Ham and Shrimp Dumplings) (5 times recipe) |
| *Entrées* | Szechuan Peppercorn Chicken (2½ times recipe) |
| | Sweet and Sour Steamed Flounder Balls (2½ times recipe) |
| | Szechuan Twice-Cooked Veal (2½ times recipe) |
| | White Rice (5 cups raw) |
| *Dessert* | Strawberry Sherbet or Seasonal Fresh Fruit (4 times recipe for Mango Sherbet) |
| | Tea |

This dinner could be made for fewer people. If you use the quantity indicated in the recipes (1 pound of veal, etc.), this amount of food would be sufficient for eight hearty appetites. I have chosen this menu for a larger group of people because it is reasonably easy to handle. If you prefer to do this as a buffet, omit the soup course.


1 DAY BEFORE

1. Go over all recipes and make a detailed shopping list. Make separate categories: butcher, fruit and vegetable store, fish market, and supermarket.
2. Wash all vegetables, drain, and refrigerate.
3. Make marinade for the lamb and refrigerate. (This marinade appears in the Roast Pork recipe as one of the variations.)
4. Make sweet and sour sauce, and refrigerate.

5. Make Sweet and Sour Steamed Flounder Balls and refrigerate.
6. Simmer veal in sherry; cool, slice, cover well, and refrigerate.
7. Boil chicken breasts, drain, cool, shred, cover well, then refrigerate.
8. Make Sauces A and B for the chicken, cover, and refrigerate.
9. Make Strawberry Sherbet and freeze in a 7½-quart mold or several smaller molds.

Approximate preparation time: 6 hours for twenty people, or 4 hours for eight people.

MORNING PREPARATIONS — DAY OF THE DINNER
1. Soak mushrooms.
2. Cut all vegetables and place in separate bowls, then cover and refrigerate.
3. Make seasoning sauce for veal; mix all binders.
4. Marinate lamb chunks 6 to 8 hours before dinner
5. Complete remaining preparations for all dishes. Place the ingredients for each recipe (those not requiring refrigeration) in the order they will be used on a corresponding tray; for this plan you should set up a total of 5 trays.
6. Set up necessary cooking equipment: rack and roasting pan for the lamb, a pot for the soup, a pot for the rice, a salad bowl for the chicken, a 4- to 6-quart saucepan for the flounder, and only one 14-inch wok.
7. Select the serving pieces and platters; if you do not have large-enough serving dishes, use 2 for every dish. Set the table.
8. Refrigerate the wine.
9. Pour chicken stock in soup pot.
10. Measure 20 teaspoons tea leaves in tea pot.
11. If using fresh fruit instead of sherbet for dessert, prepare fruit, put fruit in serving dish, and refrigerate.
12. Reread all recipes to make sure that you haven't omitted any ingredients or steps.

Approximate preparation time: 2 hours.

1 HOUR BEFORE SERVING DINNER

1. Remove all prepared ingredients from the refrigerator and set them up on each corresponding tray.
2. Make White Rice.

½ HOUR BEFORE SERVING APPETIZER

Preheat broiler; remove lamb from marinade and set up a rack resting on a shallow roasting pan.

10 MINUTES BEFORE SERVING LAMB

1. Broil lamb chunks until pink inside, about 4 minutes on each side. Cut one to check.
2. Turn off oven.
3. Put lamb on serving platter and serve.

30 MINUTES BEFORE SERVING DINNER

1. Preheat oven to 225°.
2. Shred cabbage for Szechuan Peppercorn Chicken and refrigerate.
3. Bring soup to a rapid boil; add vegetables and bean curd. Pour soup into a tureen and serve at the table, or pour into individual bowls in the kitchen.
4. Place serving dishes and rice in the oven to warm.
5. Open the wine.
6. Put a low flame under the sweet and sour sauce.
7. Join your guests for 5 minutes.
8. Return to the kitchen and thicken the sweet and sour sauce.
9. Stir-fry veal and empty contents of wok into a heated serving dish. Keep warm *uncovered* in the oven.
10. Add Flounder Balls to sweet and sour sauce. Bring sauce to a boil, add vegetables. Bring sauce to a boil again, then empty contents of saucepan into 2 or more heated serving dishes. Sprinkle with nuts. Do not keep warm in oven.
11. Heat Sauce A for the chicken. Add Sauce B to Sauce A and mix

with chilled shredded chicken and cabbage. If possible, have someone help you mix the Szechuan Peppercorn Chicken while you are finishing off the Sweet and Sour Steamed Flounder Balls; that would help coordinate and simplify serving them at the same time as the Szechuan Twice-Cooked Veal and White Rice.

#### 30 MINUTES BEFORE SERVING DESSERT
1. Take sherbet out of freezer and place in the refrigerator.

#### 10 MINUTES BEFORE SERVING DESSERT
1. Boil water for tea, pour water over tea leaves, and let steep for 5 minutes.
2. Unmold Strawberry Sherbet or remove fruit from refrigerator, and serve with tea.

### SPECIAL OCCASION: DINNER FOR EIGHT

| | |
|---|---|
| *Appetizer* | Minced Squab with Lettuce Leaves |
| *Soup* | Seven-Ingredient Winter Melon Soup |
| *Entrées* | Veal with Shallots |
| | Boneless Stuffed Duck, Canton Style |
| | Spiced Filet of Sea Bass with Broccoli (variation on Spiced Filet of Sea Trout with Broccoli) |
| *Dessert* | Fresh Papaya Slices |
| | Tea |

For eight people, follow proportions indicated in each recipe, except for using 1½ times the Minced Squab.

#### 1 DAY BEFORE
1. Go over all recipes and make a detailed shopping list. Make separate categories: butcher, fruit and vegetable store, fish market, and supermarket.

2. Wash all vegetables, drain, and refrigerate.
3. Let duck defrost, if frozen, in the refrigerator.

Approximate preparation time: 2 hours.

MORNING PREPARATIONS — DAY OF THE DINNER

1. Bone squab and duck; make stock with carcass, neck, and giblets of both.
2. Marinate bass and refrigerate.
3. Dice and marinate veal, then refrigerate.
4. Soak dried mushrooms and black beans.
5. Cut all vegetables and place in separate bowls, then cover and refrigerate.
6. Mix seasoning sauces and binders.
7. Complete remaining preparations for all dishes. Place all ingredients for each recipe (unless requiring refrigeration) in the order they will be used on a corresponding tray; for this plan you should set up a total of 4 trays (you do not need any for the duck).
8. Make stuffing for the duck.
9. Set up necessary cooking equipment: two 12- or 14-inch woks, a roasting pan with rack, a pot for soup, and a hot tray (if you don't have a double oven).
10. Select serving pieces and platters, and set the table.
11. Refrigerate wine.
12. Measure 8 teaspoons of tea leaves in tea pot.
13. Pour chicken stock into soup pot.
14. Reread all recipes to make sure that you have not omitted any ingredients or steps.

Approximate preparation time: 4 hours.

3 HOURS BEFORE SERVING DINNER

1. Stuff duck and set timer.
2. Heat 2 to 3 cups oil in wok and fry marinated fish. Remove fish from the oil with a wire strainer and drain on paper towels. Do

not wash wok. Use same wok to finish stir-frying fish when ready to serve.

3. Peel and slice 3 to 4 papayas. Squeeze fresh lemon or lime juice over slices and arrange in a serving dish.

## 2 ½ HOURS BEFORE SERVING DINNER

1. Preheat oven to 300°.
2. Remove all prepared ingredients from the refrigerator, and set up on each corresponding tray.

## 2 HOURS BEFORE SERVING DINNER

Put duck in the oven and set timer for 1½ hours.

## 10 MINUTES BEFORE SERVING APPETIZER

1. Arrange lettuce leaves on platter.
2. Stir-fry Minced Squab mixture, place over lettuce, and serve.

## 30 MINUTES BEFORE SERVING DINNER (10 MIN-UTES BEFORE SERVING SOUP)

1. Place 2 serving dishes on the hot tray to warm.
2. Make soup and serve.
3. Check the duck and reset timer for ½ hour at new oven temperature (375°).
4. Join your guests for the soup course.
5. Return to the kitchen and stir-fry the veal. Empty the veal into a serving dish and place on the hot tray.
6. Finish stir-frying the bass and place on a heated serving dish.
7. Serve the Boneless Stuffed Duck, Veal with Shallots, and Spiced Filet of Sea Bass with Broccoli together. Cut the duck at the table.
8. Open wine.

## 10 MINUTES BEFORE SERVING DESSERT

1. Boil water for tea, pour over tea leaves, and let steep for 5 minutes.
2. Take papaya out of refrigerator and serve with tea.

## BANQUET DINNER FOR TWELVE

*Soup*       Fresh Spinach Soup with Ham and Shrimp Dumplings

*Entrées*   Banquet Lo Mein
              Sizzling Shrimp with Rice Patties
              Seasonal Stir-Fried Vegetables (with Hoisin Sauce)
              Peking Spareribs
              Szechuan Twice-Cooked Veal
              Peking Duck with Peking Doilies

*Dessert*  Mango Sherbet
              Almond Cookies
              Tea

(For twelve people, follow proportions indicated in each recipe, except for the soup, veal, and sherbet, all of which should be 1½ times recipe.)

**1 MONTH TO 1 DAY BEFORE**
Make Peking Doilies and freeze.

**1 DAY BEFORE**
1. Go over all recipes and make a detailed shopping list. Make separate categories: butcher, fruit and vegetable store, fish market, and supermarket. Choose vegetables in season for the vegetable dish.
2. Wash all vegetables, drain, and refrigerate.
3. Simmer veal, cool, and refrigerate.
4. Make sauce for shrimp and refrigerate.
5. Bake rice patties and break apart, but do not deep-fry.
6. Shred lobster, duck meat and skin, and roast pork for lo mein.
7. Make Ham and Shrimp Dumplings.
8. Hang duck up to dry before going to bed.
9. Make Mango Sherbet.
10. Make Almond Cookies.

Approximate preparation time: 5½ hours.

MORNING PREPARATIONS—DAY OF THE DINNER

1. Marinate shrimp and spareribs, then refrigerate.
2. Boil noodles, drain, and mix with oil.
3. Marinate duck in sherry for 2 hours or longer in the refrigerator. Hang up again 6 hours before dinner.
4. Cut all vegetables and place in separate bowls, then cover and refrigerate.
6. Complete remaining preparations. Place all ingredients for each recipe (unless requiring refrigeration) in the order they will be used on a corresponding tray; for this plan you should set up a total of 6 trays.
7. Set up necessary cooking equipment: two 12- or 14-inch woks, a roasting pan with a rack, a steamer, a pot for the soup, and a pot for the rice.
8. Select serving pieces and platters and set the table.
9. Refrigerate wine.
10. Heat 2 to 3 cups of oil in wok to 325°. Fry spareribs and drain well on paper towels. Do not pile them on top of each other. Let cool but do not refrigerate.
11. Pour chicken stock in soup pot.
12. Prepare fresh scallions and place in ice water.
13. Place sauce for duck in small serving bowl.
14. Measure 12 teaspoons tea leaves in tea pot.
15. Reread all recipes to make sure that you have not omitted any ingredients or steps.

Approximate preparation time: 3½ hours.

1 ¼ HOURS BEFORE SERVING DINNER

Preheat oven to 375°.

1 HOUR BEFORE SERVING DINNER

1. Put duck in the oven and set time for 30 minutes.
2. Remove all prepared ingredients from the refrigerator, and set them up on each corresponding tray. (Duck does not need a tray.)

3. Remove doilies from the freezer and wrap in a damp towel.

4. Set up 2 cookie sheets lined with paper towels, 1 for the rice patties and 1 for the second frying of the spareribs.

5. Check on duck, following times and oven temperatures in recipe.

20 MINUTES BEFORE SERVING DINNER

1. Set up a hot tray to warm serving dishes, or warm them in the oven if you have a double oven.

2. Put a low flame under the chicken stock.

3. Preheat oven to 250°.

4. Stir-fry noodles, place on a serving platter, and keep warm, uncovered, on the lowest rack of the oven.

5. Open wine.

6. Make soup and serve.

7. Place metal serving platter for the shrimp on the lowest shelf of the oven, nearest the flame.

8. Stir-fry Szechuan Twice-Cooked Veal and serve.

9. Fry Rice Patties, drain, and keep warm on metal serving platter in oven.

10. Stir-fry shrimp; empty onto a dish. Put sauce in wok, thicken, then add vegetables and return shrimp to wok. Pour shrimp and vegetables over hot platter containing fried rice patties and serve Sizzling Shrimp with Rice Patties.

11. Check duck; if timer has gone off, turn over duck and reset timer.

12. Refry spareribs for the second time, draining well on paper towels. Pour oil out of wok into a bowl resting in the sink. Leave 1 tablespoon oil in wok. Do not wash wok. Add scallions and sauce, thicken, and add spareribs again. Serve Peking Spareribs.

13. Stir-Fry Seasonal Stir-Fried Vegetables and serve.

14. Boil water in steamer.

15. When duck is ready, place on a platter and present whole. Then return to kitchen and carve skin and meat. While you are removing skin and meat, steam the doilies.

16. Arrange duck skin and meat on a platter and serve Peking Duck with Peking Doilies, scallions, and dipping sauce.

### 30 MINUTES BEFORE SERVING DESSERT
Remove sherbet from the freezer and place in the refrigerator.

### 10 MINUTES BEFORE SERVING DESSERT
1. Boil water for tea, pour over tea leaves, and let steep for five minutes.
2. Unmold Mango Sherbet and serve with Almond Cookies and tea.

## COCKTAIL PARTY FOR FORTY

Cantonese Fried Chicken with Szechuan Peppercorn Powder and Soy Sauce–Vinegar Dip (12 pounds)
Pearl Balls (4 times recipe)
Deep-Fried Wontons with Plum Sauce Dip and Mustard Sauce (4 times recipe)
Barbecued Spareribs (15 pounds)

### 1 MONTH TO 1 DAY BEFORE
Make Szechuan Peppercorn Powder, Soy Sauce–Vinegar Dip, Plum Sauce Dip, and Mustard Sauce.

### 1 DAY BEFORE
1. Go over all recipes and make a detailed shopping list. Make separate categories: butcher, fruit and vegetable store, and supermarket.
2. Enlist the aid of 2 people in addition to yourself.
3. Set up an area for the Pearl Balls with all necessary ingredients. Complete all preparations. Steam for 20 minutes in 3 batches. If you have a 2-layer steamer, check after each batch to make sure there is enough water in the bottom. Allow to cool and place on cookie sheets, separating layers with wax paper. Cover and refrigerate.
4. Make the marinade for the spareribs.

5. Make the marinade for the chicken.
6. Cut up the chicken.
7. Make Wonton filling.

Approximate preparation time: 4 hours.

MORNING PREPARATIONS—DAY OF THE PARTY

1. Marinate spareribs for at least 8 hours.
2. Marinate chicken for 4 hours.
3. Set up necessary cooking equipment: two 14-inch woks, a steamer for the Pearl Balls, and two roasting pans with racks in which to rewarm the spareribs when they are ready to be served.
4. Make Wontons; start the first frying at 2:00 P.M. Drain well on several layers of paper towels. Do not pile them on top of each other. Do not refrigerate or cover.
5. Do the first frying of all the chicken pieces.
6. Strain oil into containers; then pour back into woks.
7. Roast spareribs in 2 batches, reducing the cooking time by 10 minutes.
8. Select about 12 serving platters; set the buffet table.
9. Cut up spareribs with a heavy cleaver and mallet and put them back on the racks. Cover with aluminum foil.

Approximate preparation time: 6 hours if working alone; about 3 hours if working with another person.

1 HOUR BEFORE SERVING

1. Put all sauces and dips in bowls on table.
2. Place first batch of Pearl Balls in steamer with 3 inches of water.
3. Fry chicken a second time and drain well on paper towels. Arrange chicken pieces on platter and garnish with parsley.

20 MINUTES BEFORE SERVING

1. Preheat oven to 425°.
2. Turn flame to high and steam Pearl Balls. (That allows 5 minutes for water to come to a boil.)
3. Heat oil in 2 woks to 375°.

10 MINUTES BEFORE SERVING

1. Put half the amount of spareribs in the oven and set timer for 10 minutes.
2. Fry Wontons a second time and drain well on paper towels. As soon as half the Wontons are ready, place on a serving platter and serve with Plum Sauce Dip and Mustard Sauce. Continue to fry the rest of the Wontons.
3. When the first half of spareribs are ready, remove from the oven and place on a serving platter. Place second batch of spareribs on racks and set timer again for 10 minutes.
4. When first batch of Pearl Balls is ready, remove from steamer and place on a serving platter. Then put second batch of Pearl Balls in steamer, checking to see if there is enough water in the bottom of the steamer. Set timer for 15 minutes.
5. When second batch of spareribs is ready, place on another platter and serve.
6. When timer goes off for second batch of Pearl Balls, empty contents of steamer onto another platter. Then steam the final (third) batch of Pearl Balls. Set timer for 15 minutes.

By the time the third batch of Pearl Balls is steamed, all the appetizers will be ready.

# INDEX

Boldface numbers refer to main entries.

Karen Lee, a native New Yorker, began her studies with Mme Grace Chu eleven years ago, later becoming her assistant. She started her own cooking school in 1972 and has taught in many parts of the country, including New York, Connecticut, Missouri, and Arizona. She also caters Chinese banquets and has demonstrated in private homes, gourmet shops, resorts, and major corporations, and on network television. An avid cyclist and jogger, Ms. Lee runs at least twenty miles a week. Her eight-year-old son sometimes accompanies her at the track.

Aileen Robbins Friedman is a freelance writer and editor and a professional opera singer.